nking
Children's
Rights

Second Edition

Rethinking Children's Rights

Attitudes in Contemporary Society

Second Edition

Phil Jones and Sue Welch

Bloomsbury Academic
An imprint of Bloomsbury Publishing Plc

B L O O M S B U R Y
LONDON · OXFORD · NEW YORK · NEW DELHI · SYDNEY

Bloomsbury Academic

An imprint of Bloomsbury Publishing Plc

50 Bedford Square	1385 Broadway
London	New York
WC1B 3DP	NY 10018
UK	USA

www.bloomsbury.com

BLOOMSBURY and the Diana logo are trademarks of Bloomsbury Publishing Plc

First edition published 2010
Second edition published 2018

© Phil Jones and Sue Welch, 2018

British Library Cataloguing-in-Publication Data

A catalogue record for this book is available from the British Library.

ISBN: HB: 978-1-3500-0125-1
PB: 978-1-3500-0124-4
ePDF: 978-1-3500-0127-5
ePub: 978-1-3500-0126-8

Library of Congress Cataloging-in-Publication Data

Names: Jones, Phil, 1958 April 22– author. | Welch, Susan, author.
Title: Rethinking children's rights : attitudes in contemporary society /
Phil Jones and Sue Welch.
Description: Second Edition. | New York : Bloomsbury Academic, An imprint of
Bloomsbury Publishing Plc, 2018. | Includes bibliographical references and index.
Identifiers: LCCN 2017048201 (print) | LCCN 2017049972 (ebook) |
ISBN 9781350001275 (PDF eBook) | ISBN 9781350001268 (EPUB eBook) |
ISBN 9781350001251 (Hardback : alk. paper) |
ISBN 9781350001244 (Paperback : alk. paper) Subjects: LCSH: Children's rights.
Classification: LCC HQ789 (ebook) | LCC HQ789 .J66 2018 (print) | DDC 323.3/52–dc23
LC record available at https://lccn.loc.gov/2017048201

Cover image © Michael H. / GettyImages

Series: New Childhoods

Typeset by Newgen KnowledgeWorks Pvt. Ltd., Chennai, India
Printed and bound in Great Britain

To find out more about our authors and books visit www.bloomsbury.com.
Here you will find extracts, author interviews, details of forthcoming events
and the option to sign up for our newsletters.

Contents

Introduction to New Childhoods Series

The amount of current attention given to children and to childhood is unprecedented. Recent years have seen the agreement of new international conventions, national bodies established and waves of regional and local initiatives all concerning children.

This rapid pace has been set by many things. From children themselves, from adults working with children, from governments and global bodies, injustice, dissatisfaction, new ideas and raw needs are fuelling change. Within and, often, leading the movement is research. From the work of multinational corporations designed to reach into the minds of children and the pockets of parents, through to charity-driven initiatives aiming to challenge the forces that situate children in extreme poverty, a massive amount of energy is expended in research relating to children and their lives. This attention is not all benign. Research can be seen as original investigation undertaken in order to gain knowledge and understanding through a systematic and rigorous process of critical enquiry examining 'even the most commonplace assumption' (Kellett, 2005, 9). However, as Kellett has pointed out, the findings can be used by the media to saturate and accost, rather than support, under-12s who are obese, for example, or to stigmatize young people by the use of statistics. However, research can also play a role in investigating, enquiring, communicating and understanding. Recent years have seen innovations in the focus of research, as political moves that challenge the ways in which children have been silenced and excluded result in previously unseen pictures of children's experiences of poverty, family life and community. The attitudes, opinions and lived experiences of children are being given air, and one of the themes within this book concerns the opportunities and challenges this is creating. As this book will reveal, research is being used to set new agendas and to challenge ways of living and working that oppress, harm or limit children. It is also being used to test preconceptions and long-held beliefs about children's lived experiences, the actual effects rather than the adult's opinions of the way parents see and relate to their children, or the actual impact of services and their ways of working with children.

In addition to the focus of research, innovations are being made in the way research is conceived and carried out. Its role in children's lives is changing. In the past much research treated children as objects, research was done on them, with the agenda and framework set purely by adults. New work is emerging where children create the way research is conceived and carried out. Children act as researchers, researchers work with questions formulated by children or work with children.

This series aims to offer access to some of the challenges, discoveries and work-in-progress of contemporary research. The term 'child' and 'childhood' is used within the series in line with Article 1 of the United Nations Convention on the Rights of the Child which defines 'children' as persons up to the age of 18. The books offer opportunities to engage with emerging ideas, questions and practices. They will help those studying childhood, or living and working with children to become familiar with challenging work, to engage with findings and to reflect on their own ideas, experiences and ways of working.

Phil Jones
UCL Institute of Education,
University College London, UK

Part I

Debates, Dilemmas and Challenges: The Background to Children's Rights

1

Introduction to *Rethinking Children's Rights*

Introduction and key questions

The concept of rights for children has emerged over recent years as a powerful force. In many societies it is a catalyst for changes in the ways adults and children live and work together. The pictures emerging from research reveal that the impetus, or dynamic, created by child rights is being engaged with in order to transform lives in positive directions. In addition, research also reveals that frictions, problems and failures are occurring in creating such changes and that these are harmful to children and their communities.

The cornerstone for most contemporary definitions, developments or discussions is the United Nations Convention on the Rights of the Child (UNCRC, 1989). The Appendix, (pages 279–85), offers the 'UNICEF Summary of the Rights under the Convention on the Rights of the Child', and the full version is at www.unicef.org.uk/ChildsRights. Chapter 2 considers the nature and definition of children's rights and the various ways they have been articulated and understood. One such example, with children as an audience, is offered by the Children's Rights Alliance for England (CRAE):

> Our human rights are the basic things we need in order to live with dignity, develop and reach our potential, such as food, housing and health care and the right to express ourselves, hold religious beliefs, and be free from violence and abuse. (2017, http://www.crae.org.uk/childrens-rights-the-law/what-are-human-rights)

As Chapters 2 and 3 will discuss in more detail, children's rights have tended to be divided into different areas of rights to help grasp the many different aspects they cover. One framework approaches rights in terms of liberty rights and welfare rights; another often-used analysis sees the UNCRC, for example, as concerned with discourses of provision, protection and participation. This doesn't mean that some are more important than others, as Chapter 3 discusses. An important concept in thinking about the UNCRC is that all the rights within it matter, and that they can't be cherry-picked when it suits adults. After three decades of responses to the UNCRC is it possible to rethink these rights in the light of contemporary research into what has occurred so far? This book attempts to answer this question by examining key aspects of the journey made to date and by looking forward to the future possibilities of the impetus that is being created by children's rights. In this chapter we will look at the following, introductory areas:

> Do societies see child rights in different ways?
> What do the different responses to the UNCRC reveal?
> What issues are emerging in relation to rethinking children's rights?
> How can negative responses to the rights agenda be used to help rethink children's rights?

Do societies see child rights in different ways?

A convention developed by a body such as the United Nations involves certain kinds of perspectives on rights. These are international in scope, and the UNCRC has been ratified by most individual nations. Ratification means that an individual government undertakes to implement the UNCRC recommendations in its laws and policies and to report to the United Nations Committee on the Rights of the Child on the progress being made. Butler explains aspects of this from a legal perspective:

> The Convention on the Rights of the Child makes reference to itself as legally 'binding' (Article 50). That is how the discipline of international law interprets the convention…It does not mean that all ratifying nations are legally bound to legislate the children's rights in the convention as domestic law. It means that ratifying nations are legally bound to participate in the monitoring procedure spelled out in the convention. They are legally bound to show that they are seriously trying to legally implement children's rights, to file reports on their success in implementing those rights, to be examined by the UN Child Rights Committee, and to receive recommendations from the committee. They are not legally bound to follow the recommendations or to actually pass domestic legislation. (2014, 2–3)

The Committee issues reports, and other non-government organizations also use the UNCRC as a framework for making their own reports on a country's response to child rights and on the lives of children. Chapter 2 will review how definitions, ideas and practices concerning child rights have emerged and will show how they are reflected in relation to the specific details of the UNCRC. The purpose of this book is to foreground experiences in the United Kingdom with references to responses in various countries as an approach to understanding the nature of the emerging relationships between child rights as a concept and their implementation in practice.

One of the emerging themes involves the kinds of responses that have occurred within different countries as the international convention comes into contact with the enthusiasms and frustrations created by national governments or localized practices and attitudes. The UNCRC may make a series of statements in its articles, but these are only as good as the way an individual country or society responds to them.

Different phenomena come into play within these responses: the idea of child rights, for example, does not exist in a pure vacuum of ideal and child-centred philosophy. Within individual countries, and in cultures and communities that make up those countries, research is revealing different issues that are foregrounded in children's lives and the ways in which ideas of child rights have developed their own localized meanings and drivers for change. These driving forces, ideas and interpretations are created by interactions between the nature of the society and communities children live within and the wishes or intentions of children, young people and adults, acting individually and in groups. The UN recognizes this, asserting that individual states need to realize the UNCRC to 'the maximum extent of their available resources' (UN, 1989 introduction). The UN's Committee on the Rights of the Child reviews progress, identifies barriers and issues periodic reports on how well it thinks a country is responding (see http://www.ohchr.org/EN/HRBodies/CRC). In some countries, governments have created mechanisms to review and support the implementation of the UNCRC. Organizations working for, and with, children also address positive developments and lack of progress. All of these processes often draw on research. Viewed this way, it becomes useful to see what research can tell us about the ways the notion of child rights is changing and developing: what people want and intend – the variations of difference created by the different contexts. Table 1.1 gives some sense of this diversity of research and the contexts of child rights.

This approach doesn't see 'child rights' as a monolithic one-size-fits-all phenomenon, with a basic set of commands that mean the same in every community and for every child irrespective of differences of age, gender, race, ability or sexuality. Rather, it sees child rights as something that has a variety of meanings: some work at international or national level, others at the local level of a particular school or health centre in a specific community which a child lives within. This book will identify and consider some of the questions arising from this perspective:

What can be learnt from the many different ways that child rights are being seen and interpreted?

Table 1.1 Research and examples of different contexts of child rights

Area of rights	Research questions	Discussion in this book
Poverty	In what ways is research into child rights and poverty being drawn on to lobby for change?	Pages 216–18
Protection	What is research showing us about how to better protect children?	Pages 209–10, 226–7, 251, 260
Child labour	What dilemmas about children and work is research addressing?	Page 66
Inclusion and children with disabilities	What are different states' responses showing us about how best to realize children with disabilities' rights?	Pages 134–40

What can we learn from the experiences of children and adults to date, now that actual responses in policy, law and practice have been attempted over the three decades since the UNCRC came into being?

In this way, the emphasis on the UNCRC is matched by a recognition of the many other initiatives, forces and ideas at work to champion, develop and test the ideas and practices in the lived experience of many communities and individuals.

Lundy (2012), for example, analysed the ways in which 27 European states had responded to the UNCRC's articles connected to children's right to education by examining policy documents: 'specific issues to be addressed by the states party are: the right to education, including vocational training and guidance (Article 28); the aims of education (Article 29) with reference also to quality of education; the cultural rights of children belonging to indigenous and minority groups (Article 30); and education on human rights and civic education' (2012, 397). Her analysis identifies areas that are common across many states, but also how the responses and development needs of the different states vary, reflecting our earlier point about the diversity of contexts. In terms of the relationships between the UNCRC, education and children with disabilities, for example, she notes some themes that are connected and which run across different state responses under a 'Summary of Committee's recommendations for governments' in terms of the Committee's policy recommendations. The following are two, connected, examples from this 'Summary':

- *Access* Research to identify the root causes of non-participation and low attendance; positive incentives to attend school for low income families; specially adapted curricula; prohibiting use of fees and providing financial support for books, transport etc.
- *Disability* Inclusion of children in mainstream schools; legislation prohibiting discrimination; develop early identification and intervention programmes; resources for specialised teacher training and equipment; stability in teacher employment; removal of physical barriers to enable effective access; public awareness campaigns. (2012, 401)

However, there are also variations. She notes, in relation to children with disabilities and rights, that

- some states, including Bulgaria, Hungary and Latvia were criticised for 'high levels of institutionalization of children with disabilities'
- others, for example, the Czech Republic and Ireland were 'commended on good legislative protection but encouraged to continue with their efforts to ensure that children were in fact integrated in mainstream settings'. (2012, 401)

Weakness in implementation was linked variously to ongoing prejudices towards children with disabilities, connected to

- lack of resources (France)
- lack of availability of integrated provision (Luxembourg). (2012, 402)

She notes that in each case, the committee makes recommendations such as

- public awareness campaigns,
- legislation prohibiting discrimination in access,
- investment in teacher training. (2012, 402)

This way of examining children's rights, and a convention such as the UNCRC, helps us to see that there are differences within societies and between different countries. These are affected by a variety of contextual factors. As this book will show, we are learning about the ways in which such factors can be understood as creating positive relationships between rights and children's lives but also how they limit or stop children's rights from being realized.

What do the different responses to the UNCRC reveal?

The following offers a sample of the UNICEF summary of the UNCRC made for children, followed by a brief illustration from recent research in the United Kingdom made by children regarding their critique of the UK government's response to the convention.

Key points: Perspectives on children's rights and children

Excerpt from UNICEF's summary of the UNCRC for children:

Article 1 Everyone under 18 years of age has all rights in this convention.

Article 4 Governments should make these rights available to children.

Article 12 Children have the right to say what they think should happen, when adults are making decisions that affect them, and to have their opinions taken into account.

Article 19 Governments should ensure that children are properly cared for, and protect them from violence, abuse and neglect by their parents, or anyone else who looks after them.

Article 28 All children and young people should have a right to a primary education, which should be free.

Article 31 All children have a right to relax and play, and to join in a wide range of activities.

If every child, regardless of their sex, ethnic origin, social status, language, age, nationality or religion has these rights, then they also have a responsibility to respect each other in a humane way.

(www.unicef.org.uk)

The above material is one of many examples of the ways in which different organizations in many countries have created versions of the UNCRC which

use language and images to make the convention more 'accessible'. The following image is from a UK playground, for example, illustrating an attempt to help children access the UNCRC.

However, as the following examples of research show, access is more complex than providing 'child-friendly' materials. The first example concerns two instances of research by Children's Rights Alliance for England's (CRAE), conducted in 2008 and seven years later in 2015.

Example of research 1: 'What do they know?' CRAE Report on the UNCRC (Davey, 2008) and CRAE's 'See it, say it, change it' (2015)

'What do they know?' (2008)

The Children's Rights Alliance for England's (CRAE) 'What Do They Know?' report (Davey, 2008) contained the views and experiences of children and young people relating to the implementation of the UN Committee on the Rights of the Child. The research was conducted by young people and involved 1,362 children and young people who filled in an online survey and 346 children and young people in focus group interviews. A delegation of 12 children and young people presented this evidence directly to the UN Committee on the Rights of the Child in June 2008 at its pre-session working group in Geneva.

> At present, it is clear that (UNCRC)....implementation in England, both in legislation and practice, often leaves much to be desired. Children and young people, both in the online surveys and in the focus group interviews, gave very clear messages about what is important to them: knowing and being able to use their rights; being part of a family (meaning different things for different children); being respected, listened to and taken seriously; not being stereotyped; getting a good education; and living in a good area with a strong sense of community.

The research revealed that very few children and young people knew what their rights were, and, of those who did, few knew how to act if rights were being denied or violated. The following gives brief illustrative examples of some of the key points raised, and of children and young people's specific comments:

In 2002 the UN Committee on the Rights of the Child recommended more effective mechanisms to ensure the systematic, meaningful and effective participation of all groups of children in society. In 2008, however, the UN Committee expressed disappointment that 'there has been little progress to enshrine Article 12 in education law and policy'. In our education survey, it was noted that although most schools operated a school council, only one in three children and young people (30%) felt that their views were always listened to by their school, and that primary schools were often better at involving children in decision-making than secondary schools.

They think because we're small and they're big they know better ... and they just treat us like we're nothing, like we're just a puff of cloud or something. (Child under-11; Davey, 2008, 15)

Although some children and young people were very aware of a growing change in attitudes towards hearing what they had to say, many felt that children and young people's participation in these exercises was often tokenistic:

Can't remember how many times I've been sat in the chair, and someone's asked what do you not like about Durham and nothing's changed. (16- to 18-year-olds)

Yeah, they ask you your say and then they say they're listening, but then they don't take no notice of it so you think, what's the point of saying it? (Child in care; Davey, 2008, 16)

The research revealed that one of the changes identified by the respondents 'raised most often by younger children' was for the UK government to ban smacking and for support to be offered to parents to find alternative ways of raising children 'that did not involve the use of physical force':

I would also stop smacking because if you do something violent to your child, they'll do it to their child, and it will go on which I think now would be bad, because then it will teach the whole world to smack and be violent. (Child under-11)

Davey notes that the constant requests parallel demands from the UN Committee on the Rights of the Child in 1995, 2002 and 2008 for the UK government 'to remove the "reasonable chastisement/ punishment" defence and to prohibit all corporal punishment in the family' (Davey, 2008, 39). The UK government has consistently refused to stop such violence, although many other countries have done so. Further details on this issue can be found on pages 197–9.

'See it, say it, change it' (2015)

The project was overseen by a steering group of children of different ages, reflecting diversity in terms of class, race, gender and sexuality and included children with disabilities. Its stated aim was to review the state of children's human rights in England, including 'the ways in which children's rights are not being met and recommend changes that need to be made to the UN Committee and the UK Government' (2015, 5). An online survey, responded to by 850 children aged 5–17 and 16 focus groups, involving 137 children of a similar age range, were used. The focus groups deliberately engaged with children whose voices the steering group felt were often 'not heard', including children with disabilities, those who had contact with the police, had lived in state care, were in poverty or were from minority groups including travellers. The research included topics of respect, freedom, family life, living in state care, education, health and wellbeing, play and leisure. The following offers a sample of the views expressed:

- 'Coming from a deprived area in London and growing up in poverty, I feel like I am not treated with respect and equality but instead I am dismissed and pushed aside due to my class background. I feel this in all aspects of my life. I feel like the current political system is apathetic towards my views and needs based purely upon my place in society' (Female, 17) (2015, 12).
- Nearly 40 per cent of children who answered the survey said that there was not enough support for mental health issues. They identified a range of issues that had an impact on children's mental health. The top ones were:
  Bullying (83 per cent);
  School pressure (76 per cent);
  Issues at home (75 per cent);
  Exams (74 per cent).
- 'All of these things increase the amount of stress on the child and may cause them to feel unhappy and depressed. These things can increase the likelihood of disorders such as anxiety and illnesses like depression as they target the child's mental health and drastically lower their self-esteem' (Female, 14).
- Children who responded to the survey reported feeling stressed and anxious a lot of the time. Over a third of children said they are stressed all of the time or most of the time (2015, 33).
- There was little evidence that children are consulted on play facilities in their local communities. When asked the question

'have you ever been asked for your views about play and leisure facilities?':

70 per cent had not been asked for their view on what activities are on at their local leisure centre;

66 per cent had not been asked about provision at their local youth club;

60 per cent had never been consulted about new equipment in their local playground.

- Only 9 per cent of children who answered the survey said their views are always listened to when changes are made to play facilities in their local area (2015, 46).

Reflections on the research

Activity 1

Reviewing the two samples of research in Example 1, what are common themes?

Activity 2

Looking at the 'Excerpt from UNICEF's summary of the UNCRC for children', find examples from the research extracts that relate to the different articles summarized there. What does the research show about why realizing that right is important to children's lives?

Activity 3

One organization, CRAE, is responsible for both pieces of research, with a gap of seven years between them. Discuss why it is important to keep undertaking such research and reviewing children's experiences and views?

Example of research 2: scepticism in professionals

Lyle (2014) was employed by the Welsh government to train key stakeholders in education in Pupil Participation and her research reports on this work. The initiative included teachers, head teachers and local authority advisors, 'to ensure that the UNCRC, in particular Article 12 (the child who is capable of forming his or her own views has the right to express those views freely in all matters affecting the child) of the UNCRC is understood and taken seriously by schools' (2014, 223). In contextualizing her research, Lyle notes a variety of responses by the Welsh government in relation to children's rights. This included the creating the post of an independent Children's Rights Commissioner for Wales in 2001 to safeguard and promote the rights and welfare of children, and, in 2004, the Welsh government (WG) setting out its core aims for children and young people, mapping them onto the articles of the UNCRC (WG, 2004). She notes that Wales has been described as the first country in the United Kingdom to put the UNCRC as the basis of all its work across government by passing the 'Rights of Children and Young Persons (Wales) Measure' (WG, 2011). In March 2012, the Children's Rights Scheme was developed and subsequently approved by the Welsh National Assembly. It was designed to ensure the UNCRC is taken into account in all policy and practice involving children and young people. One aspects of related practice is that

> every local authority is required to set up a Children and Young People's Forum to ensure local organisations listen to children and to provide representatives for the Council of Funky Dragon (the children and young people's assembly). Funky Dragon meets regularly with Welsh Assembly Ministers to provide input to key policies and is a good example of participatory action that ensures young people are active participants in the development of policy, not just consulted on policy. (2014, 217–218)

However, she noted that 'during that training, it became evident that there was widespread scepticism about the Welsh government's policy and resistance to its implementation in schools' (2014, 223). Her research included the responses of the adults she was working with to the training, and she discusses an aspect of this in the following way, it was

> commonly assumed children were incapable of forming their own views because they are not old enough; therefore, age becomes a key objection to the UNCRC in schools, especially in the early years and infant classroom (age 4–7). (2014, 220)

Examples 1 and 2: reflections on the research

Activity 1

Reviewing Examples 1 and 2, how would you summarize the issues the research reveals relating to the implementation of the UNCRC?

Activity 2

What do you think could be concluded about the importance of children being aware of the UNCRC and how to act on their rights?

Activity 3

Why do you think some adult responses to the UNCRC might be to be 'sceptical' or to hinder or stop children being aware of their rights and how to act on their rights? Consider what alternative responses adults might have – for example, thinking of how to enable younger children to understand their rights. After you've noted your own ideas read the following 'Example of research' and then return to this reflection and think about your response.

The following is an example of recent research that challenges the kinds of traditional, negative stereotypes of young children's capabilities found by Lyle. Such work responds to the UNCRC by looking at how to change ideas and practices, including the creation of new pedagogical approaches.

Example of research: young children and rights and a 'bottom-up' perspective

Research conducted by Harcourt and Hägglund (2013), looked at very young children's experience of rights. Two early childhood settings were invited to participate in the study: one in Sweden and the other in Australia. The researchers describe the situation in Australia where, despite efforts in some sectors to implement Article 12, participation by children was limited in practice and that young children were especially excluded. Within education for example, they assert that there had been no involvement of young children in key areas of policy and guidance for practice. Such neglect and lack of effort by adult policy makers and designers is especially common in many states in relation to young children (Carr et al., 2002; Smith, 2011). However, recent developments, such as the work that Harcourt and Hägglund have developed, challenges ideas that young children cannot be consulted and involved in rights-related matters, directly contradicting adult ideas such as those encountered by Lyle (2014): that they should be excluded due to their levels of experience, development or their capacities for communication. This is manifested in a number of ways, from how politicians act, through to training, for example:

> *The provision of adequate and systemic training and/or sensitisation on children's rights among professional groups working with and for children, are rare. This then impacts on the capacity of young children to realise their rights in early childhood settings. (Harcourt and Hägglund, 2013, 288)*

Harcourt and Hägglund's work was informed by what some call a *bottom-up perspective* (Katz, 1992; Harcourt and Keen, 2012), which involves 'recommending critical indices of quality from the child perspective that could serve to inform adults and policy-makers through the evidence provided by the child experience' (2013, 289). The children in the Australian setting were invited to discuss the topic of rights with the researchers in self-selected small groups and the researchers note that some of 'the rights that children were constructing for themselves – as opposed to those gifted to them by adults in the UNCRC – were different and related very much to their lived experiences' (2013, 292). Topics included the following:

- Reforming adult decision making that did not account for children's views;
- global issues such as famine and war;
- being safe and secure;
- a sense of justice.

The following examples are from this research with four to five-year-olds:

Kai: Children have the right to live. We waste too much food and all the people in other countries don' t have food. We need to send food on a plane to help. (2013, 294)

Picture drawn by Josh about rights
With permission of Professor Deborah Harcourt

Josh: I have tree rights. I have the right to climb a tree with my hands.
(2013 294)

Further discussion of this research is featured in Chapter 2 (pages 72–4).

Reflections on the research

Activity 1

The research by Harcourt and Hägglund refers to training and 'sensitization' as key to adult–child relationships and children's rights. How do you see this 'sensitization' as being important in relation to the role of adults in young children's awareness and experience of their rights?

Activity 2

The research by Lyle and by Harcourt and Hägglund connects to issues about *age* and *capability*. How do you see the expressions made by Josh and Kai within the research by Harcourt and Hägglund in relation to the teacher scepticism about young children's capabilities noted by Lyle in the earlier example of research on pages 13–14?

Looking at Lyle's (2014) findings and the research by Harcourt and Hägglund (2013) together is an example of how it can be useful to bring together different research findings to gain a critical understanding of the lived realities of children's rights. Chapters 2 and 3 will continue this critical reflection on how research can help us deepen our learning about the nature and realization of children's rights. Critiques relate to the way policies and practices have been formulated – from a macro or international – level to the smaller scale of local policies and practices. Many years on from the UNCRC, for example, is it important to ask what can be learned from these critiques? This book will introduce some of these criticisms and explore the questions they ask. In addition, the ideas of child rights have also been tested by beliefs, attitudes and the lived contact with individuals, communities, national and transnational forces that are directly or indirectly opposed to child rights. A key consideration here is whether we can see certain patterns or issues which are emerging? One reason to identify these is to ask what can be learnt from the patterns in order to improve children's lives, and to see whether child rights as a concept, or as a set of emergent practices, needs rethinking?

These are the ideas that are central to the work of this book. We will establish some of the cornerstones of the initial child rights movement and pay attention to key developments such as the UNCRC in Chapter 2. However, we will also look at some patterns in the different responses: critiques, challenges and antagonisms to the ideas and practices of rights as well as the excellence of initiatives and drivers of change. In reviewing the contemporary situation in Chapters 2 and 3, our intention is to look at child rights to see what is working for children and those who live and work with them, as well as what needs rethinking and changing in order to see children's relationship with rights in new ways. The following sections introduce three key emergent patterns of issues within the contemporary response to rights:

- The rights dynamic
- A rights agenda
- Rights-informed approaches to relating to children

What issues are emerging in relation to rethinking children's rights?

Emerging issues: the rights dynamic

Positive developments following on from initiatives such as the UNCRC have included the many ways in which a *rights dynamic* has been created. This dynamic concerns the ways in which ideas about rights have acted as a catalyst or tinder within countries and societies. The impact has included laws or policies that have been created, or altered, as a response to the dynamic energy created by child rights ideas. As this book will illustrate, these are within different arenas and spaces: from the justice system to policies and practices in play, education and medicine. This macro level of intervention then permeates through to the training of professionals and to the micro level of practices that relates to children in specific courts, schools or hospitals.

This rights dynamic also affects the ways debate and discussion occur. The relationships between laws, policies and practices change and develop, or specific laws and policies are created in response to new ideas about child rights. In this way, the concept and increased visibility of child rights is an emerging force that is used when international and national decisions are made in political arenas concerning the formation of laws or policies, for example. Looked at from this angle, the child rights dynamic provides a pressure for action enabling complex issues to be debated and understood. As Chapter 2 will discuss, this creates an impetus for change, particularly in rights-influenced directions.

On a micro level, the rights dynamic can be seen as a lever to promote developments in local policy and practice. The rights dynamic here becomes a force within a setting or space where services are provided for children, or where children live. The energy created by knowledge of a rights perspective can affect how adults working with children see and review their work, for example, influencing how they create spaces and provision for children. Chapters 6 and 7 will look at how this dynamic, created by knowledge and promotion of rights, is present within children's experiences of families and in settings working with children.

As the book will reveal, the actual reflection and impact of children's rights in laws and policies are extremely varied. The level of awareness by children and adults alike is affected by a number of factors, including the ways that a society sees the position of children from political, economic, cultural and religious perspectives. In its 2008 survey, based on responses of over a 1,000 children, the Children's Rights Alliance of England (CRAE) reported that, though under Article 42 of the UNCRC governments are obliged to widely disseminate information to children and young people about their rights, in England a 'majority of respondents said they knew very little about the UNCRC' and of those that had, '82% had not received this information through their school' (CRAE, 2008, 17–18). A survey conducted by the same organization in 2015 revealed little had changed. Of the 819 children who responded to the survey and the question 'have you heard of the CRC?', 46 per cent said they had not heard of it and a further 10 per cent were not sure. When asked "how much do you know about the CRC?", only one in five said 'a lot'. The majority of children (56 per cent) said they only knew 'a little' (CRAE, 2015, 10).

The following offers a contrasting picture from Norway, drawing on two research projects.

Example of research: the rights dynamic at work – Norway

(i) Children's understandings of the UNCRC

A different situation is revealed by research undertaken in Norway (Sandbaek and Hafdis Einarsson, 2008) that looked at children's awareness of the UNCRC. This gives a relatively positive picture of children's awareness of their rights. A total of 1,274 children and young people from different regions within the country and from different backgrounds participated in the survey; 1,139 answered questionnaires, while 135 attended qualitative interviews. The respondents were asked whether they had heard of the convention and, if so, through which channel. Some questions concerned the content of the convention and whether the children thought it was important to them. A further question asked whether they believed they enjoyed rights in various everyday arenas such as their home, school, in leisure activities and in wider society. In sharp contrast to the Children's Rights Alliance of England's research findings, half of the Norwegian children had heard of the convention. There was some variation between the different regions of Norway, from 43 to 67 per cent. The report discusses the different ways in which children were aware, noting, for example, the respondents' references to a short version of the convention in poster form issued by the Norwegian Ministry of Children and Equality:

> *Two of the girls remembered seeing the poster and one said: 'Oh yes, that one! It's hanging in the classroom.' The children at a day care centre ... recalled what it said, that 'all children are entitled to have fun, to play, to have a place to live and to be fed'. (Sandbaek and Hafdis Einarsson, 2008, 14)*

One of the questions asked what the children thought the UNCRC was about. The research presented the following examples of children's perspectives based on the qualitative interviews and open boxes in the questionnaires given to pupils:

- I think it says that children in Norway should be happy at school and at home.
- I think it's about finding out what it's like for children in Norway, and it's about children's rights.
- That children should have all rights like going to school, having a home, being fed etc.
- I think it says that children should be happy and not afraid, but feel safe.
- Children's rights, that all children are entitled to decide and to be fed, go to school and to be loved.
- It's about children having rights to have a say and to have an opinion without being punished.
- It's about rules for children. It's sort of a book of the rights of children.
- I think it's about the rights of children in countries that are members of the UN.

(Sandbaek and Hafdis Einarsson, 2008, 15)

Example of research: the rights dynamic at work – Norway

(ii) Legal implementation of the UNCRC

Lundy et al. (2012) conducted research into the implementation of the UNCRC in 12 different countries, using a combination of documentary analysis and interview. The following is an illustrative example of their findings from Norway:

> According to interviewees, Parliament's decision to incorporate the CRC was accompanied by an accord to transpose it into relevant sectoral laws. Norway has continued to make changes to its legislation across a variety of areas. In particular, it has integrated the general principles of the CRC (mainly Article 3, the best interests principle and Article 12, the right to be heard) into legislation within a range of areas, including laws on pre-school education, parental responsibility and notably immigration. Section 3 of the Kindergarten Act, for example, enshrines children's right to:

- express their views on the day-to-day activities of the kindergarten,
- be given the opportunity to take active part in planning and assessing the activities of the kindergarten on a regular basis,
- have their views to be given due weight according to their age and maturity. (2012, 59)

The research also indicated that 'The Children's Act 2005' also integrated the 'best interests principle' from the UNCRC, while Section 33 'recognises the evolving capacities of the child' (2012, 59). They note other areas:

> The Patient's Rights Act 1999 states that a child's parents or others with parental responsibility must hear the child's views before consent is given. It also says that children from 12 years onwards are entitled to give their opinion on all matters affecting their health. Significantly, the best interests of the child is also integrated in the Immigration Act 2008 (Section 38). Interviewees considered this a particularly important achievement given that competing public interest considerations make it difficult to advocate for children's rights in the area of immigration. (2012, 59)

Reflections on the research

Activity 1

In 'Example of research 1', what roles and actions does the research reveal adults and adult organizations have in relation to children being aware of and accessing their rights?

What relationships might there be between the kinds of implementation described in Example 1 and what the research in Example 2 reveals about what children know?

Activity 2

Compare the comments from children in Example 2 with Table 2.2 (page 52) in Chapter 2. It is possible to see the accuracy of many of the children's statements in relation to the UNCRC as well as children's own perceptions and language. The research report notes: 'These quotes show that while children linked the Convention to their own situation, several viewed it in a general perspective as something that applies to all children' (Sandbaek and Hafdis Einarsson, 2008, 15).

Activity 3

An earlier comment in this chapter discussed the importance of enabling children and adults to know about and to understand children's rights, arguing that 'the energy created by knowledge of a rights perspective can affect how adults working with children see and review their work, for example, influencing how they create spaces and provision for children'.

Compare the situation revealed by the research that showed English children were often unaware of rights, with the picture created by this research from Norway. How do you think knowledge of rights and the impact of rights are connected?

Refer to the discussion of different models of rights education in Chapter 7 (page 257). What differences might there be for adults and children living and working together in a country where children knew very little about their rights and one in which the children were informed about child rights and their implications?

A rights dynamic, then, concerns how child rights as a concept can create an impetus for change, their presence acts as a catalyst, a meeting point and a pressure for action.

Key points: emerging issues – the rights dynamic

- The way 'child rights' as a concept has provided a language and framework to see children in ways that emphasize their role as rights holders, and to draw attention to areas such as inequality and the need for radical changes.

- The dynamic energy created by child rights as a critical position to lobby for positive change in children's lives and the communities they are a part of.
- The impetus that the idea of child rights has had on macro levels of international and national government.
- The impact of child rights in rethinking and changing the day-to-day lives of children in the spaces they inhabit and in relation to the people and institutions they connect with.

Emerging issues: a rights agenda

If a rights dynamic concerns the ways child rights can animate and create an impetus for change, the idea of a rights agenda concerns the pattern of issues which have emerged within the movements for change. This child rights agenda has fuelled much enquiry and research involving children and their lives. In their review of children's rights literature Reynaert et al. argue that the UNCRC has contributed to a changed agenda in the ways that children are viewed and responded to in areas such as research and policy: the children's rights movement considers children as social actors, as active agents and autonomous, independent human beings in constructing their lives in their own right (2009, 521). They argue that the agenda for change was affected by this conceptual shift: 'the competent child with participation rights also took root in policymaking' (2009, 522). They note that one of the examples of the actions taken to realize this agenda at state level was via the creation of 'an institution such as a children's ombudsperson' who 'can play an essential role in protecting children's rights at policy level, and is considered as an important innovation in the slipstream of the UNCRC' (2009, 522). They, along with many others, argue for the importance of rights to be understood in context, rather than being delivered in a 'one-size-fits-all' approach, and for the need to understand and engage with the many different experiences and lives of children: to 'take into account the living conditions, the social, economical and historical contexts in which children grow up, which can be very diverse, and which are the environments in which children's rights are to be realized' (2009, 528).

This does not mean that rights can be waived or altered in ways that diminish the intention of a convention such as the UNCRC, but rather that particular ways of interpreting that right can make it as relevant as possible for the different contexts of children and for different children in those contexts.

The following examples help to illustrate the ways in which the particular focus of such agendas for action, change and research informed by rights varies according to local situations. These are two examples from Africa.

Child rights agenda: example 1

The first example is from an organization that calls itself the 'Child Rights Agenda' (CRA), a Nigerian network of organizations aiming to advance the rights and interest of children. It summarizes rights in relation to all children having 'the inalienable rights to grow up, free of poverty and hunger, to receive a quality education, to be protected from infectious and preventable diseases including HIV/AIDS, to grow up in a clean and healthy environment'. The agenda here is translated into objectives. These are as follows:

Objectives:

1. To provide an end to all forms of discrimination and exclusion against children since every girl and boy is born free and equal in dignity using multidimensional approaches with the support and participation of various key stakeholders.
2. To promote the value of literacy for every child and within the communities they live in. (www.projects.tigweb.org/cranigeria)

Child rights agenda: example 2

The United Nations Office for the Coordination of Humanitarian Affairs reports on another perspective on child rights creating an agenda for action in West Africa. The summary describes a meeting co-ordinated by the regional office of Save the Children Sweden and the Economic Community of West African States (ECOWAS) in 2002. Members of the armed forces of 13 West African countries and of non-governmental organizations ended a five-day meeting in Dakar, Senegal, with a call to reaffirm a commitment to 'international legal standards that protect children' affected by armed conflict:

A declaration approved by the participants in the meeting called on ECOWAS to ask member states to commit personnel, time and energy to mainstreaming children's rights and child protection (including the non-recruitment of children into armed forces, and responsible sexual behaviour towards children) in military training for all members of security forces. Another recommendation coming out of the Dakar meeting was for member states to ensure reporting mechanisms that allow military and civilian personnel to report abuses of children's rights during conflict. (United Nations Office for the Coordination of Humanitarian Affairs, 2002)

This emerging child rights agenda is also repositioning children's experiences as worthy of consideration from a child's own perspective. As Chapter 4 will show, one example of such a shift has been from a position where interest chiefly lay in adults' perceptions, opinions or concerns regarding children's lives and experiences, to one that is more concerned with acting from a position informed by children's own perspectives. This idea often uses the metaphor of children's voice. It involves work whereby children are given tools to examine and express their ideas and opinions. An example of this is children accessing decision-making processes such as meetings or committees within organizations or areas of provision that feature in their lives. Another example involves decision-making processes using materials that enable children to understand, communicate or take part. This aspect of the child rights agenda often demands children's involvement in decision making and in the implementation of their ideas within areas such as service provision. These aspects of this agenda will be described further in Chapter 7. This shift has seen the child rights agenda to be one that is increasingly led by children's own perceptions of child rights and by children's ideas about changes needed in their lives. Originally, much of the impetus for change, the perspectives on what changes needed to be made, how change was progressing and the analysis of discoveries and barriers to rights-based actions were mostly, or completely, based on the opinions and ideas of adults. The examples of research in Chapter 4 illustrate that a part of the difference resulting from the child rights agenda involves the presence of children's own perceptions, experiences and demands within the forces that create and affect their worlds.

In his paper on 'Social Inclusion as Solidarity: Rethinking the Child Rights Agenda', Bach (2002) summarizes a theme present within a number of commentators on emergent responses to child rights: the importance of connecting an agenda that emphasizes rights with a commitment to challenging social exclusion.

Calls for inclusion as valued recognition are growing as the dilemma of the 'rights revolution' becomes clear – a context where rights are expanded and exclusion is entrenched. A social inclusion agenda could address this dilemma by promoting social solidarity across expanding social, ethnic and cultural differences that increasingly characterize and divide so many societies, often in destructive ways. Policy analysis should reveal ways that social, economic and political arrangements systematically undermine social solidarity by devaluing certain people and groups, even though their rights are assured. (Bach, 2002, 4)

The key point Bach is making concerns the need to ensure that rights do not become an isolated arena, that the complex forces at work that exclude, silence and disenfranchise children are recognized and addressed. The child rights agenda is one that needs to engage with areas of 'social, economic and political' concerns in a way that promotes inclusion and equity.

Emerging issues: rights-informed approaches to relating to children

A key element of the emergent rights agenda is enabling a rethinking of the way relationships are created. This includes the ways in which organizations that govern, or that provide services, form a relationship with children. This book will focus especially on this as a principal issue within the ways in which rights are affecting children's lives. This can involve a child rights-informed approach to how policies are created, and a rights-informed approach within the policies made that relate to how workers conduct interactions with children. The former might involve children in the creation of a setting's policies, while the latter might concern the way adults engage with children in areas such as choice or involvement in decision making within everyday contact.

This connects with an important aspect of the ways in which the rights dynamic has begun to affect children's lives: it is enabling children to be seen and to be treated differently by adults. It is part of the shifts in the ways children and young people see themselves, their relationships with each other, the adults they encounter and broader organizations that connect with their lives, such as national or local government. A theme within this shift has concerned children's representation of themselves, the empowerment of children and the valuing of children's perspectives on a range of issues. It emphasizes and recognizes the ways that children can actively take part in areas such as decision making and recognizes children's autonomy and capacity.

A number of ways of working have become allied with this change. On the one hand, the influence of the philosophy and concepts of children's rights can be seen to be allied with the emergence of the new sociology of childhood. This is typified by emphasis on children as active, engaged agents in their own lives, challenging former stereotypes that saw children as passive or incapable. One of the forms this has taken, and a framework that runs through this book's consideration of rights, can be seen as rights-informed ways of relating to children. The following key points notes some ways that will be explored within this book and which research is telling us are being used in many societies.

Key points: rights-informed ways of relating to children

- Ways of involving children in decisions about their bodies, spaces and futures.
- Ways of perceiving children's lives and experiences from a child's perspective rather than from the perspective of adult ideas and opinions about what children see, want or need.
- Specific services that are designed with children in mind rather than adult services with no, or little, adaptation for children.
- Spaces designed and created for children with input into the design, regulation or use of those spaces by children.
- Looking to see how children can be seen and engaged with as active, capable and as experts in their own lives.
- Changing adult roles and relationships with children in services and provision that try to address inequalities.
- Emphasizing child-orientated ways of participating or communicating, such as play.
- Identifying and addressing the particular ways in which social divisions within society concerning areas such as poverty, race, gender, disability and sexuality affect children, rather than seeing their impact on children's lives as identical to their impact on adults.
- Enquiry through research into children's experiences and ideas about a part of their lives or service.
- Reviewing the nature and role of policy and practice and rewriting documents and guidelines from a rights perspective.

- Changing decision-making processes to include children in decisions about themselves, events or issues that affect them or within organizations that work for or with them.
- The role of advocacy within representation of children's views, opinions and decisions.

Rights-informed ways of relating to children in healthcare

An example of the impact of the ideas of rights-informed ways of relating to children is guidance material published by the UK General Medical Council on communication with children:

> Effective communication between doctors and children and young people is essential to the provision of good care. You should find out what children, young people and their parents want and need to know, what issues are important to them, and what opinions or fears they have about their health or treatment. In particular you should:
>
> a. involve children and young people in discussions about their care
> b. be honest and open with them and their parents, while respecting confidentiality
> c. listen to and respect their views about their health, and respond to their concerns and preferences
> d. explain things using language or other forms of communication they can understand
> e. consider how you and they use non-verbal communication, and the surroundings in which you meet them
> f. give them opportunities to ask questions, and answer these honestly and to the best of your ability
> g. do all you can to make open and truthful discussion possible, taking into account that this can be helped or hindered by the involvement of parents or other people
> h. give them the same time and respect that you would give to adult patients.
>
> You should make it clear that you are available to see children and young people on their own if that is what they want. You should avoid giving the impression (whether directly, through reception staff or in any other way) that they cannot access services without a parent.

You should take children and young people's views seriously and not dismiss or appear to dismiss their concerns or contributions. Disabled children and young people can feel particularly disadvantaged in this respect. (http://www.gmc-uk.org/guidance/ethical_guidance/children_guidance_14_21_communication.asp)

In 2010, the British Medical Association published a 'Children and Young People Toolkit' to support doctors, children and their families. It consists of a series of cards, 'about specific areas relating to the examination and treatment of people in England, Wales, and Northern Ireland who are aged under 18 years, and in Scotland under 16 years. Separate Cards have been produced identifying factors to be considered when assessing competence and determining "best interests", and sensitive areas including child protection and access to sexual health services' (2010, 3). The rethinking of relationships, of which these are examples, has been manifested in new structures and bodies, reflecting a rights approach to the creation of new spaces for children to participate in. As Pain says, 'there are many ... spaces and avenues of power where children and young people are denied access or a voice' (2000, 151). The emergence of new spaces marks a shift in a variety of attempts to respond to the rights agenda's demands of participation. The following table samples some of these new spaces which are discussed later in this book.

Key points: rights-informed new spaces

In local and national government:

Children's parliaments or councils.

(See page 125)

In law:

The ways in which a child rights approach can be used to reassess areas such as youth justice and the way the law features in children's lives.

(See page 167)

Early years and education:

Representation of children on decision making or governing bodies such as schools councils.

> *Seeing educational settings and practices as spaces to implement and interpret children's rights.*
>
> (See pages 15–17 and 162–6)
>
> In hospitals and social care:
>
> *Provision that is created to serve children in the creation of places and linked practices that are especially suited to children's use of health and social care services.*
>
> (See pages 183–6)

A further examination of material involving rethinking children's rights and the idea of 'rights-informed ways of relating to children' can be found on pages 102–6, in relation to new ideas about children's consent.

How can negative responses to the rights agenda be used to help rethink children's rights?

Other responses to the child rights dynamic and agenda are less positive. As this book will show, in thinking about the development and implementation of a rights agenda a constant series of 'negative' themes, or problems, emerge. Identifying the ways in which they have manifested themselves can help clarify how areas need to change – both at a macro and micro level. Some of the key issues which feature in this book are summarized below:

Key points: children's rights – problems and challenges

- Adult power used to prioritize the needs of adults, rather than those of children, in thinking about and taking action in relation to, child rights.

- Countries separating children into those who are 'worthy' of rights, and those who are not.
- Countries separating rights off from other processes, such as poverty or racism, that have a negative effect on children and the families and communities they live in.
- Entrenched customs and practices that resist changes that would benefit children.
- The creation of the appearance of responding to children's rights – a 'rights veneer' but, in reality, making no real change or having little real impact on children's lives.

Emerging issues: a divided response

One kind of response can be summarized as a divided response to rights. Here adults separate off some children as worthy of a particular right, but see others as not worthy of the same rights. Hence, this is where rights are seen to be applicable to some children, but not to others. This is not to deny that in some spheres it is appropriate to make certain rights available to children based on their age or maturity. The Children's Rights Alliance for England, for example, draws attention to such differences when it talks about the differences between voting rights and protective rights:

> While CRAE strongly supports the extension of voting rights to 16 and 17-year-olds, this must not be confused with debates about 'age of majority'. There are a whole range of protective rights that 16 and 17-year-olds have, within domestic and international laws, related to child abuse, labour, involvement in war and juvenile justice, for example. These rights recognize the difficult circumstances and challenges facing many teenagers, not connected to their capacity as individual people to vote. (2000, 15)

The idea of a divided response becomes problematic when it concerns situations where rights are not given to some children or are removed. The removal of rights in this context is seen to be based on adult opinions or prejudices about the way children can, or should, live their lives, and where these opinions are not rooted in any evidence of benefit to children and/or primarily serve adult interests. Chapter 3, for example, looks at the ways in which the United Kingdom deliberately maintained an opt-out to allow it to deny children their rights. It traces how pressures to remove this opt-out have resulted in a changed position and some degree of benefit for such children.

for many years the UK government had *deliberately* retained an opt-out of the UNCRC. This opt out allowed child migrants and asylum seekers to be locked up without judicial scrutiny. So, whereas the UNCRC obliges nations to place the 'best interests' of a child first, the opt-out meant that the UK government did not need to apply it to these children. Therefore, officials could lock them up, sometimes for weeks or months pending deportation. (Chapter 3, this volume, page 96)

Other research has identified the ways prejudices based on professional assumptions and frameworks can limit children:

Our research suggests that developmental psychology has the biggest current impact on teachers' conception of childhood that is pervasive and undermines the potential of the UNCRC to impact on practice in schools. In contrast, new inter-disciplinary narratives of childhood that critique developmental approaches to understanding children can offer a different and more positive view of children today that has the potential to impact on teachers. (Lyle, 2014, 229)

Chapter 4 looks at issues concerning the ways in which divisions based on adult stereotypes of age and competency are being challenged by new research into the capabilities and rights of children.

Particularly for disabled children, the deference to adult gatekeepers for decisions, opinions and viewpoints is longstanding. The existence of the UNCRC and terms of the UNCRPD do not necessarily mean that the provisions are manifest 'on the ground'. We were acutely aware that our research needed to focus on the rights of disabled children, in particular, to facilitate their right to have their opinions and thoughts be heard, and to demonstrate to the adult gatekeepers that it was possible to conduct research actively *with* disabled children rather than merely about them, from adults' perspectives. (Chapter 4, this volume, page 137)

Emerging issues: tensions, spaces, relationships

Tensions exist between the different spaces and relationships within which children live their lives. One of this book's key themes concerns the tensions between children's experiences of spaces where rights-informed policies and laws operate and where they do not. This is a complex arena, as it concerns what can, and cannot, be governed by state law and policy. Aspects of children's home life is one example of this: how are children's rights present within the spaces of their home and in their family relationships?

Henricson and Bainham (2005, 81), for example, have summarized the kinds of tensions present within these different relationships and spaces. In discussing the rights of parents and the rights of children, they illustrate an example of this kind of tension. They argue that the overall situation is one where human rights commitments require the government to formulate policies that take account of the rights and needs of children and parents, but these needs are often competing. Covell et al. (2017) comment on this tension in relation to children's education and the 'persistent and misguided belief in the nature of parental rights'. They illustrate this from the perspective of the UNCRC:

> According to the Convention, the rights of children are of fundamental importance while those of parents are connected to their responsibilities...Article 28 of the Convention clearly states that children have the right to education on the basis of equal opportunity. Article 5 requires states to 'respect the responsibilities, rights and duties of parents...to provide, in a manner consistent with the evolving capacities of the child, appropriate direction and guidance in the exercise by the child recognized in the present Convention'. (UNCRC, 1989, 298)

In short, parents do have rights but these are in relation to fulfilling their responsibilities and guiding children in exercising their rights. Nonetheless for many politicians, as for conservative lobbyists, the rights of parents in education continue to outweigh those of children. Not only do parents have the legal right to remove their children from the public education system, but parents in virtually all jurisdictions may withdraw children from classes that are offensive to parental 'values under formal and informal "opting-out" provisions...The child's right to education as well as to information and participation in decision making effectively is trumped by false notions of parental rights' (Covell, 2017, 329).

This identifying of tensions between children's rights, parents' rights and society's 'welfare' is often referred to within the emerging response to child rights. Further examination of this and what it reveals about responses to children's rights can be found in Chapter 5 (pages 162–4) and 6 (page 196).

> Many Health Professionals (HP) and parents (P) felt that children(C) had limited involvement as most decisions were made by adults and then implemented. For example 'At the end of the day I do think we as a team force a

lot on the kids and whether we use different words or options a lot of the decision is with us. It's either the parent or it's the team. Very rarely it seems to be the kid' (HP5). Likewise, a father explained, 'The decision-making is, "Can I go down the playroom or not?" or "Can I play this PlayStation?". They have very limited power of decisions in hospital. Everything else, it's a very, very controlled environment for them. All those decisions are made for him by everybody else around" (F3 of a seven-year-old boy). (Chapter 5, this volume, page 169)

The years since the UNCRC have seen tensions emerge regarding the relationships between other spaces in children's lives and how their lives are governed. Such issues concerning differences, rights and children's spaces are considered in Chapter 6.

A culture of 'blame' encourages carers to respond in particular ways to every possible danger for children. These dangers are not only physical but also emotional, social and sexual, coming in the form of unsupervised environments, strangers, media (particularly the Internet) and association with peers. An example of this can be seen in the results of a Playday (2013) opinion poll which included 1,000 parents of children between 5 and 16 years old in the United Kingdom. The findings highlight how children's freedom to play outside is substantially reduced compared to that experienced by previous generations with parents' fears of traffic and strangers put forward as reasons for not letting children play unsupervised. They also highlighted the fear of being judged by their neighbours if they allowed their children to play out without supervision. (Chapter 6, this volume, page 201)

A further examination of material involving rethinking children's rights and issues concerning 'tensions, spaces, relationships' can be found in relation to children and surveillance Chapter 3, this volume, page 108.

Emerging issues: a child rights veneer

Patterns within the emerging response have shown how it is possible for a rights veneer to be created. This rights veneer can be seen in many societies. As with the rights dynamic, it occurs at different levels. The idea of a rights veneer is that structures or processes set in place give the appearance of engaging with a rights agenda, but do not actually do so. This may be deliberate, but often it is not a conscious intention, revealing just how difficult it can be to alter deep-seated and long-held views, attitudes and practices. On a large scale this could be concerning policies and laws that are not effectively enacted, while on a small scale it might involve having a clear, rights-based position on paper and then in practice working in ways that ignore, or invalidate, the position. Chapter 5, for example, looks at research that challenges the rights veneer and rhetoric of the UK government in relation to the UN Committee on the Rights of the Child's critical review of their lack of progress (see pages 95–7). The treatment of children in terms of their rights to be involved in decision making in education varies. Some societies have developed a positive response to the rights dynamic, in areas such as children's involvement in decision making within education. Others, such as the United Kingdom, have been criticized for their lack of progress by comparison, and the lack of structured, embedded engagement with children as decision makers. A further examination of material involving rethinking children's rights and the idea of a 'rights veneer' can be found in relation to research and children's participation on pages 100–1.

The presence of the UNCRC and negative responses

This chapter has introduced the key themes within this book. On the one hand, it has identified concepts and practices that have developed over the past two decades such as the rights dynamic, the emergence of a rights agenda and rights-informed ways of relating to children. It has also reviewed challenges and criticisms in relation to child rights.

Alston and Tobin (2005) comment on the development of the response to the UNCRC and its impact in ways that parallel the discussions in this chapter and in the book as a whole. In their review, they note the important ways in which the dynamic for change is both reflected in and energized by the UNCRC. They refer to positive elements and the enormous progress in children's lives, as well as the negative, persistent presence of violation, harm and oppression of children. This echoes commentators who have expressed grave concerns about the gap between rhetoric and reality. Alston and Tobin cite Moorehead's conclusions that the UNCRC has become 'something of a sham', primarily because it is violated 'systematically and contemptuously' by many countries, and that 'no countries violate it more energetically than those that were quickest to sign' (Moorehead, 1997, pangaea.org/street_children/world/ unconv3.htm).

More optimistically, they note the role of the UNCRC as an agent of change and that the presence of child rights is a crucial challenge in achieving urgently needed change:

> Increased government resistance to the scrutiny applied by the Committee on the Rights of the Child, is in many respects an indication that the process is starting to bite in the ways that it should. Efforts to reduce the age at which childhood is considered to end in relation to criminal responsibility or for other purposes, are in part a function of the pressures generated by the Convention to move to a standard benchmark of 18. Arguments designed to justify the detention of refugee children are being made with increasing vehemence, precisely because the Convention challenges such practices directly.(2005, 8)

This book reviews current thinking and research that is adding to that challenge in different spheres of children's lives.

Summary

This chapter has

- looked at the different ways in which societies see child rights,
- examined research into different responses to the UNCRC and the contemporary situation of child rights,
- reviewed different kinds of rights-informed ways of relating to children,
- emphasized the importance of connecting ideas and practices relating to children's rights with concepts such as social exclusion,
- explored how negative responses to the child rights dynamic be used to help rethink children's rights,
- looked at ideas of divided responses to child rights and the idea of a rights veneer.

2

Children's Rights: Definitions and Developments

Introduction and key questions

This chapter will outline some of the key concepts associated with children's rights, looking at international and national perspectives to help identify the ideas developed by the UNCRC and other organizations concerned with children's rights. It includes a review of how the ideas and practices concerning children's rights have emerged as well as a summary of key points contained within the UNCRC. Subsequent commentaries and criticisms identify issues around interpretation and implementation as well as more fundamental criticisms. As Chapter 1 commented, the idea of 'children's rights' provokes many different kinds of response ranging from a whole-hearted enthusiasm to a fear that children will run out of control. The response is likely to be based on the interpretation of two different but over-lapping concepts: rights and childhood. This chapter examines these two concepts before going on to consider the issues for children and adults that arise from debates about rights and childhood. It attempts to answer the following questions:

Is there a common understanding of the term 'right'?
Is there a common understanding of the term 'child'?
What does the history of the UNCRC tell us about the tensions in thinking about children and rights?
What issues and tensions have emerged since the development of the UNCRC?
What does research tell us about the state of children's rights internationally and in the United Kingdom?

Is there a common understanding of the term 'right'?

The relatively recent popularity of human rights issues, particularly in the Minority World, suggests that there is an inherent value in using a rights discourse and that there is some common understanding and acceptance of concepts and values associated with the term 'right'. Chapter 1 has already introduced the idea that there are a variety of meanings at different levels, and this chapter will discuss the complexity of rights issues that are bound up with the values that underpin the organization of societies and the power relationships within them. The position taken in this book is that the concept of rights is socially constructed in different ways and there are no 'natural' or absolute rights: that is, different values and perceptions of the relationship between individuals and the rest of society lead to different ideas about the status and meaning of a 'rights discourse'.

The concept of 'human rights' tends to be associated with the Universal Declaration of Human Rights (UDHR) that was formulated in 1948. However, it is important to consider the basis for the formulation of these rights and make the distinction between the abstract concept of human rights and how this has been interpreted in the UDHR. How the UDHR itself is interpreted and implemented is a further area of difference.

The philosophical question of 'How can we best live together?' has one answer in a rights discourse. Tasioulas (2012), in discussing the contemporary philosophy of human rights, identifies the 'grounding values of human rights' as incorporating 'both the notion of human dignity – the equal intrinsic objective worth of all human beings – and the diverse elements of a flourishing human life, or universal human interests' (2012, 7). The notion of 'equal worth' means that rights are granted on the basis of humanity not on the basis of particular status and the focus of rights is based on the potential constituents of a flourishing human life, interests that Tasioulas suggests 'include, but are not limited to, basic needs and freedom' (2012, 7).

The problems of universal acceptance of the basis of human rights can be found in relation to both parts of these values. First, not all societies place 'human dignity' and 'a flourishing human life' as central to their thinking about morality in relation to 'How can we best live together?' Societies that adhere to values associated with the pre-eminence of a deity are more likely to value subservience to the will of the deity and base their morality on the rules associated with their religion. In this case a discourse based on human rights is fundamentally challenging.

Second, even when there might be consensus on the idea of a rights discourse as central to a morality of how we should live together, there are different ideas about what the constituents of 'universal human interests' might be. Tasioulas identifies basic needs and freedom as two constituents but others might add more.

If the concept of human rights is to mean anything in practice, the rights need to be identified and codified in some way that enables those claiming a right to place an obligation or duty on others to ensure that the right is fulfilled. The UDHR is an attempt to get universal agreement on what rights can be claimed by individuals and ratifying states assume obligations and duties under international law to respect, to protect and to fulfil human rights. The UNHRC identified that all states have ratified at least one of the 18 core HR treaties and 80 per cent of states have ratified four or more treaties. While this indicates some degree of consensus, it also indicates the inevitable disagreements stemming from the differences discussed earlier.

These differences are the basis of tensions and debates and will be discussed here. The first tension concerns two main areas of rights: liberty rights and welfare rights.

What are liberty rights?

In Europe and America the first real move towards consideration of rights came in opposition to power wielded by monarchs who were able to do anything they wanted and impose their will on any of their 'subjects'. The resulting ideas around 'the rights of man' were concerned with the rights of individuals to pursue their own lives without interference – liberty rights. This meant that no one should be compelled to do anything against his or her will and the state would only have the authority to intervene with the will of the people – essentially reducing the power that the state could have over what were now thought of as its 'citizens' rather than 'subjects'. Individuals would have the right to lead their lives as they wished: they would be autonomous human beings.

The legal systems that developed identified the limits of individual freedom in cases where 'pursuing your own ends' would adversely affect others; for example, there would be laws against taking someone else's property or injuring others. These ideas were developed in France, by Voltaire, and, in America, by Franklin, Paine and Jefferson, and led to revolutions in both these countries and the emergence of the Bill of Rights in America. These 'liberal' ideas have developed in different ways over time, but the essence is the promotion of individual autonomy and independence with minimal state interference.

It may seem inconceivable now that these rights movements didn't include all sectors of society as having rights, as the basis of human rights is the equal worth of all humans. However, groups such as women and people from ethnic minorities have had to fight for their rights during the last century. Mill (1859), while arguing for women's rights in the nineteenth century, reiterated that we should 'leave out of consideration those backward states of society in which the race itself may be considered as in its nonage' (1859, 23), a view that we would find totally unacceptable today, although another consideration that 'those who are still in a state to require being taken care of by others must be protected against their own actions' (1859, 22–23) is still a widely held opinion and is the basis for restricting children's liberty rights and, in some societies, the rights of women and other minority groups.

Example of liberty rights

'Prevent' is a programme developed as part of the United Kingdom's response to terrorism, designed to prevent children and young people from being drawn in to terrorism. In July 2015 it became the duty of local authorities, schools, nurseries and social services departments to have due regard to the need to prevent people from being drawn into terrorism. These bodies must refer those they believe to be vulnerable to the police, who decide whether to refer them to a panel to prepare support 'packages' to reduce their vulnerability. This is explained in the Prevent Strategy document (HMG, 2011):

> Schools can help to protect children from extremist and violent views in the same ways that they help to safeguard children from drugs, gang violence or alcohol. Schools' work on Prevent needs to be seen in this context. The purpose must be to protect children from harm and to ensure that they are taught in a way that is consistent with the law and our values. Awareness of Prevent and the risks it is intended to address are both vital. Staff can help to identify, and to refer to the relevant agencies, children whose behaviour suggests that they are being drawn into terrorism or extremism. (p 69)

The Institute of Race Relations, in response to this duty, has identified some of the tensions between 'Prevent' and children's liberty rights. The following are two examples of case referrals.

> A 15-year-old boy was referred to police under the Prevent programme after he came to school with leaflets promoting a boycott of Israel. The police officer said that the boy's views on sanctions against Israel were 'terrorist-like beliefs'. The boy's form tutor allegedly said he would report him although he was 'uncomfortable' about it. The boy has had run-ins with teachers and with the Prevent officer based in the school to 'deal with this sort of extremism', and the dinner lady reported him to teachers for asking if the dinners were cooked with ingredients from Israel.
>
> A teenager in Manchester was identified as potentially requiring de-radicalization after attending a peaceful protest against the Israeli deputy ambassador. (Webber, 2016, 4)

How might these examples be restricting the liberty rights of children and young people?

What might the examples show about the relationships between adults, children, prejudice and power?

What are welfare rights?

Assumptions behind the idea of 'liberty rights' were that each individual would be responsible for him- or herself, and his or her family, and that individual effort would result in a 'good life'. Great value was placed on individual autonomy and responsibility. This assumes that all individuals have the same start in life and have equal capacities to make a good life and act as agents in their own destiny. Acceptance that this isn't the case, because some people are born into families that have more social and financial capital than others, led to discussion of another type of rights: welfare rights. These rights identify things that need to be in place to help everyone to make best use of their liberty rights. Areas within this framework include the following: a basic standard of living, health care, education, positive working conditions, rest and leisure, and participation in cultural life. It may be argued that these stem from the fundamental principles of human rights that these are all human interests. While liberty rights call for an absence of state action, leaving individuals to their own autonomy, welfare rights call for state intervention to provide financial benefits, healthcare, education and so on for those who need them and to take action to ensure that the actions of employers, or others in powerful positions, do not endanger an individual's welfare rights. Consequently, there is a tension between these two types of rights, particularly because the state has to interfere with liberty rights through compelling people to pay taxes in order to fund welfare provision or to limit the actions of individuals and companies. While liberty rights promote individual autonomy and responsibility, welfare rights stress the interdependence of individuals and shared responsibility for each other's welfare. Interestingly, the preconditions that Mill (1859) identified as being the basis for children (and others who need care) not being granted liberty rights are those that would mean they should be granted welfare rights; however, the extent to which these should be provided by the state rather than the family would be the focus for debate.

Example of welfare rights

The Joint Parliamentary Committee on Human Rights (2014) considered how well the government's policies reflected the provisions of the UNCRC. This was during a period of austerity after the financial crash of 2008 when cuts in services were made. The overt argument made by the government was that this was in order to 'balance the books' but this was challenged in terms of the ways children are treated by the UK government.

The committee commented that

the impact on children of this current period of austerity has been greater than for many other groups. Certain categories of children may have been protected from the worst impacts of austerity, but other groups – in particular migrant children, whether unaccompanied or not, and children in low-income families – have been hit by cuts in benefits and in the provision of services... we are disappointed that children – in particular, disadvantaged children – have in certain areas suffered disproportionately... The Government needs to work harder to minimize as much of the effect on children of cuts to funding as possible. The Government should also have monitored more closely the impacts of these cuts with a view to modifying its policy in those areas where children were clearly suffering more than other groups.

(The Joint Parliamentary Committee on Human Rights, 2014, p 31)

Here the Committee is highlighting the negative effects of government policy that is attempting to 'balance the books' by making cuts to welfare.

Article 4 of the UNCRC which is concerned with the role of states in supporting children's rights says

States Parties shall undertake all appropriate legislative, administrative, and other measures for the implementation of the rights recognized in the present Convention. With regard to economic, social and cultural rights, States Parties shall undertake such measures to the maximum extent of their available resources and, where needed, within the framework of international co-operation. (UNCRC, 1989)

How is this relevant here? How might 'maximum extent of available resources' be interpreted?

What kind of welfare rights do you think might be affected?

If it is important to 'balance the books', how might this be done without affecting welfare rights?

What might others who are affected by cuts think to these alternatives?

What kind of liberty rights might be affected?

> ## Key points: liberty rights and welfare rights
>
> - Liberty rights are concerned with ensuring individuals can act autonomously with minimum interference from the state.
> - Welfare rights are concerned with enabling individuals to make the best use of their liberty rights through state intervention.
> - There is a tension between these two types of rights as one resists state intervention and the other requires it.

Rights and duties

While both liberty rights and welfare rights prioritize different kinds of rights, and give different emphases to the roles of individuals and the community, they both focus on human beings and their interests as the central concern. Different societies and political systems deal with these tensions in different ways. Rights discourse has largely developed within the Minority World with different societies giving more weight to one type of right than another: for example, socialist societies such as Venezuela tend to emphasize welfare rights, whereas liberal societies such as the United States tend to emphasize liberty rights.

As discussed earlier in the chapter, in contrast to the focus on human rights as the centre of morality, communities with strong religious beliefs or with strong hierarchical structures may have a different central focus: some divinity or supreme ruler. In these societies or communities, the Minority World concept of human rights can be seen as subservient to the concept of duty: the duty of individuals to follow the teachings of the religion or the dictates of the leader of the hierarchy. The distinction between adults and children in this respect results in adults being further up the hierarchy. Children learn their overall duties from adults and may have specific duties to adults, for example, to obey their instructions and carry out specific tasks. Women may also be considered to hold a subservient position to men, with duties associated with that position. When this position is bound up with religion, and inequalities in status are seen as part of a 'natural' or 'god-given' order of duty, a rights discourse is very challenging. States that are in this position that are signatories to the UNCRC are likely to interpret and implement the convention within a discourse of 'duty'.

Example of research: duties and rights

White (2007) analyses the *somaj* (local community) in Bangladesh where this concept of duty is identified through the common saying, 'In childhood girls are under the authority of their fathers; at marriage under the authority of their husbands; in old age under the authority of their sons' (2007, 512). She goes on to explain how these male 'guardians' are the full members of society and women and children only belong to the *somaj* by virtue of their relationship to them. Children's welfare is protected by the guardian of the family, and the primary responsibility of the guardian is to 'make a person' by transforming the infant into a fully socialized human who fulfils the requirements of their specific gender role (2007, 513). Anyone who is excluded from the community, for example through family breakdown, illegitimacy or by breaking rules, is without the protection and provision that the guardian is responsible for.

White concludes that there are strong 'contradictory and exclusionary, as well as solidary and inclusionary, aspects of the ways communities are imagined and conduct themselves in Bangladesh and these can impact badly on children who fall outside the charmed circle of 'guardianship', as well as meaning significant pressures on those who come within it.' (2007, 518)

She points out that engaging in a rights discourse with these communities is meaningless, but to engage in a discourse based on the duties of guardians has enabled rights workers to improve conditions for children while being sensitive to cultural norms.

Reflection on the research

This research shows that although the concept of rights isn't universally accepted, the language of 'duty' and 'responsibility' can be used to engage those in powerful positions to consider how children's lives might be improved.

The positive 'solidary' and 'inclusionary' features of the *somaj* that White refers to ensures that all those who conform to the norms of the *somaj* are provided for. However, the negative 'contradictory' and 'exclusionary' features mean that those who are outside the *somaj* do not get the benefits of guardianship.

Although White concludes that using a rights discourse is meaningless in these communities, there are indications that a rights discourse is developing. An example from Action Aid (2011) illustrates this:

Atika Begum from Islamkathi union of Tala Upazila in Satkhira was the first dalit woman to become Union Parishad (the lowest tier of local government) member in 2011 election. Gendered norms and discriminatory practices have long left women outside the governance structure, eroding their self-belief and determination. Atika as a woman had to face dual discrimination – as a woman and as a dalit, who are labelled as the so called 'untouchables' – and fight against all odds to contest election, 'Discrimination, identity crisis, unemployment and hunger, eviction, non-accessibility to public services and injustice are synonymous to community. Since my childhood I have experienced all these.' This overwhelming exclusion and systemic denial of rights motivated Atika to run for the election and fight for rights and entitlements of dalit.

What differences might there be in the *somaj* if a rights discourse was used. Think about the positive and negative effects this might have for those within the *somaj* and those who are excluded.

Chapter 3 discusses the concept of duty further in relation to the Charter on the Rights and Welfare of the African Child and Freeman's (2000) analysis of the tensions around 'duty' in the development of the UNCRC.

Moral and legal rights

An important distinction needs to be made between moral rights and legal rights. While moral rights identify those things we feel should be rights, stemming from the human rights principles of human dignity and interests, they don't become legal rights until codified into an agreed treaty, convention or set of state laws. So, although we might consider that everyone has a right to food, water and shelter based on human interests, unless there are legal imperatives that oblige individuals or states to provide these, the safeguarding of that right will depend on the voluntary actions of others.

Consideration of what constitutes a moral right varies from individual to individual and across societies and states because of the differences in values and interpretations of the human rights principles identified earlier. It is influenced by religion and culture and is likely to change over time and in different social and economic circumstances. However, in order for a moral right to become an enforceable universal legal right, there needs to be agreement. The difficulty in reaching international agreement is illustrated in the lack of consensus over international treaties identified earlier. Acknowledging the difficulty of agreement, Ignatieff (2003) suggests that, rather than seeing human rights as 'moral trumps', they should be considered as the basis for political discussion that takes into account political and social contexts, stressing the need for intercultural understanding.

As a rights discourse develops in places such as Bangladesh, rights may not be seen in the same way as they are in the United Kingdom for example. Ignatieff is suggesting that emphasis is placed on dialogue to make progress in understanding the social, political and economic context of each state rather than identifying one as being 'better' or 'worse' than another.

Key points: moral and legal rights

- Moral rights are concerned with what we think individuals should have a right to, but there is no commitment to make sure this happens.
- Legal rights are enforceable through laws, providing a duty to ensure the right is enabled.

This section has identified the problems in accepting human rights as a universal moral concept and in interpreting and implementing attempts to codify human rights principles into legal frameworks. It has outlined two main types of rights: liberty rights and welfare rights and identified tensions related to rights issues

- between autonomy and the interdependence of individuals on each other,
- between the provision of welfare rights and the maintenance of individual liberty rights, and
- between a rights discourse and a discourse based on duty.

It has highlighted the difficulty of a rights discourse without a legal framework.

These are summarized in Table 2.1.

Table 2.1 Rights, duties and different kinds of society

	Liberty rights	Welfare rights	Duties rather than rights
Examples of coverage of rights	Rights to life, liberty and property; freedom of thought, conscience and religion; rights to vote and take part in collective decision making.	Rights to an adequate standard of living, education, positive working conditions, rest and leisure and participation in cultural life.	Duties to others or to a deity are emphasized on the basis of tradition or religion.
View of society and the kinds of relationships that are implied	Liberal democracy Collection of autonomous individuals with agency, each striving for the best for themselves. They may support others, who can't support themselves, through charitable endeavours but this would be a choice not an imposition.	Collectivism. Interdependent individuals who work for and benefit from each other. All members of society are regarded as equal.	Individuals are subservient to a higher authority based on tradition or religion. Relationships between individuals are based on the tenets of the underlying belief. This may be hierarchical, with those having the greatest knowledge and understanding of the belief system having the most power.
Role of the state	Minimal role to ensure safety of citizens from outside threats and to resolve disputes. Otherwise there is a requirement for the state not to interfere.	Strong role to ensure all citizens are provided for by sharing resources and contribute by fulfilling the required roles or No state, as communities develop their own support systems.	Strong role in ensuring duties are carried out.
Associated values	Individual autonomy and agency, tolerance, individual responsibility.	Equality, sharing and cooperation.	Morality on the basis of the belief system.

Is there a common understanding of the term 'child'?

Chapter 1 introduced the idea that the concept of 'childhood' has changed and is still changing across time and culture, affected by the social, political, historical and moral context. This section will consider how differences in thinking about childhood affect the status of children, their relationships with the family and the rest of society and which rights they should have. As Quennerstedt and Quennerstedt describe, 'Advocating human rights for children and new social theorising about children were consequently part of the same movement in which children's status as human beings and children's place in society were reconsidered' (2014, 118). Alanen and Mayall (2001) argue that the concept of 'child' has tended to be seen as a contrast to that of 'adult', so our notions about what being a child means are bound up with what we think being an adult means. This contrast has been traditionally used to identify the adult as an ideal state that the developing child should eventually reach. This 'ideal' adult is seen as having a number of characteristics that make them worthy of being rights holders: competence, independence, rationality and autonomous agency. In contrast children are stereotyped as incompetent, dependent, irrational and passive. Developmental theories then chart the 'normal' patterns of growth in these areas from birth to adulthood. This kind of thinking leads to an adult–child relationship where adults have power over and responsibility for children and a society where children are of lower status than that of adults. This way of thinking and acting tends to see the child in terms of 'deficiencies'. In this way they may be seen to need welfare rights to provide them with basic needs and give them protection. Challenges to this way of thinking, through research and theory in the sociology of childhood, questioned these dichotomies in assumptions about the child and adult.

- Constant change and growth beyond childhood challenges the concept of the 'ideal adult'.
- The 'competence', 'rationality' and 'autonomous agency' of children and adults are variable, changing over time and circumstance. Research showed how children can be seen as competent, rational and autonomous agents while economic, political and social contexts may limit some adults.

Table 2.2 Rights and child–adult relationships

View of the child	View of the adult	Child–adult relationship	Implication for rights

Someone who is
A passive
  recipient of
  adult protection
  and provision
Lacking adult
  competences
  of rationality
  and agency
Dependent
  on adults
In need of control
	Someone who is
	Strong and
	  capable and
	  knows what
	  is best
	Able to make
	  rational
	  decisions
	  and take
	  responsibility
	Independent in all
	  aspects of their
	  life
		Unequal power
		  relationship
		Adult as protector,
		  provider and
		  decision maker for
		  the child
		Child responds
		  positively to adult
		  control
		Where the child
		  does not respond
		  positively to
		  adult control
		  the relationship
		  becomes one of
		  challenge and
		  conflict
			Emphasis on
			  welfare rights
			  not liberty rights

Someone who is
An active
  participant in
  their family and
  community
Developing and
  resilient with
  many strengths
Economically
  dependent
  on others but
  contributes in
  many ways to
  the family and
  community
	Someone who is
	An active
	  participant in
	  their family and
	  community
	Able to make
	  rational
	  decisions
	  and take
	  responsibility
	  but also makes
	  mistakes and
	  has a lot to learn
	Economically
	  independent
	  but is also
	  dependent on
	  others socially
	  and emotionally
		A mutually respectful
		  relationship with
		  an appreciation of
		  the strengths and
		  weaknesses of
		  each other
		Adult is sensitive
		  to the growing
		  capabilities of the
		  child and supports
		  and involves
		  them in making
		  decisions
		Children are
		  encouraged to
		  contribute and
		  take responsibility
		  within the family
		  and community
			Welfare and liberty
			  rights

- Ideas about the social and emotional interdependence of both children and the variability of both adults and children in physical and economic independence challenged the distinction between children and adults in this respect.

These challenges provided a way of rethinking the relationships that might exist between children and adults and the rights children should have; this has already been introduced in Chapter 1 in relation to a 'rights dynamic'. Table 2.2 illustrates the implications of different ways of thinking. There is some parallel here with the rights debates in emphasizing either autonomous agency or interdependence.

Quennerstedt and Quennerstedt (2014) stress growth in all aspects of life, including being a 'rights holder' and point to the need for education to take account of this area of growth and change alongside all other areas. Viewed in this way the distinctions between children and adults and 'children's rights' and 'human rights' becomes blurred. They suggest that it is perhaps more useful to consider social, political and moral contexts that limit the agency of adults and children as individuals or particular groups. For example, living in poverty affects the health and education outcomes of both children and adults. In turn, this can limit their agency in making decisions about employment, housing and so on. The following example of research illustrates how the complexities of the concepts of 'rights' and 'the child' are played out in a real-life situation.

Example of research: asylum-seeking children

Smyth (2013a) analysed the Common European Asylum System in relation to children's rights to liberty. The Common European Asylum System gives guidance on how those seeking asylum should be treated, particularly with respect to how adults and children may be detained when they enter the country while their claim to asylum is investigated. The Convention on the Rights of the Child has developed stringent standards for what happens to minors to ensure that they are protected from detention and, if they have to be kept in a secure environment, that they are protected while they are in there. Smyth points out that

> the detention of asylum-seeking children is more problematic than that of adults because the impact of detention on a child's rights are more profound – the right of the child to development, family unity and education being cases in point – and the child is more susceptible to abuse, victimization and violation of his/her protection rights while in detention than adults generally. (2013a, 114)

The Common European Asylum System has been redrafted to make clearer to European States how they must deal fairly with those seeking asylum. However, Smyth (2013b) found that although some rights were being acknowledged, others were not.

She attributes this to the fact that the legislation comes out of a broader political context whereby the standard of human rights is compromised by the perceived need to deter asylum seekers. So, while there is an acknowledgement that everyone has human rights and children have additional rights because of their additional needs, these can be ignored in order to deter asylum seekers. This can be seen in two ways.

First, it is seen in the act of giving to the child asylum seeker/ refugee with one hand and taking from asylum seekers/refugees generally with the other, such that the latter action cancels out the former.

...Second, the compromise is seen in an ambivalent attitude towards the child, whereby the legislation variously constructs an image of the child as needy and vulnerable and prioritizes the child's status as a child over and above his/ her migration status and an image of the child as being just an adult in miniature, possibly even an adult in fact and prioritizing the child's migration status over and above his/her status as a child. (Smyth, 2013b, 302)

Reflection on research

How does Smyth's explanation of the compromise in the document fit into the discussion in this section of the chapter? Think about

- the social, political and moral context
- the dichotomies associated with children and adults

Smyth goes on to suggest,

The challenge for any legislator is to maintain this balance, accommodating the child's agency and providing for the child's protection, without the child's agency being used as an excuse for diminished protection. (Smyth, 2013b, 303)

Think about this as you read the following sections and the research example in Chapter 3 about asylum-seeking children.

Key points: concepts of 'childhood' and 'the child'

- Ideas about childhood that emphasize the 'otherness' of children in relation to adults and traditional views that stereotype children as 'deficient' in relation to adults result in limiting views of the rights children should have.
- Ideas that appreciate the similarities between children and adults as human beings alongside the very different ways that individuals experience the world acknowledge the tensions around children's rights.

What does the history of the UNCRC tell us about the tensions in thinking about children's rights?

The twentieth century saw the upheaval of two world wars and major political, social and economic changes across the world. The previous sections pointed to the complexity of thinking about rights and about childhood and these were influenced by these changes. This section will revisit ideas about rights and childhood in relation to the development of the 1989 UNCRC.

The current positions, in different parts of the world, of children's rights is a result of international debates about human rights and children's rights which have largely taken place in parallel. The changes over time reflect changes in thinking about liberty rights, welfare rights and who should have access to rights: children being a group that was considered to have special consideration. Earlier discussion referred to the fight that women and ethnic minorities had during the twentieth century in order to obtain the vote. This is indicative of the way that liberty rights have largely been determined by the most powerful in many communities: white males. While in democratic countries liberty rights are granted to all adults, in reality minority groups are still unlikely to be able to take full advantage of these rights either because they don't have the benefit of welfare rights that support access to liberty rights or because they are deemed to be inferior in some way.

Table 2.3 Influences on the development of the UNCRC

Significant events in progress towards the UNCRC (based on Smith, 2016)	Influence of thinking about 'the child' and 'rights'
1919 Eglantyne Jebb launched the Save the Children Fund in response to the post-War misery of thousands of children around Europe. This was followed in 1920 by the International Union for Child Welfare.	Philanthropic, romanticized view of childhood. Children in need of care and protection. Children as victims.
1924 The League of Nations adopted the Geneva Declaration of the Rights of the Child drafted by the International Union for Child Welfare. This established children's rights to • the means for material, moral and spiritual development; • special help when hungry, sick, disabled or orphaned; • first call on relief when in distress; • earn a livelihood alongside freedom from economic exploitation; • an upbringing that instils a sense of social responsibility.	Children in need of care and protection. Children as victims. Children as adults in the making. Children as a potential economic asset. Welfare rights rather than liberty rights. Declaration of moral rather than legal rights.
1948 The UN General Assembly passed the Universal Declaration of Human Rights, which refers in Article 25 to childhood as 'entitled to special care and assistance'.	Moral rights with no legal status. States were unable to agree because • Islamic countries were concerned that Islamic Shari'a law might be undermined; • Libertarians argued that welfare rights have to be paid for, and this intrudes into the liberty rights of individuals being able to use their money as they wish. Children in need of care and protection
1959 The UN General Assembly adopted the Declaration of the Rights of the Child, which recognizes rights such as freedom from discrimination and the right to a name and nationality. It also specifically enshrines children's rights to education, healthcare and special protection.	Post-Second World War realization of the importance of freedom from discrimination and the right to identity. Children in need of care and protection. Children as victims. Welfare rights rather than liberty rights. Declaration of moral rather than legal rights.

Significant events in progress towards the UNCRC (based on Smith, 2016)	Influence of thinking about 'the child' and 'rights'
1979 The UN declared 1979 the International Year of the Child. The UN General Assembly agrees that a working group comprising members of the UN Commission on Human Rights, independent experts and observer delegations of non-member governments, non-governmental organizations and UN agencies should be set up to draft a legally binding convention.	Ten years of discussion about 'the child' and the rights they should have.
1989 The UN General Assembly unanimously approved the Convention on the Rights of the Child, which enters into force the following year.	Liberty and Welfare Rights. Children as active participants. Children as vulnerable. Children as rights holders. Moral rights but states held accountable for progress.

Table 2.3 identifies the key events leading up to the formulation of the UNCRC in 1989 and points to the thinking about rights and children that are reflected in its development.

The discussion at the beginning of this chapter indicated the difficulties that some states may have with a rights discourse and the difficulty of translating human rights principles into a codified framework. The consequent lack of international agreement to the 1948 Universal Declaration led to a more limited 1950 European Convention on Human Rights (Council of Europe, 1950) that sought to identify a set of rights that would be legally binding across the nation states within the Council of Europe. Interestingly, given the objections to the Universal Declaration of Human Rights, the contents are mainly negative rights that prevent the state from interfering with individual liberty rights, and there is little reference to welfare rights. Individual member states ratified the convention (but could adapt some protocols to fit their individual circumstances) and ensured that their laws took account of the convention. Any individual within a Council of Europe nation, after pursuing his or her case to the highest level within his or her own country, is able to appeal to the European Court of Human Rights. In contrast, when the UNCRC was formulated there was no provision for appeal to a higher court. However, as will be seen in the next section, this is changing.

Key points: the 1989 United Nation Convention on the Rights of the Child

The 1989 Convention on the Rights of the Child consists of 54 articles; 41 of these articles identify the human rights to be respected and protected for every child under the age of 18 years and require that these rights are implemented in the light of the convention's guiding principles:

- Non-discrimination (Article 2),
- The best interests of the child as the primary consideration (Article 3),
- Survival and development of all children (Article 6),
- Participation of children in decisions that affect them: 'the views of the child being given due weight in accordance with the age and maturity of the child' (Article 12).

The 41 articles that identify children's rights are often referred to in three main groups: the three Ps. These are as follows:

- Provision to ensure children's survival and development (welfare rights),
- Protection from abuse and exploitation (welfare rights),
- Participation in decision making (liberty rights).

However, it is clear from the convention that rights should not be thought of individually but as a whole.

A summary of the convention can be found in the Appendix.

What issues and tensions have emerged since the development of the UNCRC?

Although the 1989 UNCRC was a definitive document, difficulties in reaching agreement in drafting resulted in many areas in which there is deliberate room for development and refinement and it resulted in a convention that is a statement of basic principles rather than a detailed exposition of rights. Consequently, it has been interpreted and implemented differently in different states, reflecting different ideas about rights, children, families and society. Ratification involves states ensuring that their laws and policies are in line with the principles and articles of the UNCRC and they have systems to monitor implementation. Two years after ratification and then every five years, states report to the Committee on the Rights of the Child (CORC) on the progress they have made. The CORC receives the reports and interrogates representatives from the state and NGOs about the report and, after long deliberations, issues Concluding Comments identifying what they consider the state needs to do. The UN Human Rights Office for the High Commissioner explains how this should work.

> Concluding observations are meant to be widely publicized in the State party and to serve as the basis for a national debate on how to improve the enforcement of the provisions of the Convention. They therefore constitute an essential document: Governments are expected to implement the recommendations contained therein. (United Nations Human Rights Office of the High Commissioner, *Fact Sheet No. 10*, 5)

As well as informing individual states about issues pertinent to that state the reports and concluding comments enabled the CORC to identify emerging criticisms and tensions. Illustrations of the work of the CORC can be found elsewhere in the book (see page 63).

Early criticisms and tensions

In the early period of the UNCRC, there were a number of criticisms and tensions, some of which have been at least partially addressed while others continue to be problematic.

Early criticisms of the convention were as follows:

- The lack of appreciation of the different contexts that children experience.
- The lack of an 'appeals' procedure equivalent to that associated with the European Convention on Human rights.

As a result, three further Optional Protocols have been introduced. While the content of the UNCRC is non-negotiable the Optional Protocols are additions that states can choose to ratify. These are as follows:

- Optional Protocol on the Sale of Children, Child Prostitution and Child Pornography (OPSC) in force from January 2002 (UN General Assembly, 2001),

- Optional Protocol on Children Involved in Armed Conflict (OPAC) in force from February 2002 (UN General Assembly, 2000),
- Optional Protocol on Communications (OPSC) establishing an international complaints procedure for children. In force from April 2014. (UNHRC, 2011)

These protocols acknowledge some of the very different lives that children experience and the need to identify areas where there is a need for special provision. The third protocol also acknowledges that there is a need to strengthen the mechanisms for children's voices to be heard.

By 29 January 2016, a total of 196 states had ratified the UNCRC, 162 states had ratified or acceded to OPAC, 171 had ratified or acceded to OPSC and 24 had ratified OPSC. The United Kingdom has ratified OPSC and OPAC but has not yet ratified OPSC although the Joint Committee on Human Rights Report 2014–15 recommended that his should be a priority.

While these go some way to addressing the criticisms, there are still difficulties:

- the protocols are optional,
- two important areas of 'special circumstance' are addressed but many remain for example, 'street children', early marriage and female genital mutilation.

As well as being a means of monitoring how individual states are making progress, the monitoring process of CORC results in a continuous dialogue about interpretation and implementation and enabled the committee to identify issues across states. It became clear that the compromise in attempting to address some of the tensions identified in earlier sections such as

- acknowledging both the vulnerability of children and their active participation,
- the difficulties in addressing 'moral rights' without legal status,
- the tensions between a 'rights discourse' and concepts of 'duty' and responsibility',
- the tension between liberty and welfare rights.

led to differences in interpretation and implementation of the Guiding Principles. The following research example illustrates an area where there are significant differences in the way that the UNCRC is interpreted.

Example of research: difference in interpretation

Archard and Skivenes (2010) identified differences in the way Norway and the United Kingdom have interpreted the 'best interests' principle and incorporated it in legislation. They point to a number of differences and similarities and use these to identify problems associated with interpretation of the principle.

They identify key considerations and, through discussion of these, suggest implications for policy and practice.

The key considerations are as follows:

- The use of the term 'best interests' and the difficulties associated with one definitive view of what this means in relation to a child.
- The weighting that is given to the child's interests or welfare and how the interests of others (e.g. parents) should be taken into account.
- Difficulties in finding clear and agreed understandings of what, as a matter of fact, is in a child's interests given the wide variety of perspectives on this that are influenced by moral and cultural views and the impossibility of being able to predict the future.
- The principle of best interests must be put into an appropriate relation with the requirement that we hear the views of the child.

In discussion of these considerations they promote a process of 'deliberation' involving everyone who might be able to contribute usefully 'to determining, impartially and reasonably, what is best for the child'.

The resulting suggestions for policy and practice are as follows:

- Ensure that legislators do not write substantive assumptions about what is best for every child into their laws, but rather indicate a non-exhaustive list of key relevant considerations that decision makers can review and evaluate in each and every case.
- Clarify while populating the forums that decide the child's best interests as to who does and who does not have rights to contribute, and on what basis those rights are claimed.
- Beware of conceding professional expertise unless there are opportunities for challenging and for agreeing such knowledge as is advanced as relevant.
- Ensure the role of legal personnel – in particular the distinction between the advocacy of a child's views and the representation of his or her interests – is clear and consistent.

- Make a distinction between objective fact and what is invoked as a substantive and contestable assumption; what falls into the latter kind must be contested; those who deliberate on what is best for the child should only invoke such values as all reasonable parties could endorse; and, any justification for a substantive assumption must be clear, transparent and appropriate.

Reflections on the research

Archard and Skivenes (2010) identify considerations and possible solutions to interpreting 'the best interests' principle:

- Look at the difficulties and consider how they might relate to earlier discussion of the tensions associated with the terms 'rights' and 'the child'. The suggestions for policy and practice acknowledge the different views those concerned might have.
- How do you think the differences, including the child's own views, might be taken into account in practice?

As the differences in interpretation of the Guiding Principles became apparent, the CORC has attempted to address these. Through a series of General Comments and Themed Discussion Days, further guidance on interpretation and implementation emerged.

These are summarized in Table 2.4.

These 'clarifications' cannot eliminate the source of tension but it does mean that continuing dialogue makes the tensions clearer to states.

Key points: issues and tensions since 1989

- The four guiding principles of the UNCRC continue to be interpreted and implemented in different ways reflecting the tensions around rights and the view of the child.
- Additional protocols attempt to address the need to consider children living in particularly difficult circumstances as well as encouraging states to acknowledge the need for children to be able to have a voice.

Table 2.4 How some tensions and criticisms have been addressed

Guiding principle	Tensions and criticisms	Examples of attempts to address these
Guiding principle: Non-discrimination Children must be treated without discrimination of any kind, irrespective of race, colour, sex, language, religion or other status (Article 2).	States that are structured hierarchically and/or based predominantly around religion may find a tension between their hierarchical structure and this principle.	UNCRC General Comment No. 9 (2006) on the rights of the child with disabilities. UNHRC General Comment No. 31 of the Committee on the Elimination of Discrimination against Women and No. 18 of the Committee on the Rights of the Child on harmful practices (2014). UN General Assembly (2015) The girl child.
Guiding principle: Best interests of the child In all actions concerning children, whether undertaken by public or private social welfare institutions, courts of law, administrative authorities or legislative bodies, the best interests of the child shall be a primary consideration (Article 3).	'The best interests' of children can be interpreted in different ways and can result in an adult-centred view of what is in the 'best interests' of individual children and 'children' as a group.	General Comment No. 14 (2013) on the right of the child to have his or her best interests taken as a primary consideration.
Guiding principle: Survival and development States recognize that every child has the right to life and that states shall ensure, to the maximum extent possible, the survival and development of each child (Article 6).	The concept of the right to survival and development is essentially a moral right. When there is a legal right there must be a duty to ensure that right is upheld. By using the term 'to the maximum extent possible' the	UN General Assembly (2010) General Discussion on the right of the child to education in emergency situations. General Comment on Public Spending (2015).

Guiding principle	Tensions and criticisms	Examples of attempts to address these
	convention allows states to argue that they are doing what they can both within their own state and in supporting other states which are poorer.	
Guiding principle: participation States shall assure to the child who is capable of forming his or her own views the right to express those views freely in all matters affecting the child, the views of the child being given due weight in accordance with the age and maturity of the child (Article 12).	Here we are faced with the dilemma of who decides whether a child is capable of forming his or her own views. 'Due weight' and 'in accordance with the age and maturity of the child' are debatable concepts leaving open interpretations of these that can minimize children's voices being heard.	General Discussion (2006) on the right of the child to be heard.

Current issues and tensions

Reynaert et al. consider that '... as a consequence of the adoption of the UNCRC, children's rights have got bogged down in consensus thinking' (2009, 527). While the process of interpretation, implementation and monitoring is important in identifying issues about implementation they argue that we should be looking more critically at the more fundamental aspects of the convention.

Tisdall and Punch point to difficulties with the way the convention was developed.

> A compromise document, it ironically did not substantially include children and young people in its development (as would be required, presumably by its Article 12) and its creation was dominated by Minority World countries. (2012, 257)

While it isn't possible to go back to the ten years of development and include children in formulating a UNCRC, it is possible to identify children's views on the UNCRC and how far it reflects their ideas of rights. Children and young people have been included in the monitoring process but that is limited to considering the implementation of the UNCRC within their state rather than the content and processes of the UNCRC.

Example of research: children's views

In 2010, The European Commission's Directorate General for Justice sought the views of young people from all 27 EU member states on the topic of children's rights (European Commission, 2011). Unfortunately this, again, is only giving a Minority World perspective, and it sought the views only of teenagers, perhaps reflecting the commission's views of children's competence and maturity. However, it does give some indication of the views of children on the issues children find most important in terms of their rights. One of the findings was that the majority of respondents felt that children's rights should be broadly the same as the more general human rights. However, when asked about specific rights for children the following were identified:

- Right to play/have a childhood
- Right to choose where to live (if parents divorce)
- Right to play (afford) sport
- Right to protection especially of child victims of pornography/molestation/prostitution
- Right to make mistakes/not to be punished
- Right to information
- Right to have identity protected/internet security/freedom from cyber bullying
- Right to be taught/equipped to live independently when older
- Right to more information before choosing school subjects
- Right not to have to work
- Right to be listened to
- Right to mature slowly

Reflection on the research

Looking at the rights that the respondents thought should be specifically for children think about

- What kind of rights are these: liberty or welfare rights? Which do you think are not covered in the UNCRC?

- Why might the children and young people consider these to be important?
- What differences do you think there might be if the Majority World was included in the research?
- What differences do you think there might be if younger children were included in the research?

The criticism of the UNCRC as reflecting a Minority World view continues and creates tensions reflecting earlier discussion of

- the different status of a rights discourse across states,
- the different social, political, economic and cultural contexts of children's lives.

The tensions associated with the different status of a rights discourse are illustrated through the African Charter on the Rights and Welfare of the Child (OAU, 1990). Johnson (2015), comparing the African Charter to the UNCRC, points to the stronger African provisions for the child's 'best interests', but also the inclusion of traditional or 'cultural' practices, and provisions concerning the 'duties' of the child and its implications for the child's empowerment. This reflects a particular complexity of thinking around 'rights' and 'duties' that isn't apparent in the UNCRC.

Tisdall and Punch (2012) point to the Minority World perspective that children should not be involved in paid work but should rather be located in homes and schools. The tension in implementing articles of the UNCRC associated with education in states where children are involved in work is highlighted by Balagopalan (2008). She found that school-aged children in Calcutta took part in paid work, not only as an economic contribution to the household, but also because the gradual learning of skills improved prospects of employment in the future. The informal schooling that took place alongside work resulted in the young workers gaining a degree of literacy as the education worked in conjunction with their employment. However, when she returned to the same group of workers after the introduction of formal schooling that dismissed the positive benefits of work, she found that the children and young people were not engaging with education in the same way. She suggests that 'these contradictions can begin to be addressed if existing research on equity and schooling includes an interrogation of the assumptions of a normative childhood that the reified space of school helps naturalise' (Balagopalan, 2008, 281). In this sort of case it seems that focusing on children's rights with a Minority World perspective does nothing to improve the lives of children.

More recent criticisms of the interpretation and implementation of the UNCRC are closely linked to the tensions in the view of the child, particularly related to the agency of the child. The earlier discussion of the term 'child' pointed to the difficulties of viewing the child in terms of dichotomies and the more productive acknowledgement that both children and adults varied in their competence, autonomous agency, independence and rationality according to the context and constraints of their life circumstances. The Guiding Principles and Articles of the UNCRC reflect an image of the child as both vulnerable and as an autonomous agent.

Reynaert et al. (2009) identify the difficulties that are emerging as the autonomous agency of children is emphasized without considering the wider context. They acknowledge the very positive effects of the challenge to the traditional notion of the passive, incompetent child but consider

> a possible effect of the discourse of the autonomous child is in fact that the responsibility to realize their rights lies with the children themselves. The child is expected to know her or his own life, needs and interests and to deal with them adequately. (Reynaert et al., 2009, 523)

Tisdall and Punch (2012) list some of the areas where researchers have attributed agency to children as an alternative to helpless victims: child soldiers, child prostitutes and street children. They challenge the degree of agency that children actually have in these circumstances. It is clear that this tension is in need of further investigation so that vulnerable children are not marginalized because of the wider context beyond their control.

This kind of criticism of the interpretation and implementation of the UNCRC goes back to the heart of debates about what, if any, rights children should have and is entwined with the difficulties that arose in trying to get agreement about human rights. As the contrasts between children and adults diminish and the commonality of difficult contexts of the lives of both children and adults is acknowledged, the tension between liberty and welfare rights becomes a common strand. Debates need to move towards how we can ensure liberty rights for adults and children in contexts of war, poverty, famine, repression and the like by addressing how the contexts themselves can be changed – a strong emphasis on welfare rights.

> ## Key points: current issues in relation to the UNCRC
>
> Current issues and tensions continue to reflect earlier difficulties of interpretation and implementation and the Minority World, adult-centred perspective.
>
> In addition there is a more fundamental criticism that debate around rights as a whole has been stifled since the introduction of the UNCRC. In particular, children's autonomous agency can be over-emphasized without consideration of the wider context, and this can result in marginalized and vulnerable children not being protected.

What does research tell us about the state of children's rights internationally and in the United Kingdom?

In this section we will look at two reports that identify how well the United Kingdom (England in particular) is doing in terms of implementing the UNCRC. Following this we will consider two pieces of research linked with the issues in the previous section and the findings of the UK reports: the first on the processes of embedding the UNCRC provisions into law and monitoring effects, and the second on the rights experience of a group of young children. These will help us to see how research can identify the state of children's rights locally, nationally and internationally.

The state of children's rights in the United Kingdom

Within the United Kingdom there are a number of NGOs that are concerned with children's rights and report on children's rights issues. The Children's Rights Alliance for England (CRAE) publish an annual report on the 'State of Children's Rights in England' commenting on progress towards the Concluding Comments of the last periodic review. The 2013 report identified areas of progress, threats and regression.

Progress

- Proposing reforms to the Office of the Children's Commissioner that will give it greater independence and a rights-based mandate.
- Making provisions for children and young people with special education needs.
- Improving outcomes for looked after children and adoption and family justice.

Threats

The government proposes to maintain policies which were found in 2008 to breach children's rights:

- It will not raise the minimum age of criminal responsibility (currently ten years old);
- It will not legislate to prohibit parents and other carers from hitting their children;
- It will not make changes necessary to ensure that 17-year-olds are treated as juveniles by the police (17-year-olds who are detained by the police are often kept with adults and not given the opportunity to have an adult representative with them (Since this 2013 report the Criminal Justice and Courts Act 2015, Section 42 has addressed this).

Regression

Some areas of regression related to economic pressures include

- child poverty
- cuts to spending on education, health, play and to be safe
- changes to legal aid

Other areas of regression are more ideological and include

- repressive legislation to tackle anti-social behaviour
- proposals to require private telecommunications companies to hold records about all communications
- a new system of restraint for use on children
- systems for protecting children against sexual abuse and exploitation are not working

- moves to cut red tape and reduce bureaucracy, examples include
  - a reduction in the extent of statutory guidance around child protection
  - the deregulation of education
  - less stringent arrangements for the inspection of secure training centres (CRAE, 2013).

In August 2015, the Equality and Human Rights Commission published a shadow report covering a wide range of issues related to the implementation of the UNCRC.

Issues covered in the report include the following:

- Access to civil law justice
- Violence against children
- Standards of living and social security
- Right to health (including mental health)
- Education, leisure and cultural activities
- Youth justice
- Immigration detention
- Child trafficking

These mainly cover areas that were covered in the CRAE report but there is the addition of 'child trafficking' which has become an increasing concern with children 'disappearing' from the system (See Chapter 4, pages 126–7 for more details).

Improving the implementation of the UNCRC in the United Kingdom

There is continuing concern in both these reports about the lack of progress in monitoring and improving the lives of children in line with the UNCRC and some of the concerns will emerge in other sections of this book. One of the concerns expressed in both these reports is the lack of progress in embedding the UNCRC provisions into law and policy (compared with, for example, Australia, Spain and Sweden and illustrated by the example of Norway in Chapter 3). The first of the pieces of research we will consider was commissioned by UNICEF in the United Kingdom to find out what we might learn from other countries about how best to do this.

Example of research: legal implementation of children's rights

UNICEF UK commissioned Queen's University Belfast to study the legal and non-legal measures of implementing the UN Convention on the Rights of the Child in 12 countries other than the United Kingdom (Lundy et al., 2012). The aim was to analyse the most effective, practical and impactful ways of embedding children's rights into UK domestic law. States that ratify the UNCRC need to ensure that the principles and articles are reflected in law and provision and should monitor how this is implemented in practice. This is an area that the United Kingdom (in particular, England) has been criticized for, so the research is intended to support the government in finding ways of doing this. The research concluded that states that were part of the research had adopted different approaches to incorporation so, although there wasn't one route to effective integration there were a number of themes that emerged.

- The impact of incorporation was significant in supporting the perception of children as rights holders and developing a culture of respect for children's rights.
- The principle of 'the best interests of the child' was most likely to be represented in domestic law, and most commonly in areas of child protection, alternative care and family law but sometimes in areas such as juvenile justice and immigration. Awareness of the UNCRC was perceived to be crucial in ensuring that the principle was applied in a way that was compliant.
- The principle of the right of the child to have their views taken into account was the next that was most likely to be included. However, concerns were expressed about the extent to which the participation of children was meaningful in practice, and this was often linked to a view that children's protection rights were accepted more readily than their rights to autonomy in decision making
- All children's rights implementation is underpinned by awareness of the UNCRC – not just the content and issues but an understanding of children as the subject of rights, who are entitled to be treated with dignity and respect and to exert influence over their own lives.
- Where national plans are used to establish infrastructure and to embed children's rights into administrative decision making, they can have a clear impact on children's rights awareness and implementation.

- Children's rights implementation is underpinned by comprehensive data, which needs to be collected in a systematic manner that identifies the most vulnerable categories of children, with change tracked over time.

Most countries struggle to protect the rights of the most vulnerable children in all countries in the study. The most vulnerable groups of children (separated children, asylum seekers, indigenous children, and children in conflict with the law) continued to fare less well compared to their peers. In several countries, interviewees suggested that separated children and asylum seekers were not seen as rights holders in the same way as other children, and this was linked, to an extent, to the weakness of the UNCRC in these areas.

Reflection on the research

It is clear from the research that understanding and commitment to the principles of the UNCRC are crucial to effective implementation but there are areas that are difficult for many states: developing a widespread perception that children are rights holders and protecting the rights of marginalized groups.

Look back over examples throughout this chapter and try to find connections between these points and the examples.

What might the United Kingdom be able to learn from this to help them to respond to the last set of Concluding Comments? (page 69).

The second piece of research is a small-scale study of four- to five-year-olds in an Early Years setting in Australia. In contrast to the first piece of research, which was looking at the broad area of incorporation, monitoring and implementation from a top-down perspective, this study takes a bottom-up approach to finding out how young children experience rights issues in the Early Years setting.

Example of research: rhetorical rights and lived rights

Harcourt and Hägglund (2013), already referred to in Chapter 1, identify concern about the top-down implementation and monitoring of

Children's Rights in Australia and carried out research to identify the actual experience of young children in relation to their understanding of rights. An Early Years setting for four- to five-year-olds was the focus of research and the children were involved as participants to the research. Data were collected using a variety of means of communication: drawings, paintings, narratives after discussion over a period of time about the meaning of rights.

The researchers found the following areas of concern for the children:

Concern related to rights	Example to illustrate this
Adult decision making that did not account for children's views,	In response to an imposed 'rest time': 'My body tells me when I am tired and I am not tired when they tell me it's rest time. Everyday, I am not tired'. The children took this issue to the preschool's director, after several attempts to negotiate with their classroom teachers. 'The teachers don't listen. We have told them lots of time about rest time. They hear but they just don't listen'
Global issues such as famine and war	This is a message. Just a small one. It says to the poor children, 'Wait, we are coming to help you'. They can send a message back. It might say, 'Please hurry'. We need to go on an airplane and help them. We need to get rid of the missolds [sic] too. That would be good.
Being safe and secure and	Children have the right to live in a house with windows. They need to feel safe and not scared and they have the right to eat safe vegetables.
A sense of justice.	Children have the right to ask other children who have lots of things if the other children who have lots of things to share. If they didn't share then they are not being fair. If you share this means they like you and want to be your friend.

The researchers concluded that

- this illustrates children's perception of themselves as subjects of rights,
- children seemed to link rights with action, in accordance with one's own and others' rights,

- children embedded the idea of right within relationships with others.

Reflection on the research

The context of this small-scale research was with four- to five-old children who showed interest in the topic of rights. They engaged with researchers in discussions about rights over a period of time. How common do you think these kinds of discussions are in Early Years settings?

What might we learn from this about the potential for rights education?

How do the concerns of these young children relate to the UNCRC?

Look back at the issues and tensions in earlier sections. Which might be reflected in the process and results of this research?

The earlier discussions of 'rights' and 'the child' show that getting a common understanding of children's rights is very difficult. However, although agreement may be a very long way off, the willingness to engage in debate enables change to occur, perhaps slowly, but in a way that is embedded rather than the superficiality that comes with imposition. Chapter 1's discussion of 'a rights agenda' has shown that there is an impetus for change. Ignatieff's plea of not taking the moral high ground when discussing rights seems to have been an effective strategy in the progress that has been made around the implementation of the UNCRC so far. By acknowledging that every state has issues, rather than setting up a league table of achievement, there is more scope for open debate and finding ways forward that take into account different cultural perspectives. This wouldn't mean taking a position of cultural relativity whereby 'anything goes' but would mean taking a position more inclined towards cultural sensitivity. What does seem to be important now is that issues concerning the rights of both children and adults, as individuals living in many different political, social and moral contexts, are discussed and debated through a bottom-up approach that can give a voice to those many different lives.

Activities

The following activities are designed to help reflect back on some of the key concerns over the chapter as a whole.

Chapter Activity 1

Go back through the chapter and list points made about:

- Liberty Rights
- Welfare Rights

Chapter Activity 2

Table 2.2 identifies the implications for child–adult relationships of the different ways we might think about children. Go back through the chapter and look at the examples of research. Identify the following:

- The kind of relationship that is exemplified in each example.
- How the relationship might be different.

Chapter Activity 3

The conclusion to the chapter suggests that

the earlier discussions of 'rights' and 'the child' show that getting a common understanding of children's rights is very difficult. However, although agreement may be a very long way off, the willingness to engage in debate enables change to occur, perhaps slowly, but in a way that is embedded rather than the superficiality that comes with imposition... What does seem to be important now is that issues concerning the rights of both children and adults, as individuals living in many different political, social and moral contexts, are discussed and debated through a bottom-up approach that can give a voice to those many different lives.

- Go back through the chapter and note where differences in understanding occur and consider the implications of each of these for children's lives.
- Consider how a 'bottom-up' discussion about the meaning of rights might affect ways of thinking in these situations and how this might affect children's lives.

Summary

This chapter has

- identified different understandings of the terms 'right' and 'child'
- examined the tensions in thinking about children's rights in the development of the UNCRC,
- examined the tensions that have emerged since the development of the UNCRC,
- identified ways in which research can help to review the state of children's rights internationally and in the United Kingdom.

Further reading

Archard, D. (2015) *Children, Rights and Childhood.* Abingdon: Routledge.

Chapters 2 and 3 look in depth at historical and modern conceptions of childhood. Chapters 4 and 5 go on to consider moral and legal rights and different ideas in relation to what 'rights for children' might mean.

Thomas, N. (2011). *Children's Rights: Policy into Practice. Centre for Children and Young People Background Briefing Series, no.4.* Lismore: Centre for Children and Young People, Southern Cross University.

This gives a concise summary of the development of the UNCRC and issues around it.

Research details

Example of research: duties and rights

In a peer-reviewed journal, White (2007) investigated the different images of children in Bangladesh and how they related to 'imagining' the community. This is reflected in the culture of 'guardianship' that contrasts with the concept of 'rights'. The paper is largely conceptual but draws on pieces of research.

White, S. (2007) 'Children's rights and the imagination of community in Bangladesh', *Childhood*, 14, 505–520.

Example of research: asylum-seeking children

Smyth's doctoral thesis analysed the various versions of the Common European Asylum System in order to see how it was compliant in relation to the UNCRC. Her paper on Child Liberty focuses on this aspect of the lives of children who are also asylum seekers.

Smyth, C. (2013a) 'Is the right of the child to liberty safeguarded in the Common European Asylum System?'*European Journal of Migration and Law*, 15 (2) 111–136.

Smyth, C. (2013b) *The Common European Asylum System and the Rights of the Child: An Exploration of Meaning and Compliance.* Doctoral Thesis, Leiden University. Accessed from https://openaccess.leidenuniv.nl/handle/1887/20462.

Example of research: difference in interpretation

The differences and similarities in approach to interpreting 'the best interests of the child' in Norway and the United Kingdom are investigated by Archard and Skivenes (2010) through analysis of guidance and procedures in the two countries.

Archard, D. and Skivenes, M. (2010) 'Deciding best interests: General principles and the cases of Norway and the UK', *Journal of Children's Services* 5 (4) 43–54.

Example of research: children's views

A qualitative study across all 27 states of the EU was conducted with young people aged 15 to 17, from different socio-economic and ethnic backgrounds. They discussed the issues they see as most important in terms of their rights and the rights of children in general and the various obstacles children face in exercising these rights. The discussion then went on to explore the solutions they felt would help overcome these obstacles and the respondents' explicit suggestions for what the 'adult world' could do to better protect and defend the rights of children.

European Commission (2011) *Children's Rights, as They See Them.* Luxembourg: Publications Office of the European Union.

Example of research: legal implementation of children's rights

Lundy et al. (2012) undertook a study on behalf of UNICEF into the legal and non-legal measures of implementing the UNCRC in 12 countries other than the UK. They analysed the most effective, practical and impactful ways of embedding children's rights into UK domestic law.

Lundy, L., Kilkelly, U., Byrne, B. and Kang, J. (2012) *The UN Convention on the Rights of the Child: A Study of Legal Implementation in 12 Countries,* UNICEF/ Centre for Children's Rights School of Education.

Example of research: rhetorical rights and lived rights

Harcourt, D. and Hägglund, S. (2013) carried out small-scale qualitative research in Australia and Sweden in order to establish young children's views about rights. They used a variety of methods to engage children and staff of two Early Years settings. The settings included children form a variety of backgrounds.

Harcourt D. and Hägglund, S. (2013) 'Turning the UNCRC upside down: a bottom-up perspective on children's rights', *International Journal of Early Years Education*, 21 (4) 286–299.

Part II

An Interdisciplinary Review of Recent Research and Scholarship

3

Children's Rights: Current Tensions, Debates and Research

Introduction and key questions

Sinclair (2004) has described the area of rights in relation to children as emerging from the convergence of new, and developing, ideas and debates from a number of different perspectives. These developments are identified by her as follows:

- the children's rights agenda;
- new paradigms within the social sciences that have increased our understanding of the child as a competent social actor, seeing their

capacity to be commentators in their own lives and to be involved in decision making;
- pressure from children and young people, researchers, policy makers and practitioners working with children.

This chapter will provide an overview for the rest of the book, by reviewing recent research and enquiry that can help to explore the developments in thinking and practice introduced in Chapters 1 and 2. The focus will be on the following:

What are current tensions and debates in relation to children's rights?
What are some of the implications of these tensions?
What is research showing us about tensions and debates concerning children's rights?

What are current, emerging tensions and debates in relation to children's rights?

Chapters 1 and 2 noted that it has become usual to divide the UN Convention into particular areas of concern: these are often identified in terms of liberty and welfare rights or of three kinds of rights: provision, protection and participation. However, others draw attention to different ways of critiquing and approaching the UNCRC in ways that can help illuminate aspects of child rights. Freeman (2000), for example, sees the UN Convention in terms of 'articulating' areas of rights in a particular way. These include 'general rights' – to life; freedom of expression, thought and religion; the right to information and privacy; and against being subjected to torture. Another area is seen to be rights requiring 'protective measures' such as those that protect children from economic and sexual exploitation, to prevent abuse and neglect. The UNCRC also can be seen to address the 'civil status' of children. This area includes the right to acquire nationality, to preserve one's identity, to remain with parents (unless the 'best interest' of the child indicates otherwise) and to be reunited with family. Rights are also seen to relate to what is described as special circumstances. These include children with disabilities, refugee or orphaned children. Others have argued for the importance of children's rights as articulated by the UNCRC as being 'indivisible'. This means that all the rights of the child are relevant to all children, and that they interact with each other to bring full meaning and impact. This is both a philosophical and very pragmatic response to the way rights have been articulated and responded to. UNICEF (2014), for example, states that

> as part of the framework of human rights law, all human rights are indivisible, interrelated and interdependent. Understanding this framework is important to promoting, protecting and realizing children's rights because the CRC – and the rights and duties contained in it – are part of the framework. (http://www.unicef.org/crc/index_framework.html)

This means that a commitment to children's rights is a commitment to them *all*. Each of the rights in the UNCRC has equal importance, and these rights are interrelated. So, for example, engaging with a child's right to health and development (Articles 24 and 6) can be connected to their rights to protection from economic exploitation (Articles 32 and 36). However, this contrasts very directly to the ways in which, despite being signatories to the UNCRC, some countries undermine children's rights through acts of *division*. Particular rights are cherry-picked or responded to and seen as worthwhile by adult parliaments or service providers, while others are refused outright or ignored. This notion of a divided response will be returned to later in this chapter to help us understand how rights can be undermined or left unacknowledged.

Other attention emphasizes *particular aspects* of the UNCRC. Some, for example, have argued that the UNCRC is distinguished from other rights-based initiatives in its attempt to implement policies through it inclusion of, and emphasis on, *participation* as a key cornerstone of change:

> Participation is the keystone of the arch that is the UNCRC. Without the active participation of children and young people in the promotion of their rights to a good childhood, none will be achieved effectively. (Badham quoted in Willow, 2002, vi)

This way of analysing the UN Convention on the Rights of the Child sees participation as its heart and is summarized by Hill and Tisdall as the view that children are active, engaged participants in their lives, and, in the society they are part of, as 'social actors with their own views and goals, and not just objects or problems' (1997, 28). They quote a child asserting that children should have 'the rights of agency: to take part in family decisions, rights to make our own decisions about our future, rights to live our own life and not what our parents want us to do, the right to our own opinion' (CRDU, 1994, 24). As outlined in Chapter 2, the change here involves seeing children in their own right and as having rights, not as proto-adults, or as the property of parents. However, issues regarding participation are subject to different interpretations and tensions around childhood and society.

Authors such as Freeman note that in the UNCRC's development there were 'stumbling blocks' in relation to the formulation of child rights – in areas such as participation and freedom of thought, conscience and religion. This analysis of a developmental perspective on the convention can help understand and illustrate some of the tensions within the UNCRC referred to in Chapters 1 and 2. Freeman comments, for example, that 'inter-country adoption offended ... Latin American countries' (2000, 278). Issues such as the rights of the unborn child, female genital mutilation and differences on whether children should have 'duties' were also noted by him as contentious issues which were not resolved in relation to the final form that the UNCRC took. 'Duty' as a concept found its way into the Charter on the Rights and Welfare of the African Child, but was excluded from the UN Convention. He points to these areas as ones of eventual compromise, for example on religion, 'by the adoption of a minimal text' (2000, 278). Freeman concludes that whether these compromised positions are 'necessarily good' for children can be contested.

Freeman's analysis concerns such tensions and the *initial development* of the UNCRC. Parallel issues continue to accompany contemporary interpretations and responses to children's rights. Tasoulias has usefully summarized this tension as involving, on the one hand, efforts 'to hold the substantive content of human rights standards uniform across societies' (2012, 20) and, on the other, 'the potentially enormous divergence in normative content from one society to another' (2012, 20). This, in part, can be understood as the effects of differences *between* an international convention such as the UNCRC or HRA and specific national contexts. It can also usefully be seen as reflecting the tensions *within* different nations: how political, social or religious differences, for example, within a country affect how children and adults perceive and respond to children and their rights. Ruck and Horn, writing from a legal perspective, have identified a key aspect of this as concerning 'the influence of cultural values on young people's conceptions of rights and the tensions that arise between individuals' rights and prerogatives and cultural traditions, norms, and practices' (2008, 691). Tasoulias goes on to make a point related to such dynamics: 'in terms made familiar by Cohen and feminist writers, what is in question is not merely a legal-institutional

Table 3.1 Critiques of the UN Convention on the Rights of the Child (UNCRC) and research questions

Critique of the UNCRC	Questions
The lack of engagement with children's political rights.	How can children's political rights be best represented political processes in national and local governance? What position can be adopted regarding children's voting rights, for example? See pages 32 and 196, for further discussion.
The lack of substantial involvement of children and young people themselves in formulating the UNCRC.	How can this lack be redressed? How can the unique perspective brought by children and young people as experts in their own lives be introduced to the understanding, reformulation and implementation of rights?
Does not pay adequate attention to discriminatory forces which affect children's rights: for example sexism, ablebodiedism, racism, homophobia.	How do issues such as racial and gender discrimination and patriarchy affect children's rights? For further discussion, see pages 86–90 and 250–4. What is the relationship between cultural and religious belief and children's rights? For further discussion, see pages 152–4 and 210–13.
Children's rights in relation to areas such as participation are often interpreted as reflecting Westernized concepts that see individuals as autonomous, emphasizing rights such as individual choice. Other cultural ideas which emphasize social cooperation or the centrality of community are often left out.	How can different cultural concepts be reflected in ways of looking at children's rights? For further discussion, see pages 103–10, 128 and 256.
Aspects of 'identity' not envisaged by the authors of the text are not acknowledged: the idea is that our identities are not established by birth or parents, but made by children within interactions with society: 'A right to an identity could imply anything from respect for chosen (or not consciously chosen) sexual orientation to respect for all the child's efforts to remake his or her identity' (Olsen, 1992, 217).	How can a child's developing identity, in areas such as sexual orientation, be recognized within a rights framework? For further discussion, see pages 86–90.

structure, but a human rights ethos that pervades our lives, cutting across boundaries between public and private, society and state' (2012, 25). He recognizes the 'interwoven' nature of rights: they interact and are formed within localized contexts. This is key to current debates about what happens to rights when they meet the complex realities of national and societal contexts. Contemporary scholarship is trying to understand these processes and to make use of insights that are emerging to enable children's rights to be fully realized.

Can children's rights evolve? Diversity and LGBTI children

A tension reflecting these complexities concerns the relationship of the UNCRC and children's rights to different childhoods and aspects of the diversity of children's lives in different countries. A number of authors and organizations have noted that the direct naming and engagement of rights relating to the specific situations of lesbian, gay, bisexual, transgender and intersex (LGBTI) children were left out of the UNCRC, for example. Some might argue that they are covered within the UNCRC as whole, but this simply doesn't hold up to any serious scrutiny. Article 2 includes other differences, but omits them completely:

> Article 2: States Parties shall respect and ensure the rights set forth in the present Convention to each child within their jurisdiction without discrimination of any kind, irrespective of the child's or his or her parent's or legal guardian's race, colour, sex, language, religion, political or other opinion, national, ethnic or social origin, property, disability, birth or other status. (UNCRC, 1989)

Some organizations, such as UNICEF, position this omission in a particular way, trying to compensate for it. In 2014, for example, UNICEF reported thus:

> Despite significant progress, recent estimates suggest around 80 countries around the world have laws that subject their citizens to severe criminal penalties for homosexuality. Such laws institutionalize discrimination and can lead to violence. A small number of countries and territories have recently passed legislation or enacted administrative practices which further criminalize or stigmatize homosexuality. Such legislation is sometimes rationalized as an effort to protect children but there is considerable evidence that

discrimination or criminalization of LGBT identity or behaviour actually harms rather than protects children. (2014, 3)

They note that

as yet, there is no binding international instrument that explicitly addresses discrimination against individuals based on their sexual orientation and gender identity. There is, however, a non-binding CRC Committee General Comment (GC15), where the Committee identifies sexual orientation and gender identity as a ground for discrimination. (2014, 3)

Potgieter and Reygan's conclusions from their research considering the nature of a 'safe school environment for LGBTI youth' (2012, 49), for example, point out that in South Africa, children and young people who are lesbian, gay, bisexual or transgender and intersex 'continue to be exiled as a group, even though legal instruments are in place to provide them with full citizenship rights' (2012, 39). Bhana's (2014) research in South Africa's KwaZulu-Natal argues that the political emphasis on rights has positive effects for raising the agenda for lesbian, gay, bisexual and transgender pupils at schools. However, researchers found that one-third of all LGBT students had been physically assaulted at school because of their sexuality and almost one in five LGBT students said they had attempted suicide. The researchers also found that black and Indian students were more likely to be victimized because of their sexuality than were white students. The report noted significant victimization by teachers and principals as well as by other children (Bridging the Gaps, 2012, 19).

Example of research: lesbian, gay and bisexual young people

UK research by the University of Cambridge and Stonewall in 2012 involving a survey completed by 1,614 lesbian, gay and bisexual young people aged between 11 and 19 revealed the following:

- More than half (55 per cent) of lesbian, gay and bisexual young people experience homophobic bullying in Britain's schools (Guasp, 2012, 5).
- Only half of lesbian, gay and bisexual pupils report that their schools say homophobic bullying is wrong. Even fewer pupils in faith schools at 37 per cent say their schools say homophobic

bullying is wrong. In comparison, 95 per cent of schools say bullying because of ethnicity is wrong and 90 per cent say bullying because of disability is wrong.

'The school seems eager to eliminate racism, but says nothing on gay bullying.' (Will, 16, secondary school, Greater London)
' I don't know anything about my rights as a gay person, what the law says, or anything about safe sex. We discussed the controversy over gay marriage once.' (Natalie, 17, secondary school, South West)

Gay pupils are much more likely to be bullied in schools that don't say homophobic bullying is wrong than in schools that do (67 per cent compared to 48 per cent).

'When we did discuss gay issues the teachers were very against it and were saying that all gay people had problems, which made me feel very uncomfortable.' (Dee, 17, private faith school, Yorkshire and the Humber)
'We were told that homosexuality was a sin, disgusting and unnatural in our Religious Education classes.' (Sadie, now 19, faith secondary school, East of England) (Guasp, 2012, 16–18)

Reflection on the research

This chapter referred earlier to the absence of LGBT rights in Article 2 of the UNCRC whereas a choice was made to include other areas such as race, colour and disability. Here is the text, again:

Article 2: States Parties shall respect and ensure the rights set forth in the present Convention to each child within their jurisdiction without discrimination of any kind, irrespective of the child's or his or her parent's or legal guardian's race, colour, sex, language, religion, political or other opinion, national, ethnic or social origin, property, disability, birth or other status (UNCRC, 1989)

1. How could the language of Article 2 be altered to redress the absence of LGBTI rights?
2. How might this change result in actions or changes in policy, practice and attitude that could alter the experiences of young people such as those reported on in the research?

Dalacoura (2014) quotes Massad (2007):

Massad argues that the West's apparent intent to 'protect' the rights of homosexual men and women is part and parcel of its hegemonic project, which is underpinned by exporting ideas and concepts (such as 'homosexual' or 'gay'). (Dalacoura, 2014, 1299)

However, she argues that

the spread of the idea of 'homosexuality' in the Middle East from the 19th century onwards shows that, after that point, Middle Eastern societies and their citizens begin to share with Europe common notions and ordering principles about the self, society and the world. This does not mean that Europe and the Middle East have identical experiences of modernity with regard to that issue. It means that they begin to have in common a sufficient number of concepts to make these experiences mutually intelligible and allow communication across societies and regions. (Dalacoura, 2014, 1302).

Though this text concentrates on adults, it raises issues connected to the discussion in the example.

- Discuss Massad's suggestion that to 'protect' rights in this way is connected to what he calls a 'hegemonic project, which means the 'West' uses its power and influence to dominate and 'control others' (Cambridge Dictionary) who do not share its views and experiences.
- Discuss Dalacoura's contrasting idea of sexual identity and experience as being an area of mutuality and 'communication across societies and regions'. How do these ideas connect with the discussions of diversity and LGBTI children in this chapter?

In this way, contemporary research reveals that the *invisibility and absence* of support, education and awareness of rights or the challenging of assaults on lesbian, gay, bisexual and trans children is matched by the *visibility and presence* of discriminatory, violent and rights-denying everyday behaviours of some schools, staff and other children. UNICEF (2014) argues for a 'range of measures [that are] required to create an enabling environment for eliminating discrimination against children and parents based on sexual orientation or gender identity'. Some of the measures are as follows:

- To repeal laws that entrench such discrimination, and in particular those that criminalize behaviours or 'promotion' of homosexuality, or the association of LGBT children and individuals.

- To enact laws which provide LGBT couples and their children with the legal recognition of their family ties.
- To ensure that children, irrespective of their sexual orientation and gender identity, are provided with legal protection from abusive, violent and sexually exploitative adults, including those abusive adults who are entrusted to enforce laws.
- To equalize the age of consent for both heterosexual and homosexual conduct would help reduce discrimination against, and criminalization of, LGBT children and individuals.
- To help governments face the challenge of meeting their obligations to LGBT children under the Convention on the Rights of the Child by addressing social norms and practices that discriminate and marginalize children and adults based on real or perceived sexual orientation and gender identity.
- To include LGBT children and youth in the discussion about policy.

In this way, UNICEF reflects the position, outlined in Chapter 1 and in this chapter: that rights are a domain of debate and tension connected to evolving and developing understanding and action. Its 'current concerns' publication of 2014, quoted above, illustrates this regarding how to address absences in LGBTI children's rights.

Are rights alone inadequate?

Other perspectives on the UNCRC have argued that a rights approach in itself is inadequate. Bach summarizes this approach well:

> Whether the source of exclusion is poverty, racism, fear of differences or lack of political clout, the consequences are the same: a lack of recognition and acceptance; powerlessness and 'voicelessness'; economic vulnerability; and, diminished life experiences and limited life prospects. For society as a whole, the social exclusion of individuals and groups can become a major threat to social cohesion and economic prosperity. A rights-based approach is inadequate to address the personal and systemic exclusions experienced by children and adults. People with disabilities are leading the way in calling for approaches based on social inclusion and valued recognition to deliver what human rights claims alone cannot.(2002, viii)

Here the interrelationship between a number of different perspectives are emphasized. The central tenet of this critique is that rights and processes of social exclusion need to be addressed within different arenas of children's lives in ways that acknowledge the interconnectedness of rights, powerlessness, economic vulnerability and a lack of political acknowledgement. So, for example, the exclusion encountered by disabled children relates to the processes of exclusion concerning childhood and disability. The rights agenda for change in relation to disabled children can be seen within the pressure for inclusive education rather than segregated education:

> It is about contributing to the realisation of an inclusive society with the demand for a rights approach as a central component of policy-making. This position has been informed by insights and ideas derived from disability studies. This perspective raises some important issues with regard to the question of inclusive education. First, it encourages the issue of change to be foregrounded. Unlike integration, the change process is not about assimilation but transformation of those deep structural barriers to change including the social base of dominant definitions of 'success', 'failure' and 'ability' within the academy, as well as schools. (Barton, 2003, 13)

One of the key developments in the legal arena has been the incorporation of the European Convention on Human Rights into English law in 1998, operational since 2000. The system enables children, for example, to apply to domestic courts if they consider a government or public agency has infringed their rights as specified in the European Convention. If the court finds in their favour, then the government is obliged to rectify the situation through a 'fast-track' procedure to bring about legislation in conformity with the convention (Human Rights Act, 1998, Section 4 (2), 10, Sch. 2).

At a national, or macro, level the literature points to the importance of legislation in promoting children's rights and social inclusion and to the creation of posts such as the Children's Commissioners for England, Scotland, Wales and Northern Ireland. At a local level some have said that the UNCRC's emphasis in Article 12 on children's rights to participate has been reflected in the increase in their involvement in decision making within areas of service provision such as education, leisure and health. Others have criticized the lack of real engagement in participation to influence decisions and to have their voices acted on. A number of reviews of such initiatives have discovered that, though resources are invested in researching children's views or consulting them, adults find ways to make sure that any actual changes which respond to the children don't take place. These are often not deliberate, but, nonetheless, a variety of strategies or patterns have emerged (Raby, 2014; Reynaert et al., 2009; Simmons, 2010). A common occurrence is that adult organizations emphasize publicly that the consultation takes place, but then the participatory process goes 'quiet' and any further action evaporates. One strategy seems to be that the adults simply wait until the participation is forgotten about; another is that the views are refused with a rationale offered, such as the suggestions are impractical or outside budgetary constraints. Others are that the children's views are modified into a form suggested by adults and deemed as more 'realistic' or acceptable. An accompanying adult way of handling children is that those consulted or involved in research are never told about the results of the actual consultation, or involved in discussions or negotiations about the possible outcomes as a response to the consultation. This means that children are excluded from the decision-making processes or arena and so are kept away from opportunities to find out what has, or hasn't, happened or do not have the chance to challenge what has happened.

As identified in Chapters 1 and 2, criticism has identified other ambiguities, tensions and omissions within the UN Convention. This includes its lack of enforceability unless it is incorporated through national law, the lack of promotion of children's participation through political rights and that definitions – such as that of the child's 'best interests' – may be made by adults rather than involving children's own ideas and agency and that it does not pay attention to the ways in which forces such as patriarchy within society and families affects children. These critiques can also be seen to form the agenda for enquiry and research presented in Table 3.1.

What are some of the implications of these tensions?

As introduced in Chapter 1's discussion of a 'divided response' (see pages 32–3) and the idea of a 'rights veneer' (see pages 35–6), some have argued that the actual implementation of action to realize the UNCRC has been patchy. Some nations have been more concerned with a tokenistic engagement, rather than a real engagement true to the spirit of the convention itself and actually creating meaningful change for children. The real effects or implications of a rights perspective have been considered in a number of ways. Authors and researchers consider this from different perspectives.

Alderson (2008) identifies the following qualities of children's rights developed from the UNCRC as shown in Table 3.2.

Table 3.2 The qualities of rights

Quality of rights	Detail
All rights are limited	Some areas of children's lives can be protected by rights: for example the three 'Ps' can be protected as legal concepts. Some arenas cannot be legislated for by government – so though the UNCRC states the importance of children living in an atmosphere of love and understanding, the law can protect a child from obvious neglect or abuse, but it cannot enforce love.
Some rights are aspirational	There are factors that may affect a nation's capacity to realize rights. Hence a lack of resources may have a negative impact on a country's ability to respond to an article. (see pages 44–5 and 247 for further discussion).
Children's rights occur in a context and are conditional, not absolute	The implementation of a child's rights occur within a complex network of factors. The UNCRC states that the rights of the child should be a 'primary consideration' – but they are not the only consideration. The relationship between an individual child's situation, the concept and practice of what is in his or her 'best interest', the rights of other people and the role of what is possible within the laws or policies of a country all interact. This can make the idea of an absolute position on implementing an area of rights for every child in the same way inappropriate because individual situations must be taken into account in finding a way to engage with his or her rights.
Children's rights are shared	Alderson says that the UNCRC is not about 'selfish individualism' but about the goal of equality in social justice and the improvement of standards of life for everyone in a society (see pages 102–3 and 107–8, for further discussion).
Rights are about necessities	They concern areas such as clean water, safety, play (see pages 201–3 and 260–1, for further discussion).
Rights go with obligations and responsibilities	Not all children, for example, the very young, can understand and demand rights for themselves. Hence, adults have a responsibility, and the rights in areas such as provision and protection involve duties held by others towards children's access to their rights (see pages 47–9, for further discussion).

Source: Based on Alderson (2008, 18–19)

When reviewing the way rights are being responded to, it is useful to see them within this framework: as interconnected and as a part of other ways in which children experience their lives within a society. The material from Alderson can help to see how rights, obligations and responsibilities are connected, for example, or to perceive the interwoven relationship between children's rights and the experiences of everyone within a society or community. The framework can also help to understand that, as the previous chapter introduced, rights occur within a context and within a complex of different interests. Simmons (2010) argues that the key to ensuring compliance with human rights treaties belongs not to foreign or international agents, but to domestic processes such as elite-initiated agendas, litigation, and popular pressure and opinion. Olsen (1992) has pointed out that the tensions existing within the UNCRC are illustrative of 'the broader problems of trying to improve the life situation of a group by conferring rights ... laws conferring rights will have gaps, conflicts and ambiguities' (1992, 213). One example she selects concerns primary education, which is compulsory. Article 28 says that it shall be 'directed to the preparation of the child for responsible life in a free society' (UNCRC, 1989), and the spirit of this is of understanding, peace, tolerance, equality of the sexes and friendship among all peoples. Olsen notes that to those who do not support these ideas 'this direction is likely to sound more like propaganda than education' (1992, 213). Olsen points out that there is a contradiction within the UNCRC itself here – on the one hand advocating the right to a certain kind of education, while, on the other hand, advocating a right to religious views which are in direct contradiction with the values its vision of education promotes: 'this education towards tolerance, equality between the sexes, and friendship conflicts with various religions, which the Convention guarantees to children the right to participate in' (1992, 214).

Tensions and debates: the UK opt-out of the UNCRC: an examination of a 'divided response'

One of the key criticisms of the UNCRC as a force in children's lives is that it need not be acted on in full. This forms the basis of criticism of the UNCRC in terms of its limited ability to enforce compliance with human rights legislation. Comments such as that made in the medical journal *The Lancet* are echoed by many agencies and individuals: 'realistically many governments do not take their responsibilities seriously and others are slow to implement change' (Reading et al., 2008, 24).

An example of this 'divided response', as introduced in Chapter 1 (pages 32–3), is the United Kingdom's relationship to the UNCRC. Criticisms of the United Kingdom are persistent and vocal, from a number of agencies within the United Kingdom, and from the United Nations itself, yet the government has not altered, or been reluctant to alter, its position in some critical areas for many years. The following material illustrates this by looking at the rights of children who are asylum seekers or refugees over a number of years. In 2002, for example, the United Nations Committee on the Rights of the Child's concluding observations on the United Kingdom criticized the performance of the UK government in relation to

- children in the penal system,
- children and 'irregular migrants',
- inequalities in education and health.

Criticism of the UK government's lack of commitment to addressing its divided response to children's rights has come from many different organizations. The Children's Rights Alliance (2008), a non-government organization, made a report leading up to the following, 2008, phase of the United Nations cycle of reviewing progress in the United Kingdom. This concluded that the UK government had not significantly addressed the UN Committee's criticisms in relation to children's rights and the treatment of children seeking refugee or asylum, for example. The Report of the 2008 UN Committee echoed this and, again, criticized the UK government for a lack of progress.

Its fifth report, in 2015, continued to voice these criticisms. The following is from a summary of discussions involving members of the Committee on the Rights of the Child and UK government representatives. A 'Country Rapporteur' is someone who has particular responsibilities in addressing issues related to the country being reviewed:

> Committee Experts expressed concern about the possible repeal of the 1998 Human Rights Act as it was feared that the new Bill of Rights would weaken the protection of children's rights... The principle of the best interest of the child was not a primary consideration in all legislation and policy making, in administrative and judicial decisions concerning the children, nor in the asylum and immigration decision-making in relation to families and separated children. The Country Rapporteur also raised issues of the use of

restraints and other restrictive interventions in juvenile custodial settings, the use of "pain distraction' techniques on children, the use of Tasers on children in Scotland and in Northern Ireland, lack of prospect of legal prohibition of corporal punishment, high incidence of domestic violence and violence against children and women, as well as sexual violence… There existed a general climate of intolerance of childhood, children and adolescents in the United Kingdom, especially in the media which was promoting negative stereotypes. (United Nations Human Rights, Office of the High Commissioner, 2016)

As detailed above, for many years the UK government had *deliberately* retained an opt-out of the UNCRC. This opt-out allowed child migrants and asylum seekers to be locked up without judicial scrutiny. So, whereas the UNCRC obliges nations to place the 'best interests' of a child first, the opt-out meant that the UK government did not need to apply it to these children. Therefore, officials could lock them up, sometimes for weeks or months pending deportation. The UK Border Agency officially said that they were 'determined to treat children within our immigration system with fairness and compassion' (news.bbc.co.uk/1/hi/uk). However, despite this rhetoric, following an inspection in 2008, HM Inspectorate of Prisons, for example, said that children were detained for too long and were left distressed and scared at the Yarl's Wood Centre in Bedfordshire. The following statement from their 'Report on an announced inspection of Yarl's Wood Immigration Removal Centre' (2008) gives some sense of the UK government's attitude towards the best interests and rights of children, when its own inspectorate reported:

> The plight of detained children remained of great concern… An immigration removal centre can never be a suitable place for children and we were dismayed to find cases of disabled children being detained and some children spending large amounts of time incarcerated. (2008, 5)

Some children and families were being transported to and from centres in caged vans. The report adds that

> prolonged detention was having a detrimental effect on the welfare and behaviour of children whose fear and distress was strongly reflected in our children's interviews. (2008, 5)

Interviews with the children, some aged between 10 and 11, were made as part of the inspection. The report includes the following:

- One child mentioned that she and her sister were gated apart from their mother and brother in the van. They had only one stop on the way from Dungavel IRC and her sister had had to go to the toilet in the van.
- Three stated that they wanted to go home and were missing family and friends.
- Two were unhappy with the food.
- Two were unhappy as they had been given flight dates that had then been cancelled. One of them stated that staff had given them a flight time at 2/3am.
- One, commenting on the staff, stated 'they're evil' and that there were only two good members of staff.
- One was unhappy because they were ill.
- One was worried when thinking about going back to their country of origin and said 'I feel like I'm in prison, as if I've killed somebody.'
- One was frustrated that they needed their mother to be able to do anything, i.e. dining hall and if they needed the toilet during visits. (2008, 86)

At the same time as the Commissioner's Report, a campaign was launched by the UK publication *New Statesman* around this issue. Its remit was to call on the UK government to end the detention of children for immigration reasons. The presence of the campaign and the response from the UK government's own Children's Commissioner for England are included as an illustration of tensions regarding the role and nature of the UNCRC. The *New Statesman* describes 'No Place for Children' in this way:

> Every year, around 2000 children pass through the UK's immigration detention centres. They are there because their parents have applied for asylum in the UK. Detention is physically and emotionally damaging for children … many subsequently receive refugee status, but children who have been detained remain deeply traumatised by their experiences. (O'Keefe, 2008 www.newstatesman.com/uk-politics)

A joint report in 2015 by the UK Children's Commissioners note aspects of change which occurred. The report acknowledges that, following the widely supported campaign against the indefinite detention of children in immigration facilities, the May 2010 coalition agreement included a commitment to end the detention of children for immigration purposes. Leading on from a public review, a new process for enforcing family removals was announced in December 2010. However, Table 3.3 summarizes the continued problem with exceptions, still present, noted within the commissioners' 2015 report.

Table 3.3 Children's Commissioners 2015 Review: key issues

Key Issues identified by Report
• Children are no longer detained at Yarl's Wood or Dungavel Immigration Removal Centres but can be detained as part of the family removals process at Cedars for short periods and also in entry refusal cases Tinsley House or for a variety of reasons in short-term holding facilities in ports and airports on arrival in the UK.
• Children whose age is subject to dispute may be detained in adult immigration removal facilities and may be held in isolation until their age is determined.
• Children are therefore still not detained only as a last resort or for the shortest time. The review cites a report from the Coram Children's Legal Centre (CCLC):
28 days is currently the time allocated for the Home Office to transfer asylum seekers from asylum support to mainstream benefits once they become refugees and in CCLC's experience this regularly proves to be insufficient time to make the relatively simple administrative arrangements required. The consequence of this is that many refugees are left destitute because their asylum support is cut off before they can access mainstream entitlements, causing severe hardship for the refugees affected. (CCLC, 2015, 7)

The points necessarily raise questions about the actual nature of changes compared to rhetoric in policy or guidelines (see Chapter 2, pages 69–74, for further discussions related to this):

The commissioners' response draws on other research and review material to illustrate the lack of adherence to rights entitlements, arguing that, for example:

The State Party should ensure that migrant, refugee and asylum-seeking children have access to basic services such as education and health, and that there is no discrimination in benefit entitlements for these families that could affect children or be contrary to their rights under Articles 2, 22, 26 or 27 UNCRC. (2015, 50)

They cite as illustration a recent UK case of a child, EG, reported on by Coram Children's Legal Centre (2015). The case involved a vulnerable and socially isolated asylum seeker who developed a rare brain infection and could not look after her child (EG). The baby boy starved to death and the mother died two days later. The family became destitute during the transition from asylum to mainstream support, leaving the family 'dependent upon ad hoc payments by local agencies', adding to 'Mrs G's anxiety and consequently to her difficulty in managing her children and their collective health needs'. The review expressed 'concern about the adverse consequences on vulnerable children and the resulting additional pressure on local professional agencies' when support was cut off' (CCLC, 2015, 7).

This example helps to illustrate the way that a divided response undermines a society's response to child rights and the need for rights to be reviewed and pursued within a society. Here agents such as voluntary agencies and the media are pursuing the child rights agenda in relation to a group of children who the UK government have, for many years, identified as not deserving the same rights as other children.

Activity 1

Review the material from the HM Inspector of Prisons and their interviews with parents and children (pages 97–8). The Children's Commissioner for England described the way UK immigration system treated children as 'positively cruel' and 'inhuman' calling on the government to 'live up to its rhetoric by making sure every child does matter' (O'Keefe, 2008, www.newstatemsman.com. uk-politics).

The UK government's 'Directorate Children and Young People' (DCYP) echo many of the concerns of the UNCRC, regarding protection and development, for example. The DCYP state that 'all our children and young people are supported, protected and that they feel safe' and are 'provided with every opportunity to achieve the best possible outcomes and fulfill their potential' (www.gov.uk/government/groups/directorate-children-and-young-people).

Review the material on pages 97–8 and consider how the children's experience there relate to the DCYP's assurances of:

- being supported
- being protected
- feeling safe
- fulfilling their potential

What is research showing us about tensions and debates concerning children's rights?

The following presents a more in-depth review of the existing literature and research to illustrate the way tensions relating to three key areas relating to the UNCRC and children's rights. The first regards participation; the second, provision and consent; and the third, protection.

Tensions and debates: research and participation

In terms of the right to participation, research has shown that children and young people have varied experiences of developments to date within countries such as the United Kingdom. The following example of research examines an aspect of their experience.

Example of research: children, participation and a rights veneer

Stafford et al. (2003) interviewed 200 children aged between 3 and 18 years, from different ethnic backgrounds and different social contexts. They were asked what they wanted to be consulted on, and to detail any advice they wanted to give to government and policy makers about consulting children. Comments showed an awareness of issues referred to earlier – such as consultation being a veneer of involvement, without any real impact on children's lived situation:

- If they're not going to do something, don't ask.
- People consulting should not assume young people are going to like adult ideas and give the responses adults want, but ask for young people's own ideas.
- If the Parliament was asking it would be 'Do you think this would be a good thing?,' so that's not actually us deciding things – they're putting it into our heads... We should be asked what our idea is. (2003, 365)

The children consulted advocated a reduction in the voting age, young people's referenda over age of ten on issues such as the presence of attention to lesbian and gay sexuality within education, and young people's representation in parliament (2003, 370–371).

One of the research's conclusions was that young people's experience of consultation had often been 'unsatisfactory' due to two main factors:

- It had not been representative
- It lacked impact.

The research revealed that children and young people had a strong wish to be involved and to be consulted, especially on issues directly affecting their lives: education, school, recreation, public transport and health. The children wanted to see results from the consultation and that their participation had an effect: their views being taken into account in planning policies and in decision making. Feedback on the process and results were also seen as crucial. A strong emphasis was placed on recognizing that children's agendas in participating may be different from those of adults: 'allowing children to talk about what matters to them and not dismissing as trivial, children's priority concerns' (2003, 372).

Reflections on the research

Activity 1

How do you see the comments that the young people wanted their 'views being taken into account in planning policies and in decision making' in terms of rights issues, and the notion of a 'rights veneer' as described in Chapter 1 (pages 35–6)?

Activity 2

Sinclair has said the challenge is to move beyond one-off or isolated consultations to a position where children's rights to participation are 'firmly embedded within organisational cultures and structures for decision making' (2004, 116).

Care is needed to ensure genuinely open communication in participation rather than seeking confirmation of what adults think or want (Stafford et al., 2003, 372).

How do you see these comments on rights in relation to the interview findings summarized in this box?

This example illustrates how the emergence of a 'rights veneer' needs to be challenged by monitoring to ensure that participation is not qualified by those with power, adults, to result only in changes they feel are confluent within their own agenda. This research helps to illustrate the importance of participation being embedded within processes that result in actual impact and of children being included not only in consultation but also in decision making and in dialogue about the results of their participation.

Tensions and debates: rights, provision and consent – rights-informed ways of relating to children

Lansdowne (1996) points out that the phrases used in the legislation, such as 'best interest and welfare', are invariably defined by adults. Lowden's (2002) work can be seen as an illustrative example of this issue regarding provision and children's rights. She has argued that despite recommendations, guidelines and legislation, the response to ways of relating to children in the light of children's rights, particularly in relation to consent in the provision of healthcare, remain complex and inconsistent. She points out that though both the Children Act (Department of Health, 1989) and the United Nations Convention on the Rights of the Child (1989) stress the importance of listening to children and taking their views seriously, doctors and nurses are uncertain whether, in relating to children, they should respect children's wishes or whether they risk breaking the law by doing so. She notes:

> Case law in the UK focuses on the end point of decision making, that is consent, instead of the process of sharing information through the stages of investigation, diagnosis and considering treatment options. This amounts to an all or nothing approach, which confers full legal status on competent people but does not attend to participation when patients are partly involved and can influence rather than make decisions. (Lowden, 2002, 107)

She draws attention to the following issues:

> Children's *experience* can determine their understanding more than *age*, and children with chronic conditions who have repeated treatment have understanding that does not consist of abstract thought but of illness, disability and treatment experience. (Alderson and Montgomery, 1996a, 1996b)

From this experience, young children understand the value of life and can weigh up alternatives and express consistent values based on a firm sense of identity, thus demonstrating the moral and rational basis of wise decision making. Therefore, to test competence in the *abstract* without reference to the *circumstances* may be misleading (O'Neill, 1984).

Laws that allow treatment to be forced on non-competent children appear to assume that they have no understanding worth considering. However, very young children do reason and can perceive unexplained treatment as assault and as far more damaging than the disease it is intended to treat (Alderson and Montgomery, 1996a, 1996b). This opens a credibility gap between the child's perception of harm and the adult's intention of benefit.

Lowden argues that the greatest obstacles to children being asked for consent arise from adult prejudices about their abilities and the protectionist view of the rights they can, or do, have. She concludes thus:

> At present childhood belongs to children least of all and its study remains largely a study of adults' attitudes to and practices with children. Children are not human becomings they are human beings at birth and they have particular views about their own status. Children are people in their own right and as such should be recognized as having rights (Qvortrup et al., 1994). (Lowden, 2002, 107)

She reflects that in the United Kingdom the 'historical evolution of childhood' continues to influence children's rights. This means that rights do not exist in a vacuum and that factors such as cultural attitudes towards children affect the ways relationships are formed or the ways policies are created and responded to. Lowden argues that adult beliefs about children's rights influence children's opportunities for self-determination. Her argument is that until adults develop a more pragmatic ideology regarding children's rights, a true respect for children's autonomy will not be achieved and that areas such as consent will remain an adult and legal prerogative. Here debates about rights, consent and children are connected to the tensions outlined at the start of this chapter. Lowden illustrates both how UK cultural, social and political contexts interact with rights and also shows how the presence of rights is connected to potential positive change for children and those who work with them.

Example of research: best interests, 'maturity' and consent

A parallel illustration in a different context concerning rights and consent, is offered by Parsapoor et al. (2014) in the *Iranian Journal of Pediatrics*. They question, for example, the morality of assuming that parents or guardians automatically are in a position to make decisions that are in the 'best interests' of children:

> Deliberations on the reasons why parents are selected as surrogates in medical decision-making highlight two basic presumptions in this respect that parents are responsible and caring, when it comes to their children, and that they have their children's best interests in heart. If the two above-mentioned presumptions no longer apply, it does not seem morally appropriate that parents continue to enjoy their right to surrogacy. (2014, 5)

They note that within Iranian law this can be removed:

> Based on the Article 1173 of the Civil Code of the Islamic Republic of Iran, 'If the physical health or moral education of a child is endangered as a result of carelessness or moral degradation of the father or mother who have custody of the child, the court can take any decision it deems appropriate regarding custody of the child upon request of his or her relatives, guardian or the Public Prosecutor'. (2014, 4)

They go on to review and challenge the situation in Iranian society concerning the position of children and consent in relation to inter-pretations of Islamic jurisprudence. They firstly consider the age that children can give consent in medical contexts, or are deemed to have 'maturity', in Western countries. They note that this is not uniform in the West and, also, comment on the degree of discretion around age in many countries:

> Australia
> Age maturity is set at 18

Adult discretion However, a physician can determine that a patient younger than 16 is fully capable of decision making. In this situation the child's consent is considered valid, provided that another doctor who has examined the patient prior to treatment also confirms his or her capacity in writing (Bird, 2011):

> Canada
> Age maturity is set at 16

Adult discretion However, a younger patient's consent may be consid-ered valid under specific circumstances, where his or her physician and another independent and legally qualified medical doctor verifies the patient's capacity and the necessity of the procedure based on the patient's best interests (Jackman and McRae, 2013)

Summary based on Parsapoor et al. (2014), Bird (2011) Jackman and McRae (2013)

They note that in Iranian legislation and according to Shi'a *Fiqh*, stages of capacity – or competency in legal texts – include the following:

Stage of Momayyez – Awareness -: This stage . . . pertains to the period in which a minor is believed to have partial powers of discernment and can distinguish between benefit and loss to some extent. The law in Iran does not specify a certain age for this stage and there are no strict criteria for recognition of awareness in people as this is a faculty that can only be determined through relevant customary assessments. Based on anecdotes about Imam Ali and Imam Jafar Sadiq (PBUT), this stage may begin between ages 7 and 9.

Age of Taklif: according to Shiite jurisprudence boys and girls after age of Taklif are accountable for any actions they do and such they should act in accordance with God's order and avoid his prohibitions. In Iranian legislation, based on the Article 1210 of the Civil Code of the Islamic Republic of Iran and according to Shiite jurisprudents, age of Taklif is 15 full lunar years for boys and 9 full lunar years for girls, and upon reaching this age, no one can be treated as incompetent based on mental immaturity unless his or her insanity or mental immaturity is proved (2014, 4).

The authors in their research contacted a variety of religious leaders in Iran, asking for their position on the age of *Taklif*. In particular, they were investigating issues concerning medical decision making. The response indicated that interpretations were, in part, varied:

For example, some Ayatollahs said that 'informed consent is reaching the age of Taklif as clarified by the Sharia, and did not believe there was need for any other person's consent, parents included.' Whereas others some Faqihs considered that 'if a patient is of age, but is not mentally mature and therefore lacks the decision-making capacity, his or her parents' consent is required in addition to the patient's permission or assent'. (2014, 4)

The authors' conclusions are that the contemporary situation in Iran needs to change and that areas such as 'sex-based difference in age of decision making capacity seems to be in discordance with the current medical ethics guidelines and is therefore unjustifiable' and that 'the laws regarding decision-making capacity be duly reformed' (2014, 6). Here, as with Lowden, cultural, social and political contexts interact with new debates concerning the nature and presence of 'best interests' and a re-evaluation of adult-child relations concerning their 'right' to 'decision-making from the medical ethics point of view' (2014, 2). The example shows how the presence of rights is, again, connected to challenge and to tensions within countries and cultures concerning positive change for children and those who work with them.

Reflections on the research

Activity 1

From this discussion how do you see the relationship between rights, consent and the ways children–adult relationships are formed? Again, based on this discussion of Lowden's commentary, how can her critique help see how positive changes can be made in relation to children's experience of consent giving?

Activity 2

Lowden (2002) comments,

> *Children will not be facilitated to develop competence and thus the process of 'best interests' will continue to be defined from a protectionist adult perspective.*

How do you see the role of the research and commentaries above in relation to positive change for children in relation to their being 'facilitated' to develop competence and in challenging 'protectionist' adult perspectives?

Activity 3

In relation to the material from Parsapoor et al., how would you summarize the tensions around tradition and innovation related to child-adult relationships within the points they raise?

Tensions and debates: rights and child protection – a rights agenda

Reading et al. (2008) show how a rights perspective can alter the way an arena of children's lives is responded to, by forming a rights agenda for change as introduced in Chapter 1 (pages 24–7). Their work also questions some of the divisions often made between areas which can be considered as a 'rights'-related issue and those which are often separated off as not concerning children's rights. They review the way child 'maltreatment' is looked at. They argue that the most prevalent way of looking at it is as a public health problem, or concerning harm to individuals, but less often as a violation of children's rights. They argue that the UNCRC provides a framework for:

> understanding child maltreatment as part of a range of violence, harm, and exploitation of children at the individual, institutional, and societal levels. Rights of participation and provision are as important as rights of protection. The principles embodied in the UNCRC are concordant with those of medical ethics. The greatest strength of an approach based on the UNCRC is that it provides a legal instrument for implementing policy, accountability, and social justice, all of which enhance public health responses. (2008, 3)

They argue that further incorporation of the UNCRC principles into research, laws, policy and training of professionals working with children will result in 'progress' in the area of child protection. They also link child maltreatment to a rights-based perspective on poverty arguing that in child maltreatment the risks associated with poverty and inequalities, socially vulnerable families and the intergenerational cycle of deprivation and violence are well recognized. Strategies for prevention of maltreatment are recommended to target these high-risk groups, and intervention programmes are advised to be sensitive to social inequalities and not to inadvertently widen them. However, poverty can be represented as a violation of children's rights. The universal declaration of human rights grants the freedom from want; Article 27 of the UNCRC recognizes the right to a 'standard of living adequate to the child's physical, mental, spiritual, moral and social development' and the concept of rights as capabilities for living (e.g. the capability to be alive, healthy and have self-respect) justify the argument that poverty infringes on children's rights by prevention of their optimum development (UNCRC, 2008, 3).

They cite an approach that avoids blaming individuals, and, though, it does not 'absolve them of responsibility', it sees the state as accountable for improving social justice as a 'direct intervention to prevent maltreatment' (2008, 20). Hence, they argue such a 'rights based perspective allows risk factors to be reformulated as instances of discrimination, exclusion and victimisation', with social isolation and unemployment seen as 'violation of children's rights of protection, provision, or participation either explicitly as mandated under the articles of the UNCRC or less directly' (2008, 20). Following on from this they argue that reinforcement of laws affecting discrimination and social divisions are a powerful way of approaching child maltreatment.

The following example looks at another angle concerning rights and protection, showing how research is enabling insight into the nature of children's rights, the responses in areas such as policy making and the implication for children's lives.

Example of review: rights, protection and privacy – tensions, spaces and relationships

Analysis by Dowty (2008) identifies how information technology (IT) is being used to monitor children's lives. Her review included the following range of technologies:

- the use of CCTV in schools and nurseries,
- smart card technology that allows monitoring of children's meal choices, library borrowing and registration,
- mobile phone software that allows parents to track their children,
- the growing use of national databases that collect an increasing range of data on all children.

Dowty suggests that this combination can

produce a situation where a child cannot eat chips, visit the toilet or deviate from a pre-ordained route without somebody else knowing about it. Every test result, absence or means of travel to school is captured. Personal profiling tools, behaviour records and practitioners' observations of whether a child's friendships are appropriate, their aspirations realistic or their spare time put to constructive use create a rich seam of data that can apparently be mined for signs of trouble, or to make actuarial assessments of potential problems in the future. It is now possible for children to be under intense scrutiny by one means or another, and the speed, capacity and interoperability of information systems ensure that the assembled data can rapidly be conveyed to others. (2008, 399)

Reflections on the review

Activity

The rationale behind these initiatives concerns the 'protection' of children. What do you think the dangers are of this degree of, or approach to, protection?

How do you see it relating to the ways in which children can be protected while maintaining an appropriate degree of autonomy and privacy?

What tensions can you identify in terms of thinking about who should be involved in deciding what an appropriate degree of autonomy and privacy is?

This material illustrates the importance of a rights agenda being connected to other forces at work within society: it shows how emergent thinking argues that it is vital that the rights agenda be understood within a wider framework. It also demonstrates the complexity within the implementation of a rights-informed approach to relating to children and that our understanding of how to respond effectively to areas such as protection is still evolving: how research and analysis is helping develop insights into the nature of children's rights and responses in areas such as policy making and its implications for children's lives.

Activities

The following activities are designed to help reflect back on some of the key concerns over the chapter as a whole.

Chapter activity 1

The CRAE report in Chapter 1 quoted a child saying that

They think because we're small and they're big they know better ... and they just treat us like we're nothing, like we're just a puff of cloud or something. (Child under 11)

In this chapter, Lowden's comments on consent are referred to:

Case law in the UK focuses on the end point of decision making, that is consent, instead of the process of sharing information through the stages of investigation, diagnosis and considering treatment options. This amounts to an all or nothing approach, which confers full legal status on competent people but does not attend to participation when patients are partly involved and can influence rather than make decisions.

Consider these two quotations. How do you see them in terms of the following?

- The possibilities of developing a rights-informed way of redefining relationships between adults and children,
- Children giving consent in a health context as a child rights issue.

Chapter activity 2

Look back through the different examples of research within this chapter, and the analysis of the material. Examine the ways in which you think they offer useful ways of thinking about children's rights and set agendas for new directions in thinking about children's rights. It might be helpful to use some of the ideas in Chapter 1 to help structure your thoughts. Consider the ways in which the material helps develop or rethink ideas and practices of children's rights in terms of the following:

(a) A rights dynamic: 'the ways in which a rights dynamic has been created ... [this] ... concerns the ways in which the ideas about rights have been applied in order to affect ... laws or policies. (see page 19)

(b) Rights-informed ways of relating to children: 'enabling children to be seen and to be treated differently by adults. It is part of shifts in the ways in which children and young people see themselves, their relationships with each others, individual adults, groups they encounter and braider organisations that they connect with in their lives such as local or national government avoid presenting human rights as basic, underived moral standards that either you "get" or you do not, or as reflecting what might be seen as an idiosyncratically Western privileging of the claims of freedom over other values. Instead, the possibility opens up of showing that human rights can find support from any eligible ordering of the basic interests that are the components of a good human life' (Tasioulas, 2012, 29).

Summary

This chapter has

- reviewed the ways tensions, ambiguities and gaps within legislation have been identified;
- explored the ways these phenomena reflect issues concerning the relationships between international, national and local application of rights-based approaches to children's lives;
- examined tensions and debates concerning research and participation;
- examined tensions and debates concerning research, rights and consent;
- examined tensions and debates concerning rights and protection.

Further reading

Alderson, P. (2013) 'Trends in research about children, childhood and youth', in *Childhoods Real and Imagined: Volume 2*. London: Routledge. pp. 25–43.
Offers a thoughtful review of recent scholarship.

Broadhead, P., Meleady, C. and Delgado, M.A. (2008) 'Valuing children means valuing families', in *Children, Families and Communities*. Maidenhead: Open University Press. pp. 25–35.
A clear example of consulting children about service provision in Sheffield's Children Centre from a rights perspective.

Jones, P. (2009) 'How are otherness and childhood connected?' in *Rethinking Childhood: Attitudes in Contemporary Childhood*. London: Continuum.
Considers the ways in which negative stereotypes of children have developed and how this affects their position in society.

Research details

Example of research: rights, protection and privacy – tensions, spaces and relationships

Dowty responds to policy and practice that uses IT, identifying, recording and tracking children in England under the banners of child protection, reducing risk and improving outcomes. It argues that there is a need to review such developments in the light of a child's right to privacy. It also considers whether placing faith in unproven technology may inadvertently increase levels of risk to children.

Dowty, T. (2008) 'Pixie-dust and privacy: What's happening to children's rights in England?' *Children & Society*, 22, 393–399.

Example of research: lesbian, gay and bisexual young people

Stonewall commissioned the Centre for Family Research at the University of Cambridge to conduct a survey with young people who are lesbian, gay or bisexual (or think they might be) on their experiences in secondary schools and colleges across Britain. A total of 1,614 lesbian, gay and bisexual young people aged between 11 and 19 completed an online survey.

Guasp, A. (2012) *The School Report, The Experiences of Gay Young People in Britain's Schools in 2012*, Cambridge: Stonewall and the University of Cambridge.

Example of research: best interests, 'maturity' and consent

The paper examines the scope of the autonomy of children and adolescents and the extent of their parents' authority in medical decision making based on ethical principles and jurisprudential and legal basis, drawing on case study material.

Parsapoor, A., Parsapoor, M., Nima Rezaei, N. and Fariba Asghari, F. (2014) 'Autonomy of children and adolescents in consent to treatment: Ethical, jurisprudential and legal considerations', *Iranian Journal of Pediatrics*, 24 (3) 241–248.

Example of research: children, participation and a rights veneer

Stafford et al. interviewed 200 children aged between 3 and 18 years as a response to the 'recent surge of interest' in consulting children and young people about issues affecting them. This article is based on what children have said about consultation.

Stafford, A., Laybourne, A. and Hill, M. (2003) ' "Having a say": Children and young people talk about Consultation', *Children & Society*, 17, 361–373.

Part III

Implications for Children's Lives

4

Rights and the Child's Voice

Introduction and key questions

The idea that adults should make decisions for children and should speak on their behalf has been part of the ways many children experience their lives and the spaces they live in, whether at school or attending hospital, from the design of their playgrounds to the way they are treated in law courts. Recent theory, research and practice have started to rethink and challenge the assumption that adults should automatically represent children in this way. Research has been used to assert the right of children to participate in particular ways, to have a voice that is heard and engaged with. As this chapter will show, much initial work had a number of factors in common. Research looked at how best to engage with children depending on factors such as age, culture or language. Research also began to work with children to explore their perspectives on different areas of their lives, from their views on the ways they were treated by health services to their experiences of race, gender or sexuality, for example. However, more recent research has questioned the initial approaches taken to engaging with 'children's voice'. It has begun to recognize the well-intentioned naivety of some of this work and to look more closely at the complexity and tensions connected to such research. In addition, the response to research involving children's voice is enabling insight into the ways in which findings that would benefit the lives of children, or would enable their views to be respected, are resisted or sabotaged by adults and the organizations they control. As previous chapters have indicated, we are also gaining a deeper understanding of the ways in which such research is seen in contexts that do not see themselves aligned with children's rights. This chapter will look at the development of the idea of rights and the 'child's voice' along with the implications for children and for those living and working with them. It will examine some of the recent challenges to earlier thinking and approaches to research connected to 'children's voice' and to the complexities of adult responses to such research. The key questions are as follows:

What is the meaning of 'child's voice'?
How does 'voice' relate to rights?
What is research revealing about voice, participation and rights?

What is the meaning of 'child's voice'?

The term 'child's voice' is a metaphor. It has come to represent a cluster of ideas and issues. In many instances when 'voice' is referred to in relation to children, it is used to address its opposite: children's experience of being silenced, when adults have not listened to children, or have put words in their mouths. This silencing is not voluntary on the part of the child. It is something which is either actively done by others, or which occurs through the ways in which factors in society result in children being silenced and excluded. This chapter will look at how recent challenges to these processes have developed from the dynamic created by the ideas and practices of children's rights. It will look at how research is contributing to a changing climate for children and adults concerning rights and participation. A key concept will be that of a rights-informed way of relating to children in terms of participation. On the one hand, recent years have seen a developing agenda within many countries that children should be able to express their opinions, be involved in decisions and be aware of the factors that influence any decisions that affect them. So, for example, in the United Kingdom, the Human Rights Act, 1998 (Article 10), which relates to the ECHR, incorporated into UK law through the HRA, requires the government to uphold the right to freedom of expression, while the Children Act (1989) requires local authorities both to ascertain the wishes and feelings of children they look after and to give these 'due consideration'. A number of authors rightly identify that research initiatives concerning participation and voice can have both parallels and differences, due to their different contexts. Ehlers and Frank, for example, note that 'child participation exercises in Africa have addressed themselves to a wide range of issues faced on the continent' (2016, 123). They cite positive examples such as the consultation of children on the reform of legislation in Lesotho, South Africa, and in Mozambique and in policy development in Swaziland and Zambia. However, they argue for the need for more research on areas that are 'central to children's experiences in Africa that have not been developed in any depth...poverty, development, HIV/Aids, good governance' (2016, 123), noting that though individual contexts are important there is also a need to engage with learning from other developing countries.

Structures and procedures developing from recent initiatives and research include the following:

- Frameworks and principles for obtaining children and young people's involvement within the work done by government departments,
- Children's and young people's councils,
- Requirements for service providers to involve children and young people in reviewing the way professionals work with them.

Initiatives include children's representation on school councils, consultative processes involving government policy development and implementation and practices such as youth advocacy. An example of such representation from New Zealand illustrates a long-established structure:

The Prime Minister's Youth Advisory Forum was established...in 1998. Modelled on other advisory forums, such as the Business Advisory Council, it provides 15 young New Zealanders, aged between 12 and 25, with the opportunity to meet three times a year with Cabinet Ministers, including the Prime Minister.....The selection criteria ensured the participation of a cross-section of young people from different ethnic groups, a variety of geographical, rural and urban backgrounds, and differing educational, employment and life experiences. The aim is to provide a system where a group of children and young people can speak directly and frankly to the Prime Minister and Cabinet of the day about issues that concern them. (Inter-Parliamentary Union, 2012, 16)

Researchers are identifying the complexity of this aspect of child rights. Recent research has helped recognize the advances and limitations of attempts to elicit and involve children's voices. In addition, research is revealing that although providing laws, guidance on practice and processes for children's participation are important, other connected matters must be engaged with. If the complex interrelationship of factors silencing children are not addressed, research has shown that they will hinder or halt attempts to enable children to have voice, to participate.

The complex factors silencing children can helpfully be seen in three particular ways:

- The worth of children's voices,
- The ways that social exclusion silences children,
- The dominance of adult-orientated ways of communicating and decision making.

The first centres on children's voices not being given *worth,* in terms of adults not treating their ideas or opinions as having value or legitimacy. Here the idea of 'voice' is attached to areas such as judgement, maturity, capability and power. Adults are in positions of power in areas such as decision making and responsibility, and children are excluded from holding and using power. Their exclusion can be termed as having no 'voice' or power in making decisions. This absence of voice and power is seen within large-scale decisions in government through to children's everyday lives at school or at home.

The second concerns the ways in which a variety of factors to do with *social exclusion* interconnect in the silencing of children. These concern how people are excluded within society, and these are additional forces which add to the ways in which children are not given voice. Such factors include the ways in which poverty, class, gender, race, sexuality or disability affect children's lives. Rivers and Cowie's (2006) research, for example, illustrates how the silencing of children can be combined with other factors which exclude and silence children who are lesbian or gay:

A high percentage of victimized students remain silent about their distress. The percentage of pupils who tell their teacher or anyone at home that they

have been bullied increases fairly consistently with frequency of being bullied, especially for the highest reported frequency of 'several times a week';
but even for these, only about a half of secondary pupils tell anyone at home.
Some victims may seek help from peers, teachers, or parents. However, many
withdraw, staying silent about their suffering. Since the admission of being
upset can provoke derision or hostility from peers and retaliation from the
bullies, it often seems safer for a victimized young person to silently endure
the abuse. (2006, 12)

The third is the assumption that *adult modes of communicating* are the only
way that participation can be valid. This is embedded in many aspects of
most societies: communication, consultation and decision making are made
through the adult-orientated written word or speech. Here 'voice' is seen
as something that is *articulate* only in particular ways and that articulacy
is given to a certain status: the position of the adult. Children who do not
communicate like 'mature', 'articulate' adults are not seen as having a worthwhile contribution to make. This assumption is reflected in many formal
and informal structures and ways of working: the way organizations func-
tion, the kinds of language used, the way relationships are formed and the
time devoted to an action or process. So, for example, decisions might be
made based on information provided in a way that is only accessible to adult
ways of communicating, interactions between people are handled in a way
that children do not understand, or the longer time needed to assimilate or
decide on something is not provided for.

Children are taught to assume that they do not have voice, in the sense
that they are encouraged to believe that adult's voices serve them in many
areas of their lives.

If we think about the metaphor of the child's voice it's possible to say that,
taken literally, having a voice means being able to speak or express yourself
out loud. Looked at in this way, it is about the act of being able to articulate in
certain ways, to communicate. It is also about having something to say: experiences, opinions, ideas. It also concerns being heard or listened to by others and
your words having an impact. It is about your words having an impact. The
picture from theory, research and practice can be seen as revealing tensions
to do with children's voices being silenced, devalued or ignored, compared to
their voices being articulated, heard and responded to. Table 4.1 draws together
the discussion so far to show the different aspects of these ideas of 'voice'.

On a macro level, the issue of children's voice is seen in terms of children
representing their interests, experiences and particular perceptions in areas

Table 4.1 Silence and voice

Child's silence	Child's voice
Children's lives and experiences not worth attention In areas such as the law or education, the main focus is on adult or parental interests Main focus in areas such as legislation, the law is on adult or parental interests with children being seen as dependent, as the property of parents and as being of lower status and value	Children's voice is to do with children's lives being worthy of attention and being given value
Children not seen to be able to articulate anything about themselves of any worth Adults represent children and their 'best interests': only adult opinions about children and adult ways of valuing what happens to children are valued	Children able to represent themselves and to have opinions and input that matters Children have a perspective that is different from that of adults, and that this is of equal value to that of adults
Children's role is to listen to and be looked after by adults. They are best served by adult actions based on adult experiences and judgements of children's needs or adult intentions for children's development and future	Children are active and able participants, capable of judgement and insight. They have opinions and input of value, and are experts in their own lives
Services such as education, health or social care are structured and delivered in ways that are devised and implemented purely by adults	They should have input into the services that work with them
Children are immature and what they think and say cannot be trusted	Children are capable and are able to have input in ways that encourage and develop their capacity as decision makers and valid contributors
Adults create relationships and organizational structures that assume and assure that children see their own ideas and expressions as of less value and status than that of adult	

such as the development of policy. This includes acknowledging their status as citizens with rights to be involved. Some research has investigated the way children can participate in decision making about national agendas. Other work has focused more upon their engagement with areas of their lives that affect them in relation to the micro level of immediate service provision in their daily lives. This has ranged from policy making about education and health, through to the management of particular organizations such as schools or day care services that they are served by, or in the day-to-day running and experiences of a provider such as a health centre.

How does 'voice' relate to rights?

Contemporary ideas about the child's voice often refer to the UNCRC's Article 12 and its assertions about participation. As discussed in Chapters 1 and 2, this states that children and young people have a right to a say on all issues that affect them, and for these views to be taken seriously (UNCRC, Article 12). One of the key issues here is that children are seen to have a *right* to be involved: 'children's participation is a value or rights based principle' (Franklin and Sloper, 2005). This engages voice and participation within a framework of rights and responsibilities. In addition, this is seen to be connected to the idea and practice of seeing children as citizens with rights in the present, rather than as future citizens with full membership being granted upon their reaching adulthood. There are varied definitions of what participation means in relation to children's rights, emphasizing different issues. The UNCRC General Comment (2009) tries to address this:

> A widespread practice has emerged in recent years which has been broadly conceptualised as 'participation', although this term itself does not appear in the text of Article 12. This term has evolved and is now widely used to describe ongoing processes, which include information-sharing and dialogue between children and adults based on mutual respect, and in which children can learn how their views and those of adults are taken into account and shape the outcome of such processes.

The concept explored in Chapter 1, that the rights described in the UNCRC are indivisible and interdependent, connects powerfully to the idea of voice. An illustration of this is the way the international *Handbook on Child Participation in Parliament*, for example, makes explicit its relationship with Article 13:

Article 13 strengthens children's participatory rights by guaranteeing children freedom of expression along with the 'freedom to seek, receive and impart information and ideas of all kinds'. Indeed without access to information and ideas and without the right to express all ideas, expression or participation would be rendered meaningless. (Inter-Parliamentary Union, 2012, 13)

Key Points: voice and participation

The following list shows some of the key issues connecting voice and participation rights:

- **Representation** – creating processes and spaces that enable children to represent themselves, or to have their position represented without adult bias;
- **Impact** – the idea that a child's voice (their opinions, choices or ideas) should have an impact by being engaged with, responded to and acted on;
- **Judgement** – to view children as capable of judgement and encouraging processes that inform children, give them information and support them to make judgements about issues that affect them;
- **Validity** – the idea that a child's voice has validity and meaning, that their perceptions are as valid as, or, in certain contexts, more valid than, adults' opinions and ideas.

Within these areas of representation, impact, judgement and validity, the notion is that children are often excluded from processes that connect with their lives. The exclusion from arenas such as informing government decision making or family decisions, is held to be due to attitudes and existing structures that are specifically prejudiced against children. These reflect and re-enforce the stereotypes outlined in Chapters 1 and 2, that treat children as incapable, innocent or incompetent.

On a micro level, research has looked at how that the concept of the child's voice alters the way adults see and hear children and the ways adults see and hear children in their everyday interactions with them. This has been seen in terms of the different sites, role and relationships or types of interactions, as shown in Table 4.2.

Table 4.2 Sites, roles and relationships

Site	Role (child–adult)	Traditional type of relationship or interaction (child–adult)
School	Pupil–teacher	Passive–active; consumer–provider
Hospital	Patient–doctor	Needy/ill–expert; powerless–powerful
Home	Daughter/son–parent	Cared for–carer; protected–protector; weak–strong Decision follower–decision maker; rule follower–rule maker

Research has begun to re-examine these sites, role relationships and interactions using a framework of rights-informed ways of relating to children.

Kilkelly et al.'s (2005) research with children revealed that having a say in decisions made about them was the most important rights issue identified by them. A substantial proportion of the children's comments related to school (90 per cent), and many of these concerned not having a voice in decisions within school life. Typical comments included the following:

> Sometimes school can get on my nerves cause I don't think children get enough respect from teachers and caretakers and I think some children are scarred [sic] about speaking their mind in case they get shouted at. (Girl, aged 11 years; Kilkelly et al., 2005, 186)

Recent scholarship, research and policy are focusing upon rights and the child's voice in relation to *increasing* children's participation and involvement. On a national governmental level, this is to do with the ways in which children are consulted and listened to in relation to existing, or future, policies. In relation to national and local service provision, a similar focus is placed upon children being consulted about provision and development in areas such as healthcare or play. At a local government level, there are examples of research into the different ways local councils have begun to engage with children. The following is from Eurochild's (2012) survey of 20 European countries and their examples of what they call 'participatory methods for the inclusion of all children':

> Children participation in our city is managed through Children city councils (since 2001), Children forums (since 1995), messages of children to adults, focus groups with children, meeting with adults who make decisions in the city, county. We also involve children with special needs in workshops and

meetings with adults who make decisions (Society 'Our children' Opatija, Croatia). (2012, 2)

Attention has also been given to children's voices within their family or immediate support networks: the extent of their involvement in areas such as decisions relating to divorce or within therapy dealing with family difficulties. An example from the United Kingdom's Department of Health makes a clear distinction between *consultation alone* and *participation* that results in empirical *impact* through actions that occur as responses to children's views or expressed opinions:

> Participation should go beyond consultation and ensure that children and young people initiate action and make decisions in partnership with adults, for example, making decisions about their care and treatment or in day to day decisions about their lives. (2002, 4)

Researchers such as Lewis (2010) offer a critique of the idea and practice of the 'child's voice', examining the ethics and purposes behind such engagement with children. Her work advocates a reflective approach to understanding the motivations behind accessing children's 'voice'. Her approach describes five methodological aspects of such work: recognizing, noting, responding to, interpreting and reporting from children. As with other researchers in this area, a part of her critique concerns the importance of being wary of the appearance of consultation, providing a veneer, without any real engagement with the content of the material accessed through such practice. There are three main themes that researchers and commentators have highlighted within such criticism and the rethinking of the 'child's voice'. These are between children's *consultation, participation* and the key issue of *impact*.

As mentioned at the start of this chapter, research has explored how other structural inequalities re-enforce or add to the ways children are excluded and silenced. Factors such as gender, poverty and race add to the ways in which children are excluded, and are seen as rights-related issues.

The Irish Refugee Council statement from 2006 shows how these are related in relation to asylum-seeker children, for example:

> Separated children – children outside their country of origin separated from parents or other caregivers – are invisible in Irish society. This invisibility is two-fold, first as children who often have no voice and secondly as asylum seekers, marginalised in society. If these children are largely invisible in the first instance, who will notice if they go missing? Who will advocate

on their behalf and play surrogate parent to remind the State that its obligations under the UN Convention on the Rights of the Child apply to all children within its territory, be they citizens or not. (www.irishrefugeecouncil.ie/
press06/separated_children.html [accessed 12 June 2008])

When looked at in this way, the barriers to participation experienced by all
children become added to by other forces of social exclusion concerning, in
this example, racism and attitudes towards asylum seekers. This illustrates
how factors involving voice, exclusion and discrimination are complex and
multiple and how important it is, when trying to understand and respond
to the silencing of children, to look at the different factors which combine to
affect them. The next section explores these issues further.

The danger of participation being romanticized

Others have noted that child participation is still an emerging area within
some disciplines, which have not substantially engaged with ideas such as
children's voices and their opinions being of worth within research. They
identify a need for further research which explores the nature and value of
such an approach to enquiry, but argue that there is a danger of taking participation for granted as a 'good thing', or to assume it's a 'given' rather than
thinking about why it is being undertaken and what the specific issues, possibilities or complexities of the specific research involving children.

McCarry (2012), for example, notes a 'paradigmatic shift' in childhood
research where researchers seem to no longer be concerned about justi-
fying *why* children should participate in the research process but instead
focus on *how* to carry this out. Authors such as Bühler-Niederberger have
warned against the danger of 'children's actorship being essentialized rather
than analysed and therefore affecting the quality as well as the credibility of
research' (2010, 160). Tisdall and Punch have expressed similar concerns
about the lack of criticality of 'givens', or 'mantras', in research that engages
with children's voice (2012, 251), advocating for the need to avoid romanti-
cizing children's voice and for the need to look at the specific differences and
contexts of enquiry rather than generalizing about processes, or presenting
the work with an inherent assumed value attached to engaging with children as participants rather than as objects in research. The following section
reviews this need to look at specific contexts and to question and reflect,
rather than to assume that 'voice' is a given good.

What is research revealing about voice, participation and rights?

The following looks at the three key areas, identified earlier in the chapter, which illustrate different ways in which research is exploring and developing our response to rights and children's voices:

- The worth of children's voices,
- The ways that social exclusion silences children,
- The dominance of adult-orientated ways of communicating and decision making.

The worth of children's voices

The tendency has been to link the worth and validity of a child's voice to adult opinions about appropriate 'levels' of competency and capability. Chapter 5 looks at issues concerning capability in more depth. This section will look at the different ways in which voice, in particular, is connected to worth and lack of worth. Worth can be related to the precedence given to areas such as consultation or participation and to the value given to resources such as finance and support for time, personnel and sustaining processes that are connected with children's participation. The following extract (Davey et al., 2010) is from research involving focus groups with children who had experience of participation initiatives and those who had not. One of the findings within the report relates to this perspective on worth. Here the particular approach was on local councils.

It is often the case that a decision to involve children in a consultation is dependent on factors such as timing, funding and whether there is capacity within a staff team to fully support children's engagement. Children were very aware of these constraints and in fact, there was a lot of scepticism as to whether attempts by councillors to seek the views of children were actually genuine or merely part of a tokenistic 'tick box' exercise.

> I think that the councillors do go out to tick a box sometimes because they think, because of all this political correctness and stuff, we've got to get such and such young person and make sure that we're a diverse ... and it's like, I'm going to go out just to tick my box but they don't actually get taken

into consideration, they don't put a lot of thought into it.(Interview with an involved group of children, 2010, 35)

Ideas that children's views are of worth are consistently undermined by cultural beliefs reflected in domains such as the law, or media and in areas of cultural and professional practice such as parenting or health. In relation to worth, different adult domains often work together to reinforce each other. For example, the media consistently portrays and emphasizes children as being unreliable, or liars, or as being poor witnesses of their lives. The law has also undermined the worth of children's testimony through its practices and in the way laws are designed and acted upon. An example of this concerns the ongoing adult response in the media to the ways in which adults in families and in organizations which are designed to care for children abuse them. For many years the response in the media and in the law has been to see child testimony as unbelievable or unreliable. This means that adults could continue as individuals and groups, to sexually and physically abuse children, while the organizations that could have, and should have, stopped the adults, punished them appropriately and protected children, actually do the opposite, This has often involved drawing broad lines about competency based on factors such as age. Current developments in thinking, research and practice are questioning this, and the situation is changing.

Example of research: child's voice and age

Pérez-Expósito's (2015) research examined student participation in the secondary schools from two areas of Mexico City. The researchers worked with students, teachers and principals from secondary schools located within two contrasting municipalities (*delegaciones*) of Mexico City. The study involved over 800 students completing a questionnaire, accompanied by workshops and focus groups with pupils aged 14–16 from an urban and from a rural school and semi-structured interviews with teachers and principals. Pérez-Expósito's research creates a framework for identifying what he calls different 'domains' of student participation. These include binding decision making in areas such as school governance, curricular and pedagogical decisions, resolution of community problems and the ways pupils and staff work together and see each other. Linked to his research, he creates a series of questions designed to help analyse his data in terms of what he calls the *quality* of the participation:

- How authentic is the pupils' involvement?
- To what extent does the participation allow autonomous action?
- How effective is the participation? (2015, 348–351)

He breaks these down further to try to identify what each means in practice. For example in relation to the question about how 'authentic' the participation is he creates four *levels*:

(1) no pupil involvement or simulated forms of participation (i.e. manipulation or tokenism)
(2) pupils are consulted and informed
(3) pupils take part in the process with voice and initiative
(4) participation is led and controlled by the students. (2015, 355–356)

The following are extracts from the research findings, related to one aspect of the education system's ways of aiming to work with participation. All secondary schools in Mexico have to form a Student Society (SS), referred to as '*planillas*', each academic year. Pérez-Expósito contextualizes these data by referring to the Mexican Educational System's Agreement 98 (see Note 9), which states that the SS will have the following 'goals':

- To exercise among its members the practice of democratic life, as a way to contribute to their formation.
- To promote the realisation of activities that contribute to constructing in the educands a responsible personality, with a clear sense of their obligations and rights.
- To promote to the school authorities the initiatives that advance the progress and improvement of the school. (2015, 363)

Data from the urban school:

Facilitator/interviewer: So, what are the planillas for?
Pedro: Supposedly they are for improving the school.
Moses: But it doesn't work
Facilitator/interviewer ... Why?
Moses: They did nothing; they said there would be mirrors in the toilets, but it didn't happen.
All: Yes, nothing.

Data from the rural school:

Facilitator/interviewer: So, if we think about the school's problems, have you done something to solve them?
Miriam and Ana: We? Nothing.
Adrian: Supposedly that's why we vote for the planilla.
Karina: But they do nothing.
Ana: Yes, they do nothing. Well, two years ago I think we have more control.
Adrian: Yes, if we noticed something wrong we left it to the planilla and they tried to fix it. But now the planilla sucks, they do nothing, simply nothing.
Facilitator/interviewer: Have you ever taken part in an election?
Miriam: Yes, to elect some students ... We had to elect the representatives in the Student Society ... they gather together and count the votes...and supposedly there's democracy ...
Facilitator/interviewer: And why did you say 'supposedly'?
Miriam: [raising her shoulders] because it's like a game. (Pérez-Expósito, 2015, 361–362)

Reflection on the research

Activity 1

Reflect on the extracts from the data:
   Which of Pérez-Expósito's levels of quality in terms of authenticity do you think the data connects to?

1. no pupil involvement or simulated forms of participation (i.e. manipulation or tokenism),
2. pupils are consulted and informed,
3. pupils take part in the process with voice and initiative,
4. participation is led and controlled by the students. (2015, 355–356)

Why do you think this?

Activity 2

Student participation in school is relevant mainly because in most countries it is a right of adolescents, and therefore, it has to be guaranteed. But also, adolescents' participation in this setting seems necessary for the education of active citizens, and has been positively associated with the development of knowledge, attitudes and skills, also relevant in other domains (like the labour market), and with the reduction of violence in school and dropping out rates. Enhancing adolescent participation in school, then, should be part of the strategy oriented to tackle these problems. (2015, 361)

In an interview within the research the principal from the urban school was asked about whether there were 'real opportunities for students to have influence in decisions about the school'. Her response was as follows:

I think we are not used to it. ... We don't even have in mind that they take a decision through a sort of survey, to see what is the most important decision we should make in the school? How do we want to approach a given problem? How we would like that the school shows itself to the community? What are the things that make us uncomfortable? ... We are not willing to participate. This participation doesn't happen. (2015, 361)

How do you see the principal's comments in relation to the reflection by Pérez-Expósito?

How do you understand the principal's response in relation to some of the issues about power and children's voice within this chapter?

Activity 3

Compare the ways in which participation features in this research with the example of research later in this chapter: 'Ask us too! Doing participatory research with disabled children in the global south'.

What do you think are parallels and differences?

The following areas might be useful themes to help frame your analysis:

- worth and value,
- power,
- adult–child relationships,
- assumptions based on the past,
- how change happens,
- the ways in which individual experiences relate to wider cultural and political perspectives.

The ways that social exclusion silences children

Research has revealed that, while in a number of countries legislation and practice have begun to reflect children's right to express their views and to have them acted upon, broad factors that exclude sectors of the population have an impact on children's participation. A review of research by the Joseph Rowntree Foundation concluded that the indications were that

> many professionals fail to consult with or involve disabled children, even where statutory duties require authorities to ascertain children's wishes and feelings, as in The Children Act 1989, The Children (Northern Ireland) Order 1995, and The Children (Scotland) Act 1995. In addition, disabled children and young people are often excluded from wider consultations around local policy and planning, their neighbourhoods and communities. (www.jrf.org.uk/knowledge/findings/socialcare/741.asp)

Rights and inclusive education for disabled children are intimately connected. UNESCO, for example, frames the 'human right to education' as the core of inclusive education in its working document 'Inclusive Education: Public Policies' (UNESCO, 2008). Its review of research and practice summarizes this view as concerning the ways in which 'a rights-based approach establishes the rules against all grounds for discrimination in education such as gender, disability, caste, ethnicity, religion, race, economic status, refugee status and language' (2008, 3). Tomasevski (2004) described this agenda as being founded upon three principles:

- Access to free and compulsory education;
- Equality, inclusion and non-discrimination;
- The right to quality education supported by concrete conditions, inputs, processes and outcomes.

The 2008 UK Children's Commissioners' Report to UN Committee on the Rights of the Child summarized the situation in the following way, highlighting the relationship between voice, exclusion, decision making and the need for training, alongside attitudinal and structural change:

> Disabled children and young people are much less likely than those without disabilities to participate at any level, particularly those with complex needs or with only non-verbal communication. Research has shown only a small number of disabled children are involved in decisions about their care. Many

professionals lack understanding, hold assumptions and/or underestimate disabled children's competence and ability to participate (Franklin and Sloper, 2007). Other research found that it is common for professionals to record that a child's level of impairment prohibited their wishes from being ascertained (Stuart and Baines, 2004). Despite new statutory duties on public authorities to promote positive attitudes towards disabled persons and to encourage participation by disabled persons in public life, there is limited evidence of the impact of these duties on the lives of disabled people. Moreover, the duties have yet to be implemented by a number of authorities. (2008, 19)

The following is an example of research that examined ways of challenging the exclusion experienced by disabled young people by exploring effective ways of creating access to participation, decision making and impact.

Example of research and interview: Ask us too! Doing participatory research with disabled children in the global south

As this chapter has discussed, recent research has begun to help us understand more about the relationships between the broad perspective of a convention such as the UNCRC and the different contexts and situations of children's lives. Wickenden and Kembhavi-Tam (2014) explore the specific, contextual dynamics related to disabled children and young people living in the global south and active participation in research that addresses their lives. The researchers do not take this relationship nor the children's participation in research as a 'given' that need not be thought about carefully and questioned. They concisely summarize their approach in the following way:

> Researchers should be cautious in claiming the power or essential 'goodness' of participation per se and wary in interpreting and representing what children say and in claiming its authenticity or potential to empower with rather than about children recognises that given appropriate opportunities, they have and can express their own views, and these are often different from those of proxies such as parents or professionals who might previously have answered for them. (2014, 401)

Wickenden and Kembhavi-Tam note the importance of dynamics concerning disability and childhood, and of the contrast between different political and geographic factors. In terms of research concerning disabled children, for example, they note 'an inclusive and reflexive turn...Ideally, disabled people lead the research agendas, rather than being passive subjects or objects of investigation' (2014, 402). They create their engagement with disabled children within a framework that is informed by identifying and examining 'the socio-political processes which create disability and in disabled people's views about how these impact on them and can be challenged' (2014, 402). Their work is also located in terms of global parallels and differences in children's lives. Citing UNICEF (2014, 403) they note,

> Research on child disability is woefully inadequate, especially in low and middle-income countries. The resulting lack of evidence hinders good policymaking and service delivery for children who are among the most vulnerable. (UNICEF, 2013, 8)

They engage with the issue of different contexts and lives in ways that can help see why, and how, it is important to explore how dialogue can occur between the UNCRC and specific lives, but *also* how awareness between and across these different contexts can create benefits for children through research. They argue, for example, that 'there are a number of practical and attitudinal issues to be considered. If this is done well, the children's identities as disabled are not privileged over their views of themselves as interesting and ordinary young people' (2014, 413). Kembhavi-Tam undertook research in Bangalore, India, with a group of adolescents with physical disabilities. The research involved 37 participants between the ages of 11 and 18. She notes that participants 'were invited if they had a physical impairment leading to mobility limitations or had multiple physical and sensory impairments (vision or hearing)' (2014, 405).

The method is described in the following way:

> Photography was used as a key visual method to foster discussion among participants during focus groups. Participants were given disposable cameras, instructed on their use and asked to take pictures of things that (1) made them happy, (2) made them sad, (3) made them angry and (4) that they would like to change. A week later, the cameras were returned for development of the images. During the groups, the photographs were returned to each participant, and discussion was facilitated about issues relating to participation and inclusion. (2014, 405)

Wickenden undertook her research in four sites in India and Sri Lanka. The aims of the research are described as 'to investigate the feasibility of and methodological issues in exploring disabled children's perceptions of their lives, through participatory meetings' (2014, 406). Participants were aged between 8 and 18 and the participants worked in different groups, and are described in the following way: 'each group had 3 to 6 participants with a variety of types and severities of impairment, including some children with communication and cognitive difficulties' (2014, 406). A variety of participatory methods and processes are involved in the research. The following is an example:

> 'Things I like and don't like'. A large grid with a pictorial emoticon scale in column headings (like, don't mind, don't like, don't know). Initially the researchers suggested things that children might like or dislike and they then placed stickers, thumb prints or their initials to rate their feelings in the relevant rows and columns. Initially, 'easy' and obvious items were suggested so that everyone understood the task (e.g. food, going out, being with family, festivals, being on your own) and then the children contributed their own items (e.g. positive: bathing in the sea, eating out, playing with my brother, my dog; negative: adults fighting, schoolwork, wanting a job). (2014, 407)

The researchers carefully note the different contexts of the research and the lives of the children who became involved in the research. However, they also position their work as learning between the different contexts. The following illustrates their approach:

> Visual and tactile support – Pictures, symbols and signing. Cognitive psychological research shows that information is understood much more easily visually than through hearing. Therefore, activities that are supported by visual information are more easily accessible for everyone. Pictures are often used in activities with young children, but visual support is also useful for many older children (and adults). In both studies, there is a deliberate predominance of visual material (photos, pictures, charts, symbols) and this clearly contributed to the success of the sessions (2014, 411).

Interview with Gayatri Kembhavi-Tam and Mary Wickenden

Dr Gayatri Kembhavi-Tam and Professor Mary Wickenden, Institute for Global Health, University College London

Phil Jones: *How did the research contribute to your understandings of the nature of children's rights and of disabled children's rights?*

Gayatri Kembhavi-Tam and Mary Wickenden: *The UN Convention on the Rights of Persons with Disabilities (UNCRPD) does outline specific provisions in regards to the rights of disabled children. Article 3(h) (General Principles) concerns, 'Respect for the evolving capacities of children with disabilities and respect for the right of children with disabilities to preserve their identities.' Article 7 specifically deals with children with disabilities. In particular, this articles states that, '...children with disabilities have the right to express their views freely on all matters affecting them, their views being given due weight in accordance with their age and maturity, on an equal basis with other children, and to be provided with disability and age-appropriate assistance to realize that right.'*

Our work in the global south with disabled children made us particularly aware of the reality that children's rights are not always upheld. This is especially the case in regards to their right to be heard, and a right to influence decisions made on their behalf. Particularly for disabled children, the deference to adult gatekeepers for decisions, opinions and viewpoints is longstanding. The existence of the UNCRC and terms of the UNCRPD do not necessarily mean that the provisions are manifest 'on the ground'. We were acutely aware that our research needed to focus on the rights of disabled children, in particular, to facilitate their right to have their opinions and thoughts be heard, and to demonstrate to the adult gatekeepers that it was possible to conduct research actively with disabled children rather than merely about them, from adults' perspectives.

Although the UNCRPD does explicitly state that disabled children have the right to be heard, this does not necessarily mean that they are either aware of this right, nor are they provided with adequate supports and opportunities to exercise that right. More emphasis, perhaps, needs to be placed on the ways in which we can support this right, and in increasing the awareness among service providers and other organisations that this is not merely 'a good idea' but urgently necessary.

Phil Jones: *You talk about being 'wary in interpreting and representing what children say and in claiming its authenticity or potential to empower' (2014, 401). How do you see this quote and your research in terms of the ways you approach (1) creating relationships with participants and (2) with the creation and analysis of their data?*

Gayatri Kembhavi-Tam and Mary Wickenden: *The need to be 'wary in interpreting and representing what children say and in claiming its authenticity. . .' stems from the issues presented in the paper with regard to power differential, the role of the researcher as 'outsider' and person in a position of authority. Particularly in the context of research with children and disabled children in the global south, it is imperative that as researchers we take the time to build relationships with our participants before and during the course of the research, and potentially to investigate ways in which these relationships can be maintained if our research is to have a lasting impact on not only the children's lives, but also the way in which research with children and disabled children is carried out in these settings in the future. Having trusted local partners who are gatekeepers for families and children (and trusted by them) is important. Equally important is the relationship that researchers have with local partners, in order to foster an open-minded attitude in the inclusion of disabled children in research.*

As with all qualitative data, the creation and interpretation of the data collected from research with children require an open-mindedness. Being mindful of the researchers' position with the children (person of authority, outsider, someone from the 'global north', for example) is also key when interpreting the data. As we stated in the paper, the data may be 'messy' and seemingly disjointed, but the skill of the researcher lies in seeing beyond the 'mess'.

This is particularly tricky with disabled children because they are in an especially disempowered position. In general, disabled children are not used to being asked their views and so they may, even more than other children, say what they think is expected (a form of courtesy bias). Disabled children may also have unusual communication, behaviour and thinking styles. What they tell us may be said through fewer words, unclear speech, informal gestures, non-verbal forms of communication, etc., so that their meaning might not be as clear and explicit as someone using 'conventional' styles of communication. Thus guesses at meanings have to be verified as far as possible but may still remain provisional.

Verification by checking with the child (did you mean this?) is even more important than it is with other research participants.

Disabled children with learning and or communication difficulties are used to being left out, or rather, are often not used to being consulted or taken seriously. Thus when they do get this opportunity and the activities and communication methods are adapted to suit them, they often 'warm up' quickly and enjoy expressing their views. Thus using appropriate methods, listening actively and giving them enough time can lead to very positive relationships between adult researchers and participants. They are very sensitive to being patronized or overlooked. They often say 'no one ever asked me before'. However caution in interpreting their meanings is still warranted.

Phil Jones: *Creating relationships between the different projects and contexts is full of potential and problems. Looking back at the research, and on your reflections and writings about it, what are the main areas you feel are important to think about in creating such relationships?*

Gayatri Kembhavi-Tam and Mary Wickenden: *First, we feel that it is important that research in the global south is not generalized from one context to the other, based purely on the fact that it all takes place in the global south. As we said in the paper, the term global south is in itself problematic and any kind of generalization is bound to overlook important characteristics of different places and situations. Each context is unique, and although there may be similarities, what is true for disabled children in Sri Lanka, for example, is not necessarily going to be true for children in India.*

Second, we feel that when creating relationships between projects in differing contexts with disabled children, the key is to focus on the broader issues of inclusion and participation. That is, while specific research methodologies may differ from one environment to another (segregation based on gender, the inclusion of children with different disabilities in one group, age matching, language and cultural issues, gatekeeping setups etc.), it is critical that we continue the discourse on how we can facilitate the active participation of disabled children in research. Therefore the aim of our paper was to demonstrate some underlying tenants that will arguably always apply. These include: using the levers of the UNCRC and UNCRPD to underline disabled children's rights, ensuring ongoing collaboration with local partners to build positive perceptions of the capabilities of children and of them as citizens, the need to increase awareness among researchers and others of the importance of including disabled children in child focused projects, the provision of opportunities for disabled children to be involved in research and consultations, and awareness of the accommodations and adaptations needed to make this successful. Further, we need to build relationships with adults in a variety of roles who consider consulting children, such as service providers and policymakers. It is essential to enhance everyone's understanding of the importance of including disabled children and their confidence in doing so, making them aware of small but necessary variations and additions to research methodologies that would create a more fully inclusive atmosphere for all children. As is often argued in relation to inclusive practices generally, the benefits of including disabled children are not just for them but will also impact on other children and the adults around them who will grow to understand their perspectives and desire to be treated like 'ordinary children' with things to say.

Phil Jones: How do you see your work offering a direction for future research involving disabled children and their rights?

Gayatri Kembhavi-Tam and Mary Wickenden: We hope that our work and the work of our colleagues serves to increase awareness of the ways in which disabled children can and should be included in research. Necessary adaptations (physical adaptations, visual materials, slower pace, use of varied communication modes, the need for the building of relationships before data collection can take place, etc.) are not onerous, but require commitment and desire on the part of researchers working with children and disabled children as well as forward planning. We would hope that the inclusion of disabled children in research that concerns not only their lives and rights, but issues related to children in general, will become a natural process. Just as we move towards a more inclusive society for all people, so too we hope that our work offers a way to make research more automatically or routinely inclusive, thereby having a greater impact on disabled children and the realisation of their rights. There needs to be an expectation and assumption that they can and should join in rather than the persistence of the view that they cannot.

Reflections on the research

Activity 1

Think about the points made about parallels and differences between different contexts and discuss your thoughts about the research described:

- What are some of the positive values of looking at the ways in which different contexts respond to the articles of the UNCRC?
- What do you think some of the problems might be in looking at the relationship between rights in different contexts?

Activity 2

Take the following points raised in the interview by the researchers about their enquiry and look back at the summary of the research. How do you see the points they make in their interview relating to the research they undertook?

- The use of levers of the UNCRC and UNCRPD to underline disabled children's rights,
- The need to increase awareness among researchers and others of the importance of including disabled children in child focused projects,
- The provision of opportunities for disabled children to be involved in research and consultations, and awareness of the accommodations and adaptations needed to make this successful.

The dominance of adult-orientated ways of communicating and decision making

MacNaughton et al. (2007) examined ways of challenging aspects of the barriers to children's right to participate, looking at approaches to challenging adult-orientated ways of communication and involvement in participation. Their work focused on young children, and is rooted in the relationship between rights and voice:

Adults' views are valued according to their proponents' social identities (e.g. their class, 'race' and gender); and on the rare occasions when children's views appear in public debates, they are rarely regarded as equally valuable as adults' views. Thus, listening to young children is the first step to regarding children's rights as rights of citizenship, rather than as rights defined – and restricted – by age. (2007, 466)

They say that adults face two major tasks in relation to this listening and 'including younger children's voices' (2007, 466):

- to enable young children to express their opinions confidently,
- to ensure that those opinions are taken seriously.

Example of research: consultation with young children

MacNaughton et al. (2003) initiated a consultation exercise with young children from birth to eight years. They used an action-learning model to assist 23 early childhood staff to consult children about their experiences of their education and care services. This drew on a combination of methods designed to enable a child to work with the language or process the child wanted to and could express themselves through. These included pictures, photographs as well as words. Most children were in the age group of three to five years, with 8 of the 173 children aged less than two years.

The researchers worked with key questions:

What do children think they need for their well being? What do children wish for and value in their lives?

The children's views covered three arenas of their life: their experiences of family and home, of education and of care. In relation to their family and home, for example, the children's priority was to have a safe and caring family with whom to spend time, and most children felt safe with key people in their families. Many children also wanted a home in which members of the family have time together and time apart. The findings included the following:

Girl – 'I feel special when I'm with my family.'
Boy – 'I feel safe when I live in a house so the rain and thunder don't get you.'
Girl – 'My family is special because they are always there for me.'

Girl – 'Home is a place where I can be myself.'
Girl – 'I'm happy in this picture at the lucky, lucky preschool because it's not noisy there. There aren't too many kids. The teachers sit down and talk to you all the time. They let you decide what to do all the time. They don't tell you what to do.'

The authors argue that this kind of approach reinforces the growing body of research evidence that young children

- are quite capable of expressing their views on things that affect them and that they value;
- enjoy the opportunity to do so;
- can be worked with in ways that encourage and assist them to develop the knowledge, skills and confidence they need to become active citizens who can participate actively in public decision-making. (2003, 465)

They conclude that honouring children's rights to express themselves and their lives creates more effective policy; it results in a more inclusive community and moves towards healthy democracy. However, they note issues concerning power and voice are both crucial to engage with and form a key challenge to young children's voices being heard and empowered (2003, 466).

Research in Norway with slightly older children offers insight from children and young people on what they thought was effective within school systems on their views being engaged with through the schools council system. The qualitative interviews revealed that staff–pupil relationships were considered by the children to be crucial to the success of participation. The pupils cited a number of examples of good groundwork by teachers:

> At lower secondary school the pupils' council had a greater say; the teacher who assisted them was very good. She listened to what we had to say and took the matter up with the school board. We exerted a lot of influence compared with pupils at upper secondary school.
> At lower secondary school the teacher left the classroom for maybe half an hour, so we could discuss in class any problems we had concerning the teacher, or with anything else. It wasn't always easy to talk about these things with the teacher present. (Sandbaek and Hafdis Einarsson, 2008, 24)

Reflections on the research

Activity 1

Summarize the key points about important issues regarding children's voices being engaged with from the UK research with young people and the research with the Norwegian pupils.

Activity 2

How do you see the quotation from the UK research, 'honouring children's rights to express themselves and their lives create more effective policy' (2007, 466), in relation to the points made by the Norwegian pupils?

Activities

The following activities are designed to help reflect back on some of the key concerns over the chapter as a whole.

Chapter activity 1

Dalrymple's review of advocacy services draws on research into young people's experience of the provision. A number of the findings were positive, speaking of how with an advocate 'you're treated like an adult' and shifting from a position in case reviews where 'not having an advocate in the review I didn't get in what I wanted to say. It gives you confidence' (Dalrymple, 2005, 7). Others, however, saw the process of being supported to have their voices heard in a different way:

> *Personally I don't feel I can influence things. Even now everyone has closed ranks. But at the last meeting having an advocate in the room meant I felt I could (influence things) and I wasn't taking the whole lot on my own. (Dalrymple, 2005, 8)*
> *I wouldn't say it's useful 'cos it ain't – it makes it uncomfortable for kids 'cos staff want to know what's going on. They're all sweety sweet for when Inspectors or the psychiatrist comes to the house but then they change. (Dalrymple, 2005, 9)*

In their interview Gayatri Kembhavi-Tam and Mary Wickenden say that 'particularly for disabled children, the deference to adult gatekeepers for decisions, opinions and viewpoints is longstanding. The existence of the UNCRC and terms of the UNCRPD do not necessarily mean that the provisions are manifest "on the ground"'.

Each of these examples, in part, shows how adult attitudes can sabotage attempts to enable children and young people to have their say. Consider any of the research examples in this chapter and

1. reflect on how adult attitudes might sabotage the work to enable children's voices to be represented,
2. review what processes could help reduce or stop this occurring,
3. think about Kembhavi-Tam and Wickenden's point about traditions of 'deference' and how the research connects to challenging established ideas and relationships.

Chapter activity 2

In the light of your reflections and review, examine the importance of the points made by the National Youth Agency in their guidance on 'Avoiding the traps' regarding children's rights, voice and participation:

- involve children and young people in the earliest stages of planning;
- start slowly, proceed carefully and draw on pilot projects;
- take time and ensure there are the relevant resources;
- recognize and enable the wider changes in attitudes, behaviour and power required; and
- provide consistent support and staff development for steady progress to spread. (The National Youth Agency, 2005)

Summary

This chapter has

- looked at the meaning of 'child's voice',
- examined how ideas of 'voice' relates to child rights,
- explored how ways of relating to children and young people can silence and disempower and harm them,
- examined ways in which a child rights agenda challenges ideas and practices that silence them,
- reviewed research in order to look at ideas and approached that effectively involve children and young people.

Further reading

Kellett, M. (2010) 'The research process reviewed from a children's rights perspective' and 'Children and young people as researchers', in *Rethinking Children and Research*. London: Continuum.

An examination of child research from a rights perspective, not only featuring illustrative studies about the exercising of those human rights but also discussing what rights children have in the research process itself, and a review of approaches involving children undertaking and leading their own research.

Lewis, A. (2010) 'Silence in the context of "child voice"', *Children & Society*, 24 (1), 14–23.

Offers a critique of the idea and practice of the 'child's voice', examining the ethics and purposes behind such engagement with children. The article includes recommendations for researchers working in the fields of 'child voice' concerning five methodological aspects: recognizing, noting, responding to, interpreting and reporting silence from children.

Tisdall, K. and Punch, S. (2012) Not so 'new'? Looking critically at childhood studies, *Children's Geographies*, 10 (3) 249–264.

A critical review of recent approaches to childhood and research involving children, particularly concerning participation and voice.

Research details

Example of research: children's perceptions of being involved in decisions that affect them

Research involving children and young people's perceptions and opinions involving focus group work, available at www.niccy.org, including a children's and a young person's version.

Kilkelly, U., Kilpatrick, R., Lundy, L. Moore, L., Scraton, P., Davey, C., Dwyer, C. and McAlister, A. (2005) *Children's Rights in Northern Ireland*. Belfast: NICCY and Queens' University of Belfast.

Example of research: children with disabilities

The project involved disabled children and young people and was led by The Children's Society with joint funding from the Joseph Rowntree Foundation. It was developed by the United Kingdom's Department of Health's National Disability Reference Group for a programme called 'Quality Protects'. Its objectives include improved involvement and services for disabled young people and their families.

Badham, B. (2004) 'Participation – for a change: Disabled young people lead the way', *Children & Society*, 18, 143–154.

Example of research: consultation with young children

MacNaughtonet al. initiated a consultation exercise with young children from birth to eight years of age in the United Kingdom. They used an action-learning model to assist 23 early childhood staff to consult children about their experiences of their education and care services.

MacNaughton, G., Smith, K. and Lawrence, H. (2003). *ACT Children's Strategy – Consulting with Children Birth to Eight Years of Age. Hearing Young Children's Voices*. London: Children's Services Branch, ACT Department of Education, Youth and Family Services.

Example of research: child's voice and age

Mixed methods research, which included qualitative work in two schools from contrasting municipalities of Mexico City, and a representative of 828 third grade students from the secondary schools in these two areas.

Pérez-Expósito, L. (2015) 'Scope and quality of student participation in school: towards an analytical framework for adolescents', *International Journal of Adolescence and Youth*, 20 (3) 346–374.

Example of research and interview: Ask us too! Doing participatory research with disabled children in the global south

Reports on two participatory research projects with disabled children and young people in India and Sri Lanka, focusing particularly on practical issues that arose including recruitment, information and consent processes and data collection methods.

Wickenden, M. and Kembhavi-Tam, G. (2014) 'Ask us too! Doing participatory research with disabled children in the global south', *Childhood*, 21 (3) 400–417.

5

Rights and Decision Making

Introduction and key questions

Decision making occurs in children's lives within a wide range of spaces: from domestic decisions about what to do or where to be in their home or community, to educational decisions about the way a school is regulated through a school council, for example. In some parts of the world, children are increasingly involved in decisions about policy making at national or international levels. Children's active engagement in decisions relates to all areas of their rights: to liberty and welfare rights, to participation, protection and to provision. Those adults involved in such decision making vary in terms of their roles and relationships with children: these include family members, professionals such as teachers, doctors, the police and those involved in local, regional, national and international government. Children's rights have recently been at the fore of questions that are being asked about the very varied treatment and experience of children in relation to decision making in their lives. However, across all of these different arenas and varied contexts or types of interactions, recent developments and research have certain emergent themes or tensions in common. Learning can occur across and between them. The following questions will be used in this chapter to draw out these tensions and themes, rethinking decision making from a rights-based perspective:

> **In what ways does decision making feature in children's lives?**
> **What is the relationship between children's rights and decision making?**
> **What tensions exist in contemporary society about decision making in children's lives?**
> **What does research reveal about the impact of recent thinking and practice in relation to decision making in different spaces within children's lives?**

In what ways does decision making feature in children's lives?

Though a number of rights connect to decision making, Article 12 is often cited as key to participation and decision making:

> States Parties shall assure to the child who is capable of forming his or her own views the right to express those views freely in all matters affecting the child, the views of the child being given due weight in accordance with the age and maturity of the child. (UNCRC, 1989)

The language and concepts within this article creates connections between children:

- *forming* views on their lives,
- *expressing* them and that
- *what weight is due*, judged by factors indicated as being *age* and *maturity*

These actions – forming, expressing and being given due weight – are complex and much of this chapter connects with the ways these actions are interpreted and understood. The following activity starts to explore some of this complexity.

Activity

What decisions could children be involved in at

- home;
- school;
- hospital;
- playground?

What do you think 'capable of forming their views' and 'due weight' might mean?

How do you think factors such as 'age' and 'maturity' relate to ideas about children's views being given 'due weight'?

How might negative stereotypes of children affect how 'age' and 'maturity' are viewed?

What areas of decision making might a young child be actively involved in? What areas might a teenager be involved in? Discuss areas that are parallel and different – and your reasons for making those choices.

Decision making relating to children happens in ways that involves direct personal interaction with a child: for example between a father and a small child at home, or in a playground, or between a teacher and a child in a large classroom group. Decision making relating to children can also happen in ways that do not often involve face-to-face interactions: for example, in committees involving the creation of policies, or within governments involving law making. The literature also reveals the ways in which different disciplines see children and decision making, and how these ways have an impact on whether and how children are involved in decisions that affect them. These include conceptual frameworks from developmental perspectives which relate to how ideas about 'maturity', age and cognition are seen, for example, and which are reflected in children's encounters with, for example, the law or medicine. From political and sociological perspectives emerge issues about the ways in which negative traditions and stereotypes upheld by adults about children's capability and capacity affect the ways legal or health services view and treat children's decision making.

The following offers some brief illustrations of the wide range of issues and contexts within which children's decision making is currently being reviewed in practice and research. The Australian National Childcare Accreditation Council, for example, gives a flavour of approaches that are developing that lay emphasis on children as 'decision makers' *at an early age*:

Children can be involved in decisions about

- whether to play alone or in a group, be involved in a quiet activity or to be physically active;
- which materials and experiences they will engage with and the opportunity to choose those things that interest them and match their level of competence;
- what happens to them in relation to their physical care, for example, nappy changing, toileting, sleeping and eating;
- whether they want to do things independently or would like some help. (www.ncac.gov.au/factsheets/factsheet2. 1)

Other perspectives examine different contexts and situations, recognizing the diversity and complexity of decision making. The New Zealand government, for example, notes in its guide to children and decision making that 'Children in New Zealand have *unique experiences of life* based on their gender, age, ethnicity, religion, ability, locality and individual living circumstances' and argue for the importance in any arrangements for decision making of ensuring their 'ideas and interests are heard and to avoid ignoring their differences'. In their advice to professionals, they talk of the context of Māori children, for example, in the following way:

Māori children are tangata whenua. The Treaty of Waitangi recognises their right to partnership with the Crown. For government departments in particular, involving Māori children in decision-making is an expression of that partnership.

You also need to consider a number of broader cultural issues – for example: children are considered part of their wider *whānau* and should not be viewed in isolation there are differences between Māori children who live in urban settings and those who live in rural settings not all Māori children have ongoing associations with *iwi*.

You can support the participation of Māori children by using facilitators who have the trust and confidence of the group of Māori children, their *whänau* and their community using facilitators skilled in *tikanga* and *te reo* when appropriate working with the Māori community, including *iwi* organizations, social service and educational organizations and cultural groups to ensure appropriate participation processes providing for whänau and support people to be present, if appropriate (Ministry of Social Development, 2016, 9).

Tangata whenua is a term translated as local people, indigenous people and being of the land where the people's ancestors have lived.
Whānau can be translated as extended family.
Tikanga has been described as a term meaning the general behaviour patterns or guidelines for daily life and interaction in Māori culture.
Te reo is a term often used to refer to the Māori language.
iwi refers to a large social unit in Māori culture, the term has been translated as tribe or group of tribes. (http://maoridictionary.co.nz/)

Activity

How do you see this text from the New Zealand Government relating to Article 12 of the UNCRC?
How do you understand the ways in which 'cultural issues' relate to the ideas about 'difference' and 'decision making' in the ministry text?

Another important perspective sees decision making in terms of *structural political frameworks*. In a different arena of decision making, and in relation to older age groups, Combe's (2002) discussion of a survey of local government in the United Kingdom, for example, links *involvement* and *being responded to* as key to decision making. Combe concludes that the survey revealed that many councils are committed to 'including young people in decision-making' around policy priorities. Research (Davey et al., 2010) undertaken by organizations including Children's Rights Alliance for England and the Children's Commissioner for England asked children and young people about their experiences in such 'involvement' and decision making:

There was a lot of scepticism as to whether attempts by councillors to seek the views of children were actually genuine or merely part of a tokenistic 'tick box' exercise:

... I think that the councillors do go out to tick a box sometimes because they think, because of all this political correctness and stuff, we've got to get such and such young person and make sure that we're a diverse ... and it's like, I'm going to go out just to tick my box but they don't actually get taken into consideration, they don't put a lot of thought into it. (Interview with an involved group of children) (Davey et al., 2010, 35)

The young participants recommended that decision makers

take off their suits and ties and stand on a street corner and do some ... you know like detached youth workers do, they just go out in their jeans and...just go and talk to a big group of young people, and see what they're up to and see what their thoughts are but councillors wouldn't do that. (Interview with an involved group of children)

Conducting research and consultations in the street was also considered a useful way of accessing the hidden populations of children whose voices might otherwise be missed if more traditional methods of consultation were used (Davey et al., 2010, 35).

Activity

What do you think the main differences are between 'listening' to children's views and children being involved and responded to in relation to decision making? How does this relate to the comments made by the participants in Davey et al.'s research?

What are your views about the points made by the participants in terms of the need for councillors to engage with less traditional means of accessing young people's views?

Issues concerning the different levels of the engagement of children and young people in decision making are also revealed as an issue within research. Franklin and Sloper's (2006) survey of social service departments in England, for example, reflected this type of division in their results analysis:

Encouragingly, disabled children were being involved in different decision-making areas, although it would appear that quite a majority of children's involvement in service development so far has centred on what could be termed 'children's issues' – activities, equipment or décor, which are more concrete concepts and within a child's own experience. Involvement of disabled children and young people at a higher strategic level still seems to be rare. (2006, 731)

This illustrates some of the different spheres of children's lives within which decision making occurs, and how exclusion can vary between these arenas, with adults permitting access to some areas, but not to others. It also shows how factors such as the social divisions of society and the ways adults relate to children as gatekeepers for access to rights affect the ways decision making is experienced by children.

What is the relationship between children's rights and decision making?

The material examined so far has seen decision making from a variety of interconnecting perspectives: for example, in relation to politics and democracy. This section focuses upon ways of viewing children's decision making from a *rights* perspective. The US organization 'Youth on Board', for example, sees decision making *primarily* as a rights issue. They frame it in a way that makes clear the relationship between rights, decision making and childhood:

> Nowhere in the U.S. Declaration of Independence is there a stipulation concerning age. 'All men are created equal', 'all are entitled to 'certain unalienable rights'. So why is it that in this country, decisions that affect a significant segment of the populations are made by others? In far too many situations, young people are not being heard. Their rights are being disregarded or violated, and adults do not seem to hear or care about it. This needs to change. A shift is needed in our communities to allow young people's concerns to be heard and taken seriously. They have the same right as adults to voice their hopes, ideas, and fears. ('Youth on Board', 14 points: Successfully involving youth in decision making, www.youthonboard.org, 1)

Decision making, when looked at in this way, can be seen to relate to liberty and welfare rights and a child's right to participate as defined in the UNCRC. As referred to earlier, traditional practice in many societies, and in many cultures, has largely involved adults making decisions about areas of children's lives and the spaces they live in – such as education, health or leisure. Key transitions and events in a child's life can occur without any attempt to involve a child in them. Tomlinson describes the situation in the following way:

> The complexity of ideas about childhood and the ways these are drawn on by politicians is often overlooked. Where children are concerned they may be viewed solely as economic investments. Their care and welfare might be considered but their status in society as full human beings far less so ... where

the child is the centre of consideration, the emphasis has tended to be on their welfare and the role of the family rather than their status in society. (2008, 29)

She contrasts this position with one that views children as citizens 'as holders of human rights too' (Tomlinson, 2008, 29) and argues that this can be allied with the need to acknowledge 'the power of children and their participation in political and economic decision making' (Tomlinson, 2008, 29). The picture which has emerged from research into children's experiences of spaces such as home, school, hospital and the streets of the communities they live in is one in which it is routine for adults to behave in ways that assume that the following is quite normal for adults:

- to make the decisions about what children can do, and how they live within the spaces they inhabit;
- to regulate children's lives through formal laws, and the way they treat children more informally through rules and attitude, as if children either do not have the capacity, or right, to be involved in decisions about the way they conduct their lives.

Examples of this are included in the following key points.

Key points: spaces and norms in decision making processes

Space	Issue	Norms in decision making processes
Education: school	Which type of educational provision a child receives: which school to attend	Parents decide on options offered by adult education workers with no requirement for children to be involved in the decision
Law: courts	Sentencing in youth courts	Decisions are made by adult professionals with little or no effective involvement of the child in the analysis or discussion of the situation

Activity 1

Consider the decisions listed in the column titled 'Norms in decision making processes':

Reflect on your own experiences of decision making in each area – either your experiences as a child, or an adult. In particular, consider whether you as a child, or you now as an adult, experienced each of these in a way that is reflected by the 'norm' described, or whether your experience has been different? For example, in the norms concerning education – has your experience been that adults decide, or were children involved in the decision making about which type of school was attended?

Reflect on different ways in which children could be involved in decisions in each of these arenas. Ask yourself what assumptions you are making about why, how and whether children can be involved in decision making.

Activity 2

Consider the earlier quotation from 'Youth on Board':

In far too many situations, young people are not being heard. Their rights are being disregarded or violated, and adults do not seem to hear or care about it.

How do you see the connections between this quote and the material in the 'Key Points' about 'norms' and children's spaces?

Many of the examples above illustrate some of the challenges and frustrations faced by children in relation to decisions in their lives. The following examples examine children's lives in the light of a rights-based approach to decision making and illustrate how this perspective offers new opportunities and challenges long-held assumptions and ways of working.

What tensions are emerging concerning decision making and children?

The struggle, as described in Chapters 1 and 2, between traditionally held views of children that hold them as incapable or innocent and the framework emerging from the new sociology of childhood is reflected in debates about decision making and child rights. This section looks at key arenas of children's lives as examples of rethinking rights in terms of this struggle and tension. It draws on children's experiences in the spaces of child protection, education and then law to look at the complexity of issues concerning decision making and rights in some detail.

Social work and child protection

Research conducted by Alfandari related to 'recent national reform in Israeli child protection practice that comes in the wake of the UNCRC and includes a mandatory commitment to listen to and consider children's views when making intervention decisions' (2015, 7). Alfandari notes that to date there had been no systematic national data on the operation of the reform in everyday work or on its outcomes. The research drew on 21 case studies, including interviews with professionals. It concluded that though 'including the right building blocks recommended by the international literature', drawing on practices such as informed preparation, offering the opportunity for children to attend committee meetings with 'several options' for communication, the reform 'did not meet its target' to 'work directly, consistently and effectively with children in order for meaningful participation to be achieved' (2015, 8). An illustration from the data included one social worker commenting, for example, that

> I don't have relationships with most of the children here. It is all round parents' requests, only if there is something exceptional or (due to) reports from school or such things. (2015, 4)

Van Bijleveld et al. (2014) conducted an extensive literature review drawing on multiple bibliographic databases, to examine what was known about 'barriers and factors facilitating child participation within the child protection and child welfare services from both children's and social workers' perspectives'. Their approach connected child participation to the nature of their decision making within the provision of services. Their summary concludes that 'the majority' of children and young people reported that they had limited opportunities to participate in the decision-making process involving their lives or that they had no opportunities at all (2014, 133). In the major decision-making contexts, such as review meetings or family group conferences, they report that the literature shows that though a number of children and young people were in attendance, they were often only present rather than actually engaging in the decision-making process. They noted across 'all studies' that 'the intent to involve children is present, but that social workers still demonstrate striking ambiguities and reservations about the precise role children and young people should play' (2014, 129). Some workers interpreted participation rights as giving children information about what is decided but did not mean children having an influence on the actual decision making. The authors summarize that a key problem in the process of involving children in decisions was the inadequate engagement with the different, complex factors involved, for example:

> Social workers and case managers need to determine what is in the child's best interests in a context where different stakeholders have their own conflicting interests, rights and needs. For example, the case manager has to manage the child's right to participate but also acknowledge the custodial role of the parents. In addition, Article 12 of the UNCRC states that the views of children should be taken into account according to age and maturity but gives no guidance on who should assess the maturity of the child and what criteria should be used. (2014, 130)

The lack of time and the way relationships were formed were commented on.

> Child protection and welfare services should … focus on the image of children held by professionals and the ambiguities around the legal rights of children's participation. The interpretation and meaning of the legal rights should be clearer to the child protection and welfare services: the child should be seen as the service user and the child image should be less focused on protection, and more on that of a child as a knowledgeable social actor. In other words, the children should get a central position in the decision making process, right from the start. (2014, 137)

The review concludes that children want more involvement in decision making, and that from the perspectives of children and social workers, the *relationship* between the young person and the professional, and *time* to create and develop it, were the most important factors for successful participation in decision making alongside this shift in the way the 'image' of the child is constructed by professionals and children within the service.

Decision making: the complexities of policy and lived practice

Research has revealed many examples of effective, innovative practice in relation to children's decision making. However, it is also helping us to understand the many ways in which policy may be clear on paper, but actual practice could not be more different. The following is an example to illustrate this kind of enquiry. The research involved a participant observation study of face-to-face encounters between social workers, children and families.

Example of research: 'how children become invisible in child protection work'

Ferguson's analysis of the 'encounter' is described by him as aiming to deepen understandings of 'how and why children become invisible in everyday child protection practice' (2016, 1). In the following extract the researcher accompanied a social worker on her visit to a child's home after a two-year-old girl, given the pseudonym of Amelia, was allegedly left unsupervised and was found a long way from her home. Amelia's mother, in the research given the name of Mrs Brown, was a lone parent and there was another child in her family, a five-year-old called Jamie. The researcher reports that in the home visit, the researcher, the social worker, Mrs Brown, Amelia and Jamie sit together in the same room throughout the visit. The researcher notes that the social worker talks to Mrs Brown about the situation at home with no interaction at all with the children present. This is an extract reporting on what happened after the visit:

> When asked in the car straight afterwards whether she had considered speaking to the five-year-old, the worker replied: 'But yeah I, I could have done, couldn't I, really? But I didn't think about it at the time because he's only five.'
>
> I knew that this worker had interviewed a five-year-old alone in another case I had shadowed her on, so this was not a convincing reason for not doing it. As the social worker continued to drive, she must have been silently reflecting on this and, a couple of minutes after the above comment, volunteered: 'But I'll be honest, I didn't, I didn't even think about it, I don't know why but I didn't.'... As she was getting out of the car at the office fifteen minutes after the end

of the visit, referring to the five-year-old, she said, 'I don't know why I didn't talk to him?'. The worker was unable to explain even to herself how she had so totally failed to think about the children and keep them in mind. In the heat of the visit, talking with and other forms of relating to the children became unthinkable and the fact that she had not engaged with them in any way was, at the time it was happening, unknown to the worker. The children had ceased to exist to her despite being there right in front of her. They were invisible children. (2016, 12)

The researcher argues that this is not adequately explained as individual 'errors and judge them to have failed due to lacking the skills and competence to do the work' as 'the same workers in the examples given were observed on other occasions with different families practising competently' (2016, 12).

'Organizational culture' first comes into play in relation to the definitions of need and risk to children that are operating and the time available to practitioners to respond to them. The researcher makes the following comments in his analysis:

- A key dynamic in how some children become invisible in child protection work is the systemic pressures practitioners feel under to rush through their work and the limited time they have generally to make any children 'visible' (2016, 13),
- In stepping into the service user's life (and home), practitioners' responses are then shaped by the emotional demands and interactional dynamics they experience and the impact of the home or other environment where the work goes on (2016, 14).

Reflections on the research

Activity 1

Looking at the research, what factors contribute to the children's 'invisibility'? Do you agree with the way the author uses this word to describe what is happening to the children?

Activity 2

The researcher uses the term 'organizational culture' and connects this with pressures on workers. What is your understanding of how this features in relation to children's decision making discussed in the extracts above?

The use of such research is that it enables insights into the ways in which decision making and children's rights are not just about policies on paper; it is connected to resources, training, personal emotions. It can help to argue for more effective provision. This research, for example, makes the following comments about improvement:

> The more that social workers are given time to do quality work, opportunities to talk, reflect on feelings and to think critically about their lived experiences, the less risk there will be that children will become unheld and invisible. (2016, 15)

While the research doesn't directly use the word 'rights', it is a useful example of the complexity of lived practice and can be helpful in illustrating the ways in which adult power, the complex psychological, emotional dynamics at work and the ways in which personal experiences and training connect to organizational forces such as the provision of resources such as time, support for workers and professional development. These all create a matrix of powerful forces which result in the silencing and lack of involvement of a five-year-old child in what happens to them and their family within the provision of care. What should be *centred* on them becomes something that *excludes* them or in the words of the researcher makes them 'invisible'.

Decision making and participation rights in education: which school?

Children spend much of their time, when awake, in school spaces, or pursuing school-related activities in their home environment. Hence, the nature of the school space and the processes concerning schooling are key to any child. However, in the United Kingdom this crucial arena of a child's life is largely the domain of adult decision making, with children treated as the recipients of adult decisions. As this section will show, research has revealed how they are disenfranchised from the right to participate in most aspects of decision making within their main space in their life, concerning areas such as the direction and regulation of educational experience and school life. Local authorities are legally obliged to make arrangements for enabling parents to express preferences about the nature and use of this space, but are under no such obligation to consider the wishes of a child 'by, for instance, allowing the child to make submissions as to what type of educational provision would best suit him or her and at which school the child wishes to be educated' (Anderson, 2008, 20). Codes of Practice concerning school admissions, such as the following example from Scotland's 'Choosing a School', make reference to children in the decision-making process but until the age of 16 the service provider has no contact with the child in this process, and only considers the child as *possibly* having views. The child 'may have views that their parents should consider': it is an option that may be taken by parents. There is no direct action to ensure or even ask if any engagement in this decision has occurred:

From: the Scottish government's 'Deciding which school you would prefer your child to go to' (2010)
Children's views

All parents naturally want the best for their children. That natural desire is underpinned by the Children (Scotland) Act 1995, which sets out parental responsibility to safeguard and promote their child's health, development and welfare, in their child's best interests. Like the United Nations Convention on the Rights of the Child (to which the United Kingdom is a signatory), it also recognizes the rights of children to have their views taken into consideration when any major decisions are being made that affect their development and welfare. Choosing a school is clearly a very important decision, and children may have views that their parents should consider, taking into account their relative age and maturity.

Young people over 16

In addition to the rights described above, once a pupil has reached the school leaving age the pupil – not the pupil's parents – may choose which school to go to. The time at which pupils are old enough by law to leave school depends on when their sixteenth birthday falls in the year.

- Pupils who have their sixteenth birthday on or between 1 March and 30 September can leave school or decide for themselves whether they want to ask for another school from 31 May that year.

- Pupils who have their sixteenth birthday on or between 1 October and the last day of February can leave school or decide for themselves whether they want to ask for another school at Christmas in between those two dates.

If the pupil wants to change schools, then he or she should write to their local council to say so (http://www.gov.scot/Publications/2010/11/10093528/2).

Anderson (2008) has noted that the Committee on the Rights of the Child maintains that the right to participation contained in Article 12 applies to all other rights contained in the convention and to 'all measures adopted by States to implement the Convention' (UN Committee on Rights of the Child, General Comment No 5: General Measures of Implementation of the Convention. On the Rights of the Child, parts 4, 42 and 44, CRC/GC/2003/5 (2003), para 12).

Anderson's analysis helps to see the connections between the right to participation and the decision-making process in terms of problematic issues arising within many children's experience of education:

> The Committee has specifically stated that the rights to participation is important in ensuring a child's right to education, and child rights within the education system: 'education must be provided in a way that ... enables the child to express his or her views freely in accordance with article 12 (1) and to participate in school life' (UN Committee on the Rights of the Child, General Comment No. 1: The Aims of Education, CRC/GC/2001/1 2001, para 8).(2008, 18)

This means that children should be able to participate in decision making in areas such as the type of education provision they receive. Children should be involved in:

- the running of the school,
- the recruitment of staff,
- the formulation of disciplinary policies,
- curriculum development,
- policies on teaching methods and staff development.

Anderson notes that this should also be interpreted to mean that any child should be 'enjoying the right to appeal school admission and exclusion decisions' (2008, 18):

> According to article 12 of the UNCRC, individual children should be afforded the right to participate in educational decisions affecting them. In addition,

at a broader level, children's views should be sought in the development of school and government policies, procedures and rules in relation to education. (2008, 19)

The treatment of children in terms of their rights to be involved in decision making in education varies between and within different societies. Some have developed a more positive response to this aspect of children's relationship to their experience of education (Cohen et al., 2004). Others, such as the United Kingdom, have been criticized for their lack of progress by comparison, and the lack of structured, embedded engagement with children as decision makers. The UNCRC periodic review of the UK government notes in 2002, for example, that obligations relating to Article 12 were not consistently incorporated in legislation. In terms of education, it criticized the UK government, saying that it needed to take further steps to promote, facilitate and monitor 'systematic, meaningful and effective participation of all groups of children in society, including in schools' (para 30), in a way that 'reflects article 12 and respects children's rights to express their views and have them given due weight in all matters concerning their education' (UNCRC Concluding Observations: UK of Great Britain and Northern Ireland (2002), CRC/C/15/Add. 188, para 48).

Anderson comments that, despite this indictment from the UNCRC in 2002, over five years later,

the government has failed to implement these recommendations and ensure that children in England enjoy the right to participate effectively in the education system.

Still later research (Davey et al., 2010) with different groups of children in England explored their experiences and views of involvement in decision making in school. It involved 86 children aged between four and twenty in different settings. The overall findings were as follows:

- Most children were generally dissatisfied with their level of input into decision making processes in school.
- There were some excellent examples of where school councils, youth forums and individual parents/carers had proactively engaged children in decision-making processes; in general, these opportunities were not the norm.
- The low status adults often accorded to children's opinions and the lack of explanation on how children's opinions had or had not been taken into account during a decision-making process.

The research found that 'disabled children, very young children and those from a refugee and migrant background' were 'amongst the most likely to miss out on opportunities to raise concerns that were pertinent to their lives and to have these concerns addressed as a result' (2010, 42).

The conclusion of the report included the following:

Children were very aware of the unique perspective they brought to discussions on account of the fact that they were of a different generation and as such were more likely to be creative in their approach to problem solving. As citizens of their community they also stated that they had a right to be involved in decision-making processes.

Children wanted more regular meetings with adults and were particularly keen to access government structures which they deemed to be the most powerful and influential mechanisms for making change happen'. (2010, 42)

Activity

Decision making and school

- Why do you imagine adults would want to exclude children from decisions about their school?
- How do you think children could be involved in decision making in the following areas:

    1. Children deciding about their Early Years setting of choice?
    2. Children deciding about their secondary education?

Consider the findings of the Davey et al.'s (2010) research:

- what do you understand by 'unique perspective they brought to discussions'?
- in relation to education how might pupils 'access government structures'?

Research has shown how parallel processes occur in different areas of their lives. Kilkelly (2008), for example, has shown how children are excluded from decision making in a different space – that of the law courts. Her research into Youth Courts in Ireland examined children's experience of decision making in Ireland. She observed the way interactions occurred between the young person and those involved in decision making. The following are examples of her key findings:

- Those who wished to speak for themselves, and to follow what was going on, appeared to find participation difficult if not impossible.
- Some were ordered to be quiet or to let their solicitor speak on their behalf, while others' efforts to intervene went unnoticed.
- In 55 per cent of the cases no communication between judges and young people took place: the judge did not greet the young person, did not speak to them at any stage and did not explain when proceedings had been concluded.
- The young person was frequently referred to as 'he' or 'she'.
- The young person was observed frequently staring at the floor or ceiling or chatting to family members.
- Some did not realize their case was over until the next case was called.
- When interaction did take place between the judge and the young person, it was usually minimal in nature involving a basic greeting at the start and the end of proceedings.
- On rare occasions the interaction between the young person and the judge was aggressive with the young person being ordered about, insulted or reprimanded about his/her dress or posture. In a small number of cases, efforts to engage the young person were made by the judge who addressed him/her by name and wished him/her good luck at the end.
- The young people were often visibly surprised at being spoken to, but appeared overwhelmingly pleased at being spoken to by name (2008, 51–52).

Activity

Review the insights offered by Kilkelly's research:

- How do you think the practices she observed limit or deny children's rights?
- How might practice be changed to enable children's rights to be realized in the kinds of situations that Kilkelly describes?

The following example continues with the theme of professional practice and how research can help us understand the complexities of specific contexts. It looks at a specific situation in children's healthcare and examines different perspectives to help deepen our understanding of how rights connect to decision making and children's experiences of cancer and cancer care.

Example of research: children, participation and decision making during cancer care

Coyne et al.'s (2014) research explores the complex relationship between childcare, health provision during treatment for cancer and participation rights. Their work illustrates both the need and value of research that helps to understand the relationships between universal rights and very specific contexts. The research looked at one haematology/oncology unit in Ireland and aimed to examine what they call 'shared decision making' involved in the process of children's cancer care. A part of this sharing concerns 'decision making and the child's position in the three way relationship' that connects child, parents and healthcare professionals (2014, 274). They involved 20 children over a wide age range of seven to sixteen, 22 parents and 40 healthcare professionals. The types of cancer were varied, including leukaemia, sarcomas and lymphomas.

The researchers contextualized their work within the different dynamics and processes which occur in healthcare provision when dealing with children and a 'life-threatening illness' (2014, 273). This includes how

- children experience themselves and those around them in relation to processes of decision making;
- the ways professional roles such as consultant or nurses are conceived of, and how adults handle these, in relation to child cancer care and treatment;
- policies about decision making and the lived experiences of these policies relate to each other;
- adult to adult relationships occur within decision making, for example between professionals and parents.

They note the lack of attention and guidance given to this in terms of advice for those involved. The situation in the day care unit is reported as follows:

There was a policy of family centred care in place, but no policy on information-sharing nor participation in decision-making. Parents and children were invited to participate if they met the following inclusion criteria: child receiving cancer treatment more than 6 weeks since diagnosis, aged 7 years upwards and not receiving palliative care. (2014, 274)

Importantly, they look at the interrelationship of attitudes, professional practices and policies relating to children and place the children's experiences within these dynamics. Examples of these concern the ways in which 'doubts exist about the appropriateness of sharing illness related information and decisions with children' connected to adult concerns about children's 'competence to participate' and a desire to 'protect children from distressing information' (2014, 274). Decision making is seen in a very specific context, rather than being seen as a general singular issue and process.

Decision making is placed by them in relation to a diversity of responses from children and while some may desire involvement in decision making, others 'may wish to take a passive role and may prefer their parents and/or health professionals to make the decisions depending on the situation. Balancing children's right to participate in shared decision making and their need and right for protection can be at its most extreme in a healthcare situation' (2014, 274). The interviews with participants were thematically analysed and the following is an example from the three sets of interviews concerning the extent of child participation in decision making:

> *Many Health Professionals (HP) and parents (P) felt that children(C) had limited involvement as most decisions were made by adults and then implemented. For example 'At the end of the day I do think we as a team force a lot on the kids and whether we use different words or options a lot of the decision is with us. It's either the parent or it's the team. Very rarely it seems to be the kid' (HP5). Likewise, a father explained, "The decision-making is, "Can I go down the playroom or not?" or "Can I play this PlayStation?" '. They have very limited power of decisions in hospital. Everything else, it's a very, very controlled environment for them. All those decisions are made for him by everybody else around." (F3 of a seven-year-old boy). Adults felt that the choices they could offer were quite limited due to strict protocols in cancer care and that they had to 'walk a fine line' with offering choices while ensuring that care adhered to the protocol. (2014, 277)*

The researchers noted a number of nuanced differences related to the types of areas to be decided upon, the emotional aspects of decision making, whether decisions were perceived by children as 'real' or not, age and contextual factors concerning treatment 'diagnosis, urgency, and seriousness of the illness' (2014, 278). They note that children between ages seven and eleven appeared 'satisfied' with their level of decision making, but the responses of adolescents differed:

Although they were involved, some spoke about lacking any choices. For example, 'You have to take your tablets, end of. You don't get a choice, sorry if you want one you just don't get one. Just find other ways to take control; you don't get an option' (C3, aged 16). Children may complain or try to delay receiving treatments but they eventually agreed because they knew that the care 'had to be done'. One girl said, 'I'd know I'd have to take it (Liquid food supplement). I hate taking it. It's a thing that helps me gain weight and it's really thick and gooey and I have to take it, but I hate taking it' (C8 aged 12). Some adolescents did not see choices as 'real decisions' because their input would not alter the outcome. These girls said, 'There aren't decisions' (C7 aged 16) and 'I don't really get to make any decisions' (C6 aged 16). (2014, 277)

The research made some recommendations for practice, which they extrapolated from the small scale of the sample, but which may be relevant to other such units. These following are samples of the kinds of implications they draw:

- Though the context of cancer care meant that opportunities for participation were 'quite limited', the research indicated that adults need to be aware of the many ways children can participate and allow choices where possible.
- Such opportunities are identified as: including children in treatment discussions, eliciting preferences, offering choices, and incorporating preferences. They advise that these areas should be considered by 'all members of the multidisciplinary team' including nurses and consultants.
- The nature of the shared decision making should not be seen as a single process, but as complex and changing over time: children's preferences may vary during the cancer treatment 'for many reasons (e.g. stage of illness, seriousness of condition, types of decisions)' (2014, 278).
- Adults should receive education and coaching on how to assess children's preferences and how 'to facilitate their participation as communication' (2014, 278).

Reflections on the research

Activity 1

The research asked children about their views about participation. Looking at the examples of children's comments in the summary, what might influence how children think about and communicate their views?

For example:

- Do you think they are aware of alternatives to the way they experience decision making?
- Do you think age might affect this?
- How do you think the context – that the participants are involved in a treatment situation – might affect what they think, feel or say?

Activity 2

Reading the summary of the research and the recommendations, what factors do you think seem to be important in learning from the research? How might matters be made more positive?

What factors do you think are specific to the context, which factors might relate to other areas of child provision and decision making?

Interview with Professor Imelda Coyne about her research

Professor Imelda Coyne, Trinity College, Dublin

Phil Jones: How did you approach interviewing children about their experience of treatment in what could be a complex situation: for example, asking them about those treating them whilst they were involved in receiving care from those adults?

Imelda Coyne: I have interpreted this question as to whether talking about involvement might have been difficult when the children were still receiving care from the professionals. So my short answer is that we asked the children about their participation in information-sharing and decision making generally. We did not ask questions about specific decisions, such as were you involved in choosing treatment A or B which may have made them think of a particular professional. So when the children responded they never named professionals or specific incidents. Rather they talked generally about how they experienced their involvement. The confidential nature of the study was highlighted to children in both information leaflets and consent forms. They were assured that their accounts would be anonymized and confidential. Although the children were quite sick, they were keen to tell their stories about being there and how interactions went for them. When I reflect on the findings, this is not surprising since children generally felt disempowered in that they 'had to have this done' and so perhaps they welcomed an opportunity to talk about their experiences.

We were aware that asking questions about participation could raise uncomfortable feelings or anxieties during the interview, so the researcher could refer to four specific protocols that were devised to manage situations such as a child (a) displaying signs of anxiety (b) becoming ill (c) disclosing sensitive information (e.g. child protection issues) or (d) feeling emotionally distressed. The details of the protocols were negotiated with the senior staff nurses, the psychologist and social workers so that agreement was achieved. The protocols were a guarantee to the staff who cared for the children that ethical principles would be adhered to and were approved by the hospital ethics committee.

We devised information leaflets tailored for the age groups so that the children could understand in simple language what they were agreeing to and the children signed their own consent form. We designed six different information leaflets for children that were decorated with brightly coloured graphics and the information about the study was written in a simple way to ease understanding. The information leaflets were piloted with four children aged 9 to 15 who were asked to read them and make recommendations. These recommendations included using different graphics such as current movie and television characters popular with children and adolescents, e.g. SpongeBob Square Pants and High School Musical.

Information and consent forms were written in age appropriate language for younger children aged 7–11 years and older children aged 12–16 years. It was essential that the children understood what the research entailed and what it meant for them to participate. The discussion was documented in the field notes to ensure the process of consent was clear. In general, interviews with parents and children were conducted seven or more days after they had agreed to take part. The average number of days between first contact with a family who agreed to take part and data collection was 14 days. This seven-day rule (stipulated by the university ethics committee and endorsed by the hospital ethics committee) was observed to give parents and children time to reconsider their agreement to participate.

We knew that it would be challenging for children to feel like participating when they were receiving active cancer treatment due to painful symptoms and side effects. The children were often very sick and at times and needed a lot of care. Because of this, we tried to ensure that the child/parent did not feel pressurized into participating in interviews when it was not convenient for them. Interviews were held when the child was well enough or had someone else to care for them and at a time which did not conflict with planned treatment schedules. Consent was seen as an ongoing process throughout and children were provided with a 'red card' which they could use to stop the interview at any time. The opportunity to arrange interviews at a later date was offered to parents and children.

Sometimes children's protocols were changed due to illness or events and children and parents were not available for interview in the hospital. When this occurred, we followed up with parents to arrange a time for interviews when it suited the family. On some occasions, it was not possible to interview families because the children were very sick or children had changed their mind about taking part due to illness or tiredness. Some children preferred to sleep throughout their chemotherapy and so were not available for interview. On two occasions, it suited children to be interviewed in their homes and so a date and time was arranged to call out and conduct the interview.

We used a child-centred participatory approach to somewhat reduce or mitigate the challenges of researching very sick young children in an acute clinical setting. In the pilot, it became clear that asking young children about participation (which is a vague/complex concept) was challenging. So, we used a range of activities such as play (drawings), jelly-bean pots, shoebox (wishes could be posted), and images of decisions on cards. In order to stimulate discussion around decision making, laminated cards were designed with pictures and written descriptions of decisions that could be made on the ward. Also, cards representing the child and cohorts of the staff were used to explore children's preferences around who should make what decisions. For example, a child might be asked who decides what the child eats to which they can respond by answering verbally as well as placing the card with the relevant person/group. Children were also invited to draw a new card if they thought of a decision that was not already represented.

Phil Jones: How did you see your role as an adult and as a researcher?

Imelda Coyne: I see my role as a researcher, that it is vital that we access children's views directly as most research in the past has been conducted with adults about children. I am passionate about hearing children's voices and understandings and bringing their accounts to the wider public. I knew that despite decision making featuring throughout the trajectory of care, rarely has the child's perspective been included in research and hospitalized children's participation in decision making remains an area much under-researched and complicated by conflicting opinions. So, although this area is challenging, there is an urgent need to do research with children and not to use the issue of vulnerability to avoid accessing children's views directly. Getting the study approved through two ethics committees was challenging as some members thought the children could be caused further distress and the notion of vulnerability was raised many times. We addressed all the concerns and agreed to several safeguards and the study was approved. Several studies had been done in the US with children in end-of-life decision making and we used this as an example to advocate for this study to be approved. Although we got ethical approval, we had to spend several weeks negotiating with gatekeepers on the units. We held several separate meetings with all the professional staff (doctors, nurses, social workers, psychologist) to gain their support and access to the children and parents. Some professionals were concerned about children's vulnerability and needed reassurance about the safeguards and conduct of the researchers. We agreed that the researcher would check in with the nurse-in-charge every day to ensure that 'vulnerable' families were not accessed. We could see the value of this gatekeeping role as we were unaware of family's circumstances, but at the same time we were concerned that some children may be prevented from having their voices heard because of an assessment made by an adult rather than allowing them to make that choice.

As an adult and a children's nurse, I was very aware that children experience cancer treatment as harsh and can suffer a lot; so this made me feel very protective. We had frequent discussions about the interview process and follow-up calls and debriefing after each interview. We had arranged counselling support for the researchers in case of emotional distress caused by witnessing children's suffering and/or hearing their accounts. We also set up regular team meetings to ensure that any potential difficulties were addressed quickly.

As an adult and a researcher, I always cognizant that despite our best intentions, we always are influenced by our personal adult biases and adult lens to the research process and the children's accounts. Although we used child-friendly leaflets and participatory techniques to support children's participation in the research and to voice their perspectives, we could have done more. If I were to do this study again, I would work with children right from the initial idea to co-design the study, the research questions, the data collection methods and dissemination methods.

Phil Jones: How did the experience of the research and its findings of your enquiry relate to your understanding of children's rights?

Imelda Coyne: The findings revealed that although professionals say they support children's rights, they find it very difficult to translate children's rights perspective into practice on a cancer inpatient unit. I think that most healthcare professionals seemed aware of the importance of listening to children and involving them but perhaps see the child's involvement as more about ensuring compliance with their decisions. They tended to see decision making as either black and white (yes or no) rather than in shades of grey (on a continuum). Children did not appear to see decision making in this dichotomous way. Viewing participation in decision making in this way neglects to consider all the other ways children's rights could be upheld. For example, the right to be heard, to be listened to, to have views respected, to be given due consideration etc. Nurses seemed more aware of different strategies they could use to involve children in decisions daily, perhaps because they provide the 24-hour care (and that's not my bias). Professionals generally viewed children's rights as a good thing, and professed support, but then tended to use competency and numerous child characteristics to justify inclusion or exclusion from decision making (and in the best interest of the child). Adult's actions in the best interest of a child might fit the agenda of healthcare professionals and the healthcare circumstances more than the child's actual best interest. Acting in a child's best interest should mean enabling his/her views to be heard alongside the views of parents and health professionals.

I think the focus on competency is misleading and is a handy excuse for excluding children – instead the focus should be on recognizing and supporting children's agency and viewing them as competent co-constructers with others in everyday social relations. A child's competence can be illustrated as existing on a continuum from full competence in a certain issue, on a certain occasion, to inability in other issues and situations. The fact that children's participation is relational and situated is an important finding for me. We need to know more about whether children are not involved because of their preferences or because of professionals' actions. The findings did alter my understanding of children's rights in that it made me more aware of the nuances associated with children's participation and the challenges with promoting this in clinical practice. It also revealed that involving children in decision making is complex because of adults' protective behaviours, concerns about children's competence, and the child's position in the three-way relationship (child–parent–health professional). Adults need to view children as individuals with needs that vary according to each situation. The need for protection or/and participation is situational rather than temporally bounded. The situational position recognizes children's right to have a say, without necessarily having full control over decision making.

Phil Jones: Your research connects very much to children's participation rights – do you see the research connecting to other areas of rights?

Imelda Coyne: I agree that most of my research with children about decision making connects to children's participation rights and the rights of the child as outlined in UNCRC Article 12. It also connects to protection, promotion and participation rights. The rights to protection include from harm, neglect and abuse, from fear, pain and loneliness, as well as from too many medical interventions or denial of necessary treatment. Promotion includes the rights to resources such as education and care. The rights to participation include the child's self-determination, dignity, respect, integrity, non-interference, and the right to speak up and make informed personal decisions. When children's preferences for inclusion are not met, or impeded, they feel powerless and depersonalized.

My research also connects to other rights outlined in the UNCRC. These include Article 2 (non-discrimination), Article 3 (best interests), Article 5 (right to direction and guidance), Article 8 (right to preserve identity), Article 13 (right to seek, receive and impart information), Article 19 (protection from abuse) and Article 24 (right to healthcare services).

Phil Jones: You mention education and coaching for adults – do you think children might benefit from such an approach – helping them to be aware of the own agency and participation rights in this context?

Imelda Coyne: I would agree that children would benefit also and good you spotted that omission. Children need to be made aware of their own agency and participation rights. They need education, support and consciousness awareness from an early age within homes and schools. This appears to be happening as children appear more knowledgeable about their rights to be heard and to participate in matters that affect their lives. Within healthcare, we need to develop more creative means of helping children to understand their rights and how they can take part in communication interactions and decisions. Improvements to routine communications between child–parent–healthcare professional coupled with communication interventions may help children with cancer to participate in decision making in several ways. It may help children to better understand their disease and treatment so that with more knowledge they are enabled to offer their views. It may help children to become more familiar with healthcare professionals and to develop relationships with them. Having a good relationship with healthcare professionals may encourage children to participate in communication interactions. Feeling more prepared and comfortable interacting with healthcare professionals may encourage children to seek inclusion in the decision-making process, to ask more questions and express their preferences.

Phil Jones: What work needs to be done, in your opinion, to take research such as yours further?

Imelda Coyne: Including children in healthcare decision making is an area that is relatively under-researched but over time we should see more research occurring. Studies are needed into how new multimedia innovations can support information exchange between children and healthcare professionals. We need to develop multimedia interventions to promote communication, information-exchange and decision making for children. Children are more familiar with new technologies and could learn at their own pace about their disease and treatments via an information technology medium. Some work is being done in this area worldwide. For example, I am supervising a Swedish doctoral student who has developed an application to promote children aged three to five years understanding and participation in healthcare encounters and examinations. Although there is a commitment to hearing children's voices, there has been to date less progress on facilitating choices and involvement in healthcare. Interventions to facilitate choice and participations should be developed with children and should draw upon existing research which reports the needs and preferences of children with cancer about decision making.

What does research reveal about the impact of new thinking and practice in relation to rights and decision making in different spaces within children's lives?

Rights-based challenges to ideas and practices, such as those cited in the previous section, have resulted in new ways of working that seek to involve children and young people in decision making. This section examines some of these by drawing on three different examples of guidelines and perspectives on decision making and rights in order to look at the ways in which more general points emerge from the specific experiences. The examples are chosen to emphasize different aspects and levels of decision making.

Example 1: rights, power and decision making and young children

The Australian National Childcare Accreditation Council (ANCAC) describes a way of working that connects rights, power and decision making and young children. They note that in a busy work environment it is easy to forget that young children are both resourceful and have the ability to contribute to their own development. They comment that adults have 'great power over children' in terms of physical strength and size, control over resources and in terms of adult power to decide over issues such as what will happen and what is fair' (www.ncac.gov.au, 2). They place their approach to work with children in a way that recognizes this but that emphasizes the importance of adults needing to see that children need to exercise their own power, to be seen as capable and to be encouraged by the messages they receive from adults that they can become competent and capable:

> Children need to have the self-confidence and skills to explore, take on new challenges, test their theories about how the world works, make mistakes and discover unexpected consequences. This self-confidence is more likely to occur when children are provided with an opportunity to contribute to their own experiences and learning, sharing in decisions about what they do and how they do it. (www.ncac.gov.au/factsheets/factsheet2, 2)

Key points: ANCAC approach to decision making

- They see decision making as key to child rights, and they position it as a 'life skill' in need of time and practice to develop.
- They see day care setting as a safe environment to practice and rehearse decision making.
- This is accompanied by an assessment of the ways in which practical engagement between adults and children can foster decision making in children.
- They advocate involving young children in setting rules and boundaries in resolving everyday conflicts within the groups and encouraging decision making by support and positive feedback.
- They prescribe space and furnishings that enable children to make choices about what they do and with whom – to play with others, or alone, to be quiet or active.

- They encourage providing easy access to materials that allow children to obtain things they want independently, and that allow choice and decisions to match their level of competence with their play materials (www.ncac.gov.au/factsheets/factsheet2, 3).

Activity 1

How do you see these key points in relation to the relationship, made by ANCAC, between self-confidence, decision making and rights?

Activity 2

What models of relationship between adults and young children are reflected in the approach within the boxed key points?

Example 2: youth involvement in public decision making

On a broader, strategic level the Canadian Association for School Health (CASH), a federation of 12 provincial/territorial coalitions, promote the use the school as a strategic site within the community to reach children and youth as well as adults. It has been involved in developing five sets of criteria assessing the effectiveness of youth involvement in public decision making developed from a variety of sources. The following gives a brief summary of the sets to illustrate this approach to looking at efficacy in developing the right to be involved in decision making.

Key points: CASH – five sets of criteria to assess youth involvement in public decision making

Each of these five sets includes several questions, derived from research, that assess the effectiveness of youth involvement programs and activities.

1. Relationship between youth involvement and sponsor organization goals.
   (a) How do the characteristics of the sponsoring organization relate to youth involvement?
2. The nature of the youth involvement.
   (a) How will youth participate collectively; is it episodic, developmental, structural or are various youth groups being linked together?
   (b) How will each young person be involved individually?
   (c) What are the roles to be assigned to young people?
3. The processes to be used.
   (a) Are basic principles of youth participation being respected?
   (b) Are barriers being addressed?
   (c) Are enabling factors in place?
   (d) Are the developmental needs of young people being met?
   (e) Are the young people accountable?
   (f) Are adults prepared to assist young people to participate?
4. How are these criteria applied to different types of decision making? For example, youth representatives on governing board or regular committees, formal consultations of youth.
5. The evidence of the impact of youth involvement.
   (a) What evidence is there of the impact of the youth participation in the decision making of the organization or on the youth leaders? (McCall, 2009)

Activity 1

Review each of the five points and discuss how decision making and children's rights are present in each

Activity 2

Why do you think each area of the five is important to decision making?

Activity 3

Point 5 talks about the importance of 'impact' and evidence: why do you think this might be important to obtain?

Example 3: rights and decision making – a Norwegian perspective

Research with Norwegian pupils into rights and decision making asked the question: 'How can pupils have a greater say in decision making?'

The research findings presented the following proposals from the pupils:

- That we have a lesson in which the teacher writes up the pupils' views.
- If the adults try harder to understand, it will be easier for the pupils' voice to be heard.
- The teachers can set up individual appointments with pupils in the class so the pupils can give their views without fear of being laughed at.
- The teachers should ask questions more often.

The children also emphasized the teachers' cooperativeness:

- The teacher should lend a hand in improving things, but the pupils must also play their part.
- Everyone should be allowed to express their views and adults should accept that our views differ from theirs and should try to see things from our point of view.
- The teachers and (some) pupils should improve their ability to work together.
- The pupils appreciated the significance of utilising formal bodies, especially the pupils' council, municipal council, the children and young people's municipal council, and believed that they themselves should do a better job in this respect and draw in teachers to make things work better. (Sandbaek and Hafdis Einarsson, 2008, 33)

The research feedback from the children also suggested that various forms of preparation such as free class discussions or girls' and boys' meetings were useful. The answers within the research were commented on by the researchers as according with the impressions gained from other answers in the findings: 'Children and young people were eager for more influence' (Sandbaek and Hafdis Einarsson, 2008, 33).

Reflections on the research

Activity

- Reflect on the proposals from pupils reported in the research.
- How do you see these reflecting a rights perspective?

- Do you consider them realistic and appropriate? How might they be implemented and what barriers might be encountered in trying to implement them?

The Social Care Institute for Excellence (SCIE) have prepared an effective guide to enabling the participation of children and young people in developing social care. Details of how to obtain the guide can be found at the end of this chapter. It emphasizes key relationships that it argues are crucial to effective engagement with the practice of children, decision making, participation and rights.

They first emphasize the creation of an effective system or structure in order to enable young people to become active participants and then to be involved within decisions that affect them and their lives: 'Such structures include staff, resources, decision-making and planning processes' (SCIE, 2006, 7). They highlight decision making as a crucial factor in any attempt to engage with children and young people's participation. They conclude the following:

> Even where organisations are committed to a culture of participation, they do not always change their ways of working as a result. Participation can only create change or improvement when children and young people can influence decision-making processes. (2006, 7)

Key points: SCIE guide to participation

The guide suggests that organizations should consider the following areas of service development in order to establish effective structures that support participation:

- Development of a participation strategy
- Partnership working
- Identification of participation champions
- Provision of adequate resources for participation (2006, 7).

The key to achieving involvement in decision making is seen to lie in the creation of an effective system or structure. They propose that there are four elements which need to be considered to ensure that such a whole-systems approach is established:

- Culture
- Structure
- Practice
- Review

The four areas are depicted as four pieces of a jigsaw puzzle. This image usefully brings together many of the themes considered within this chapter concerning participation and child rights. It sees the development of participation not as a linear process but as an organic process that can occur in different ways within different kinds of settings. The image of a jigsaw is seen to show how each of the four elements can be considered separately, or developed to combine in particular ways.

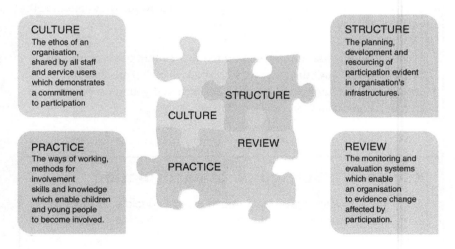

CULTURE
The ethos of an organisation, shared by all staff and service users which demonstrates a commitment to participation

STRUCTURE
The planning, development and resourcing of participation evident in organisation's infrastructures.

PRACTICE
The ways of working, methods for involvement skills and knowledge which enable children and young people to become involved.

REVIEW
The monitoring and evaluation systems which enable an organisation to evidence change affected by participation.

Source: (SCIE, 2006, 13)

They define the elements that combine to enable decision making as follows:

Culture: The ethos of an organization, shared by all staff and service users, which demonstrates a commitment to participation.

Structure: The planning, development and resourcing of participation evident in an organization's infrastructures.

Practice: The ways of working, methods for involvement, skills and knowledge which enable children and young people to become involved.

Review: The monitoring and evaluation systems which enable an organization to evidence change affected by children and young people's participation.

Activity

The guide talks about the interrelationship of the four different elements. Reflect on these in relation to children's experiences of being within an education space such as a school, or a health space such as a hospital. Consider the following:

1. How might looking at an organization's **culture** relate to changing its ways of conducting adult–child relationships (e.g. how teachers or doctors relate to children), the uses of space in terms of rules, the way it is managed or run to involve children more effectively in decision making?
2. How could looking at an orgaization's **structure** be necessary to change its ways of reviewing its work to involve children more effectively in decision making?
3. How might looking at an organization's **practice** relate to changing its ways of working to involve children more effectively in decision making?
4. How could looking at an organization's **ways of reviewing and monitoring its work** relate to changing practice to involve children more effectively in decision making?

Activities

The following activities are designed to help reflect back on some of the key concerns over the chapter as a whole:

Chapter activity 1

Consider Anderson's comment from earlier in the chapter regarding the UNCRC, children's rights and decision making:

> *The Committee has specifically stated that the rights to participation is important in ensuring a child's right to education, and child rights within the education system: 'education must be provided in a way that ... enables the child to express his or her views freely in accordance with article 12 (1) and to participate in school life.' (UN Committee on the Rights of the Child, Gen Comment No 1: The Aims of Education, CRC/GC/2001/1 (2001), para 8 (2008, 18))*

How might the SCIE's four different elements – culture, structure, practice and review – help to critique and help change the practice described in the Research Example titled 'Irish Youth Courts and Decision Making and Participation Rights in Courts' (Pages 166–7), concerning the courtrooms in Limerick, Cork and Waterford?

Chapter activity 2

Review the two examples concerning children's experiences of decision making within the UK education system (pages 162–4). Use the Canadian perspective, following CASH (Canadian Association for School Health) key points, to assess the efficacy of young people's involvement in the processes described.

CASH 3 – the processes to be used:

1. Are basic principles of youth participation being respected?
2. Are barriers being addressed?
3. Are enabling factors in place?
4. Are the developmental needs of youth being met?
5. Are the young people accountable?
6. Are adults prepared to assist young people to participate?

Do you think the Canadian perspective would see the UK ways of involving young people and children in decision making as effective?

Summary

This chapter has

- looked at the meaning of 'decision making',
- examined how ideas of 'decision making' relates to child rights,

- examined ways in which a child rights agenda challenges ideas and practices that exclude children from decision making,
- reviewed research in order to look at ideas and approached that effectively involve children and young people in decision making.

Further reading

Australian National Childcare Accreditation Council. *ANCAC Approach to Decision Making*. Available online at: www.ncac.gov.au/factsheets2.

Linked to 'Putting Children First', a simple description of decision making structures and strategies within a family day care environment.

Charles, A. and Haines, K. (2014) 'Measuring young people's participation in decision making: What young people say', *International Journal of Children's Rights*, 22 (3) 641–659.

Based on research to explore how young people thought their participation in decision making should be measured, this article reports on the development of a participative methodology and the construction of a new participation measurement scale.

McCall, D. (2009) *Selected Case Studies of Youth Involvement in Public Decision Making*. Canadian Association for School Health (CASH).

Documents on health issues and strategies for health promotion of children and youth can be found on an abstract database available on the Internet on a subscription basis. Recent research projects undertaken by the centre include heart health, school readiness, student health indicators, nutrition, youth-led health promotion and AIDS prevention. Details can be found at Public Health Agency of Canada at www. phac-aspc.gc.ca and Schoolfile at www.schoolfile.com.

Social Care Institute for Excellence. (2006) *SCIE Guide 11: Involving Children and Young People in Developing Social Care* https://www.scie.org.uk/publications/guides/guide11/files/guide11.pdf.

A detailed guide to enabling the participation of children and young people in developing social care, it offers organizations a framework for developing the participation of children and young people in the design, delivery and review of their services (www.scie.org.uk/publications/guides/guide11/ index.asp).

Research details

Example of research: children, participation and decision making in child protection

A qualitative study following 21 case studies of families referred to the committees over six months in Israel. Data were collected from interviews with social workers, field observations of the committees and a document review.

Alfandari, R. (2015) 'Evaluation of a national reform in the Israeli child protection practice designed to improve children's participation in decision-making', *Child & Family Social Work*, 1–9.

Example of research: children, participation and decision making during cancer care

A qualitative exploration of participants' experiences of children's decision making. Interviews were conducted with 20 children aged 7–16 years, 22 parents and 40 healthcare professionals.

Coyne, I., Amory, A., Kiernan, G. and Gibson, F. (2014) 'Children's participation in shared decision-making: children, adolescents, parents and healthcare professionals' perspectives and experiences', *European Journal of Oncology Nursing*, 18 (3) 273–280.

Example of research: children's views on participation

The report examines the extent to which children living in England feel they have a voice and influence in matters affecting them at school, at home and in the area where they live. This report is based 12 focus group interviews with 44 boys and 42 girls from a variety of backgrounds aged between 3 and 20 years of age.

Davey, C., Burke, T. and Shaw, C. (2010) *Children's participation in decision-making: A Children's Views Report*. London: Office of the Children's Commissioner and Participation Works.

Example of research: 'how children become invisible in child protection work'

An analysis of case study material on research which observed day-to-day encounters between social workers, children and families.

Ferguson, H. (2016) 'How children become invisible in child protection work: Findings from research into day-to-day social work practice', *British Journal of Social Work*, 46 (1) 153–168.

Example of research: literature review on child participation within child protection and welfare

A literature review examining barriers and factors facilitating child participation within the child protection and child welfare services from both children's and social workers' perspectives.

van Bijleveld, G.G., Dedding, C.W.M. and Bunders-Aelen, J.F.G. (2014) 'Children's and young people's participation within child welfare and child protection services: A state-of-the-art review', *Child & Family Social Work*, 20, 129–138. doi:10.1111/cfs.12082.

Example of research: survey on child rights

Survey connected to Norway's report to the UN on their compliance with the UNCRC in spring 2008. The Ministry of Children and Equality wished to communicate children and young people's views on growing up in Norway, seen in relation to some articles of the UN Convention.

Sandbaek, M. and Hafdis Einarsson, J. (2008) 'Children and young people report to the UN on their rights', *NOVA Report*, 2b/08. Available online at: www.reassess.no/index.

6

A Rights Perspective on Family Life

Introduction and key questions

This chapter is concerned with the place of children's rights in relation to families. It is generally believed that this is the best place for children to be brought up and government policies in different countries work on the basis that families, in particular parents, will act in children's best interests. While there is an increasing awareness and emphasis in legislation of human rights, and within this of children's rights, there is unease about the discourse of rights, particularly in relation to children and their position in families. Within the family, the impact of a rights discourse is only beginning to be felt, and is associated with fears about decreasing the authority of parents. The role of the state in ensuring that children's rights are addressed is also of concern, and it is often positioned by opponents as 'the nanny state' interfering with family life. At the heart of this discussion is the question of the relationships that exist between child, family and the state as children need to be considered in different ways with each involving potential conflicts:

- Children as individuals
- Children as part of families
- Children as part of societies, communities and cultures

The family is in the middle of the relationships and is meant to be supporting the child as an individual while ensuring that they develop positive relationships as part of families, communities, societies and cultures. However, each family will have a set of beliefs and values that influence their expectations of the child and their relationships. For example a family that has a strong religious affiliation may expect their children to follow the same belief system and act accordingly. These may not be in keeping with either the principles of the UNCRC or with the expectations of state policies. Lee (2005) cited in Quennerstedt and Quennerstedt (2014) identifies that, for some, the concept of rights for children collides with traditional views of the roles of parents. This may then lead to concern that 'rights for children may threaten and dissolve close relationships between parents and children' (2014, 118). This chapter will explore this concern. It argues that within the family there are inevitable conflicts between children's growing autonomy and parental wishes and these are exacerbated by the expectations that are placed on children themselves and their parents and carers in today's society.

Up to this point the term 'family' has been used without any further explanation, but this concept is also problematic and the value placed upon some kinds of families rather than others has been debated. The traditional view of the family of two heterosexual parents with a working father and a mother caring for the children is no longer the norm. Children may be part of very different family structures:

- Cohabiting parents
- 'Reformed' families
- Adoptive families

- Single parent families
- Families with same sex parents
- Both or no parents working
- Extended families
- Being in the care of the state – foster or institutional care

Within this chapter the term 'family' will be used to cover any household that includes a child and the term 'carer/s' (rather than 'parent/s') will be used to identify the adult/s who have legal responsibility for the care and welfare of the child in order to cover the range of families identified above. The concern here is not to debate the relative merits of different types of family, but to consider

- the place of children's rights within the family,
- the complex relationships between the child, their family and the state within the context of multiple family structures in many different contexts.

The chapter considers the issues that arise when considering the following questions:

- How does the external context influence children's experience in families?
- What rights issues arise within families?
- What is the role of the state in relation to children, their carers and their rights?
- How can we understand the relationship between children, families and rights?

How does the external context influence children's experience in families?

The different kinds of family introduced in the previous section are often set up as being deficient in some way (compared with the 'norm' of two heterosexual, married parents), for example single parent or same sex families might be judged by right wing media as 'not being able to provide appropriate role models'. However, this kind of specific denigration ignores the fact that all families face challenges and external influences that can improve or diminish a family's capacity for supporting children. The issue is not 'which type of family is the best for children?' but 'how might children in all types of family be affected by external influences?'

It is clear in Articles 3, 5, 9, 10, 18 and 27 of the 1989 UNCRC and Articles 8, 12 and 14 of the UN Convention of Human Rights that the primary responsibility for children's care and guidance should be with the family, whatever form it takes. The four main areas of rights in the UNCRC – survival, development, protection and participation – form the basis of what is expected, and the UNCRC emphasizes the holistic nature of the rights which shouldn't be considered in a fragmented way. However, the ability of families to ensure children's rights are upheld in these ways is influenced by many factors outside the control of the family. This section will consider how

- different expectations of 'the family'
- the social, cultural and political context
- and the economic context

might influence the child's experience within the family and the family's ability to fulfill the child's rights to provision, protection and participation.

The influence of different expectations of the family

Until a child becomes socially and economically independent s/he will be part of a family with carers who are responsible for them. While the law does not define in detail what the responsibility of those carers is, the UK government identifies the following list of key roles in its 'Direct Gov' information pages:

- providing a home for the child,
- protecting and maintaining the child,
- disciplining the child,
- choosing and providing for the child's education,

Table 6.1 UK government's position on rights and parental roles

Type of right	Role of parent
Provision – survival	• providing a home for the child
	• protecting and maintaining the child
	• agreeing to the child's medical treatment
Provision – development	• having contact with and living with the child
	• disciplining the child
	• choosing and providing for the child's education
	• agreeing to the child's medical treatment
Protection	• protecting and maintaining the child
	• being responsible for the child's property
	• disciplining the child
Participation	There is no indication that parents have any duty to support children's participation

- agreeing to the child's medical treatment,
- naming the child and agreeing to any change of the child's name,
- looking after the child's property (Gov.uk, 2016).

The list of responsibilities can be linked with the key areas of children's rights to draw out where the government's priorities might lie.

This list of responsibilities can illustrate some of the differences and tensions regarding expectations of the family.

First, it is interesting that this list doesn't mention children's participation and that there is an instance where child participation is actually denied as it gives those with parental responsibility the authority to choose the child's education. The following piece of research shows that this area of child participation was also a difficulty for those developing the UNCRC.

Example of research: rights, families and education

Quennerstedt (2009) analysed the UN Working Group's reports that show how the articles of the 1989 Convention were formed. She identifies the challenge that emerged during this process in relation to the rights of parents and their children. This involves the balancing of the civil and political rights of the child and the civil rights of the parents. In Article 28, the right to education, she found that the contradictions that had been evident in the drafting process disappeared as Article 28 expresses only the child's social right to education: their civil and political rights to involvement in decisions about their own education, and education in general, aren't included, possibly because they were too difficult to deal with.

Reflection on research

The list of parental responsibilities (listed on page 195) includes the responsibility of choosing and providing for the child's education. This research shows that the difficult contradictions of parental rights/duties and children's participation rights has been fudged. Quennerstedt and Quennerstect (2014) comment on this finding by asking '...who holds the right to education – the child, the parent or the state?' (116).

All three of these parties have an interest in children being educated. Children have an interest in being able to develop their talents and learn new things in order to enhance their future as well as for their immediate satisfaction. The parent or carer has an interest in the child's development towards an autonomous adult and the direction that this might take. The state has an interest in the child becoming a productive and contributing member of their community and wider society through the education that is provided. However, it may be that these interests don't coincide: for example, the child may wish to develop their artistic talents while a carer may consider that isn't a suitable preparation for employment and the curriculum laid down by the state may emphasize skills needed for the workforce of the future and pay little attention to art. In most states that are signatories to the UNCRC, education is compulsory so children have to be educated even though the education provided may not be what they would choose for themselves.

Why do you think the early acknowledgement of potential conflict of rights with regard to education was ignored in the final version of the convention?

The UK government clearly identifies choosing a child's education as the responsibility of the carer. How does this affect the child's rights to participation?

Look back at the research by Anderson (2008) in Chapter 5 (pages 163–5)

How are the expectations of carers and children in relation to education in Anderson's research different to the expectations of the UK government?

Do you think it is possible to balance out the interests of the child, parent and state in relation to education? How might this be done? How would this affect the expectations of the family and in turn, the rights of the child?

Another area within the list of government expectations that might be problematic is in the area of discipline. While it isn't explicitly included in the list of responsibilities, there is also an implicit expectation that it is the responsibility of carers to prepare children for their place in society, commonly referred to as 'socialization'. It is evident from the list that the government considers 'disciplining the child' as important in socialization. There is the possibility of that discipline impinging on children's rights to be protected when physical punishment is used when there are differences in what is considered to be appropriate discipline. For example, a slight tap to make sure a hand is removed from potential danger such as electricity or fire may be seen as acceptable but stronger physical punishment such as smacking may be seen as abuse. However, reaching a common understanding of what constitutes acceptable discipline and what constitutes abuse is difficult.

Example of research: discipline and abuse

Taylor et al. (2015) researched the experiences of ten deaf and disabled children and adults who had experienced abuse as a child. The interviews tried to draw out experiences of reporting abuse and the barriers to effective communication and action. Among the findings were instances of the confusion about what is 'normal' and 'abusive' behaviour. The participants in the research were allocated codes to identify which group they were in so the identification of respondents belwo refers to their first name and code.

> A recurring theme in participants' accounts was the poor levels of awareness of abuse or understanding of what constitutes abuse amongst the participants themselves, their family members, the wider community and even the professionals with whom they came into contact. (Taylor et al., 2015, 21)

> I think ... I'd grown up around it for like ages it was like all I know and I just thought it was normal. (Sara 1FA)
> I didn't know it was illegal. There was no information, there was no books when I was kid, or posters, nothing. There was no information, didn't have social workers. (Wendy 8FA)

> When you're immersed in an abusive environment as a child, you don't realise that it's abuse, I didn't know it was abuse, I just knew I was unhappy, I knew I didn't like how I was being treated, but I didn't realise it was abuse, I didn't know it was wrong, or that it shouldn't have been happening to me.

The response from adults shows a similar confusion or inability to identify abuse when children attempted disclosure.

> I said to my teacher if it was ok if your parents hurt you? ... and they said it was ok... that they had a right to discipline you when you were bad. (Wendy 8FA)

Reflection on the research

These issues are common to all families and the experiences of these children and adults can help us to appreciate the difficulties in identifying what kinds of behaviour are acknowledged as being abusive and the barriers to effective action.

Wendy wasn't sure whether what she was experiencing was normal. She couldn't approach anyone in the family and so she went to her teacher. Why do you think the teacher responded as she did?

How has the expectation that carers are responsible for discipline affected the experience of these children?

In contrast, the CRC's response to the United Kingdom's 2015 report on children's rights in the United Kingdom asked the government to explain how it intends to fulfill 'its obligations to remove all legal defences for corporal punishment of children in the home and all other settings' (UNCRC, 2015, 2) in line with the provisions of Articles 19 and 37.

Chapter 1 pointed to research by Davey (2008) that identified that young children were keen that this should take place and carers should be offered support to find alternatives to the use of physical force.

How might this expectation of the family influence children's experience?

The influence of the social, cultural and political context on the family

The context of family life has been, and is still, changing across the world. One of the main changes concerns the nature of the family. The list of different family types at the beginning of the chapter indicates this change and during the period of childhood an individual child may experience more than one family form and the change this involves affects children's experiences. In addition there are many other social, cultural and political factors that affect children and their families. A number of examples of these will be considered here:

- The consumer society
- Over- and under-employment
- The commodification of children as social and emotional assets
- The perception of danger and blame
- Political conflict and war

The first three of these are interrelated and are concerned with changing values that are reflected in the social, cultural and political context. Prout (2000) identifies the 'emergence of consumption (particularly leisure) as a source of identity' (2000, 307) as a significant change that has affected family life. Individuals and families are increasingly under pressure to purchase, leading to families needing to have more than one income in order to 'keep up' with the pressure to consume and what Jensen (2003) terms 'over-employment' where carers work long hours and have little time to spend with their children.

On the other hand, families with unemployed carers suffer not only from lack of income but also from lack of status that goes along with having the right kind of possessions. Media representations and advertising can reinforce the expectations that 'good families' should provide children with these material goods. In contrast, The Children's Society (2015) found that most children said that being loved and supported, having freedom and having stability and security were important things about being in a family.

Activity

1. Consider the effects of these influences on

   a child in a family that has a different set of values and doesn't value material possessions in the same way
   a child in a family where wearing fashionable clothes is not valued
   If these families were part of a wider community that shared their values how might it make a difference?

2. The findings of The Children's Society suggest children value things that would give them more emotional support. How might these elements of family life be affected by the external pressures identified at the beginning of this section? Think about children's rights to provision, protection and participation.

Wade and Smart (2003) also identify the 'commodification of children' as part of this emphasis on materialism. As families have fewer children, particularly in the Minority World, the importance of the child in the family has grown in being a resource that gives pleasure to parents socially and emotionally. This makes the process of separation or divorce (as part of the changing nature of families) very difficult as both parents are likely to want to maintain 'possession' of the child. It may also mean that parents live vicariously through their children, wanting them to live a life they were unable to themselves (Brummelman et al., 2013).

Activity

Look back at the discussion of the child in Chapter 2. What image of the child is being reflected in 'the commodification of children'? How might this affect the child's rights?

A culture of 'blame' encourages carers to respond in particular ways to every possible danger for children. These dangers are not only physical but also emotional, social and sexual, coming in the form of unsupervised environments, strangers, media (particularly the Internet) and association with peers. An example of this can be seen in the results of a Playday (2013) opinion poll which included 1,000 parents of children between 5 and 16 years old in the United Kingdom. The findings highlight how children's freedom to play outside is substantially reduced compared to that experienced by previous generations with parents' fears of traffic and strangers put forward as reasons for not letting children play unsupervised. They also highlighted the fear of being judged by their neighbours if they allowed their children to play out without supervision.

Activity

There are two elements of fear cited by parents in this research: (1) the physical fear of the danger of traffic and strangers and (2) the emotional fear of being judged by others.

How might the different types of fear be dealt with by carers?

How might both these fears affect children's rights within the family? Think about the areas of provision, protection and participation.

These, largely social and cultural, influences have an effect on families' abilities to fulfill children's rights. The final influence, political unrest and war, is one that is likely to have a significant impact on all aspects of a child's experience within the family and on their rights. The following two examples highlight the extent of this impact. Both concern Syrian refugees. The first example considers refugees who are living in the Lebanon. The 2016 Vulnerability Assessment of Syrian Refugees gives an indication of the conditions for Syrian refugees in Lebanon:

Households are increasingly adopting coping strategies that deplete assets, negatively affect the households' livelihoods, and very often are irreversible, such as selling household goods, productive assets, or housing or land held in Syria. Households are increasingly incurring debt in order to buy food, cover health expenses and pay for rent... Some households were also resorting to involving children in income-generating activities ... In some districts, the share of working adolescents reached roughly one third. (UNHCR, 2016, 1)

We are eleven people living in one tent. The water container is not large enough. No one is taking care of us. (34)

The following extract shows how the impact of the conflict in Syria has affected two children while living in Syria.

Save the Children (2012) 'Untold Atrocities' tells the stories of Ala'a and Nur

Ala'a is ten and now lives in a camp outside Syria.

When the shells started to fall I ran. I ran so fast. I ran and I cried at the same time.

When we were being bombed, we had nothing. No food, no water, no toys – nothing. There was no way to buy food – the markets and shops were bombed out.

After that we came back home. To make our food last we just ate once a day.

My father went without food for days because there wasn't enough. I remember watching him tie his stomach with rope so he wouldn't feel so hungry.

One day men with guns broke into our house. They pulled out our food, threw it on the floor and stamped on it, so it would be too dirty to eat. Then we had nothing at all. Soon after that we came here. (Save the Children, 2012, 18)

Nur is 9 and also lives in a camp. Here he describes how he has been affected by the conflict.

I do not play. Why? Because I am not young any more. I go to the bathroom, take a shower and then sleep. That is all.

In Syria I was happy, I used to play football and other games. Then the violence started and they started to make us suffer. There was nothing that they did not use to hurt us with.

Earlier they used tanks, and then they took it further and started using air strikes, bombings, missiles and every weapon you could think of. They killed us. Today there is nothing left in my home village, and most of the people have left.

I was terrified. Us along with my cousins, neighbours, aunts and people we know used to go to the shelter to hide. I used to like hiding. Hiding is better than dying.

The camp is better than being in Syria – there they are shooting at us while here there is neither shooting nor shelling. I want it to stop so we can go back, so I can play again with my friends. (Save the Children, 2012, 37)

Activity

Ala'a and Nur describe the immediate effects of the war while they were living in Syria.

What kinds of rights have been affected by the war?

Do you think it was possible for the families of these two children to protect them from any of these effects?

Once in the camps or in a safe country, the immediate effects of the war are taken away but other effects of the political impact of conflict, described by the UNHCR, are still having a major impact on the lives of children and their families. How will the conditions described in the first example impact on the lives of children? Think about all areas of rights: provision, protection and participation.

The effects of the economic context on the family

Many families across the world live in either absolute or relative poverty. Absolute poverty is when the family cannot provide for basic needs such as food, water and shelter, and we have seen how this occurs in areas of conflict. Relative poverty is recognized differently in different countries but is usually associated with the family having an income that is significantly lower than the average income for the country and is therefore unable to take part in many of the social and cultural activities that are the norm in that particular country.

Some of the effects of absolute poverty due to political conflict and war have been considered in the previous section. Here we will consider a different example of absolute poverty and its effects and research on the effects of relative poverty.

Research example: poverty and child labour

Save the Children (2007) reported on the extent of child labour across the world and identified how family poverty can lead to eight particular forms of child slavery:

- child trafficking,
- commercial sexual exploitation,
- bonded child labour,
- forced work in mines,
- forced agricultural labour,
- child soldiers/combatants,
- forced child marriage,
- domestic slavery.

One of the areas they report on is bonded child labour where the report describes how their parents take out a loan to pay for their home, medicine or maybe just food. They are then obliged to work for the money-lender in lieu of the money. The whole family, including children, must work until they have effectively paid back the money. This can take years for even the smallest amount. These bonded workers have no power to negotiate the repayment rate or the interest added to the original sum. Unable to earn money of their own, parents are often forced to take out further loans, increasing the amount they owe.

They found that

- In Nepal, there are approximately 200,000 bonded labourers, many of them children.
- In Pakistan's Sind province, almost seven million bonded labourers, including children, work for their landlords without pay.
- Around 250,000 children live and work in Pakistani brick kilns in complete social isolation.

Reflection on the research

Activity 1

In all these situations children are being exploited: they are not working out of choice and they are not working in conditions where they are protected. The reason that they can be exploited in these ways is because their work may be the only means of keeping the family alive.

The most evident right that is being violated here is Article 32, the right to work safely and be paid fairly. However there are many other rights that will be affected. Go through the UNCRC and find others that will be affected when the child is in bonded labour.

Why might families in this situation be unable to support the rights of their children?

Activity 2

In concluding their report, Save the Children asks the public to lobby their MPs to make the elimination of child slavery a priority, support fair trade initiatives that protect the rights of child labourers.

How do you think these things might make a difference to the lives of these children?

What would be needed to enable the families to protect and provide for their children?

The second example investigates the effects on children of relative poverty as opposed to the absolute poverty described in the previous example.

Example of research: the effects of poverty

In 2013 The Children's Society reviewed the available literature and found that children identified the following areas of concern about their experience of poverty:

- Economic and material deprivation that meant going without essentials and anxiety about not having enough money.
- Social deprivation as limited resources resulted in restricted access to social activities.
- School issues when there was an inability to pay for resources.
- Poor quality housing, homelessness and neighbourhoods that affected education and physical and mental health.
- Family pressures from tensions due to financial pressures and children taking on responsibilities in the home.
- Stigma and bullying due to visible signs of poverty.

Other effects, not identified by children but through data gathering were as follows:

- Social isolation and low self esteem.
- Lower health, education and employment outcomes in the long term.

The research went on to look at the way some groups are at higher risk of poverty than others and found the following groups were more likely to suffer from poverty:

- Children living in households affected by disability (40 per cent of disabled children).
- Lone parent families (43 per cent compared with 22 per cent in two-parent households).
- Large families of three or more children (36 per cent compared with 24 per cent in two children families).
- Black and minority ethnic groups (44 per cent Black and Black British, 55 per cent Pakistani and Bangladeshi, 25 per cent White households).
- Workless households (67 per cent) although 60 per cent of children in low income families have someone in work but it is low paid.
- Asylum-seeking families who are prohibited from working and only allowed a lower rate of benefit support than are UK citizens.

Reflection on the research

Activity 1

While some of these are a direct result of a lack of adequate resources, some are more indirect effects: family pressures, stigma and bullying.

How do you think that issues considered in the earlier section on social influences, such as pressures to wear the 'right' sort of clothes, own the 'right' sort of technology and engage in the 'right' sort of activities, might contribute to the effects of relative poverty described in this research?

Activity 2

The long-term effects on health, education and employment mean that as these children grow into adults and have their own children, there will be continued effects. How might the next generation of families be affected?

Look at the groups that are at higher risk of living in poverty. Why do you think this is the case?

Key points: influence of the external context on families, children and rights issues

While the circumstances of families in different countries are different, the issues around social, cultural, political and economic influences will affect the experiences of children and families' ability to ensure children's rights are upheld.

Both absolute poverty and relative poverty affect the experiences of children in different families. These short- and long-term effects might be experienced differently by different family types.

What rights issues arise within families?

In this section we will consider the rights issues that arise within the family due to the possible tensions between

- the rights and responsibilities of carers and children's rights,
- protection rights and participation rights,
- who decides what is in the 'best interests' of the child.

We will consider ways of dealing with possible tensions and return to some of the difficulties associated with a rights discourse.

In Chapter 2 we saw that there is tension between liberty rights and welfare rights. In the early days of thinking about children's rights, the emphasis was clearly on welfare rights and, as views of children's capabilities changed, their liberty rights, in particular their right to participate in decisions that concern them, were included but this is still a contentious area. Within the family the assumption is that parents will automatically put children's 'best interests' first but their powerful position in relation to their children and the demands that are made of them externally, as discussed in the previous section, make this a difficult thing to do. For example, carers are often pressed for time when carrying out many daily routines and, although it might be in a child's best interests to make decisions for themselves in relation to when to play, meet friends and so on, the carer's need to get to work, do the shopping and the like may take precedence over the child's wishes. More seriously, when there is a family breakdown, the best interests of the child may be compromised by the needs and wishes of the parents in their struggle to make the best life for themselves.

Although putting forward a case against children's agency rights, Brighouse (2002) points out that the Human Rights Convention must be understood in the context of the complexities of the responsibilities.

> You may indeed have superior power but this fact does not authorise you to use your power to your own advantage. In some cases you must attempt to relinquish this power. But in others, when it cannot be relinquished, you must understand that the person in your power is a rights-bearer, one whose interests count for as much as yours. When you use your power with respect to that person you are morally bound to attend first to their, and only after to your own, interests. (Brighouse, 2002, 36)

When put against the concept of 'the child's best interests' this makes it clear that carers need to be aware of the power relationship that they have with the child and acknowledge that their personal interests may be in conflict with the child's. Knowing the child's thoughts on the matter can only be beneficial in trying to make the best decision.

The main implication of these ideas is that in order for carers to act in the best interests of the child, they need to be aware of and respect the views of the child. This doesn't mean that the child will always do exactly what he or she wants but he or she will participate in discussions about what actions might be best. Interestingly, Thomas's (2002) research into children's participation in decision making found that 'what they wanted was above all the opportunity to take part in dialogue with adults, not for either themselves or the adults to determine the outcome' (2000, 152). Perhaps this finding might alleviate concerns from carers about losing authority unless they consider that 'authority' means acting in their own interests rather than the child's.

One area that is potentially very difficult for families is respecting children's autonomy in matters of religion. The UNCRC identifies the child's right to their own religion, and this is generally interpreted as being that of their parents. Indeed the European Convention on Human Rights identifies the rights of parents to bring up their child in accordance with their religious beliefs. However, it is interesting that 'determining the religion of the child' has now been deleted from the United Kingdom's list of responsibilities of parents (see page 195). The difficulty for parents and carers is in bringing up their child in accordance with their religion while allowing the child to develop their own views at some stage.

The following two pieces of research highlight the tensions:

- between protection rights and participation rights
- between parental rights and duties and children's rights

In the previous section we looked at the difficulties that carers may have in protecting children and how actions to protect may affect other rights. In the first research example this tension is seen in the ways carers and children deal with potential threats online.

Example of research: parents and online problematic situations for children

Smahel and Wright (2014) investigated the online problematic situations of 9–16-year-old children from nine European countries. A total of 114 interviews and 56 focus groups were used to collect data. As part of the research they investigated sources of mediation for children and this brought out issues to do with children's rights to privacy and access to information and the role of carers. One of the findings was that parents checking up on what children do online can be problematic. While younger children might accept this more, older children might find it a point of tension with parents/carers.

Girl 1: First rule of Facebook, I got told by everyone, was, never add your parents as friends because they'll see everything you're up to!
Interviewer: Are there things you don't want them to see?
    Girl 1: No, it's just like, it's a bit more private. It's you and your friends.
    Girl 2: Yes, because the way you act around your friends isn't always how you act around your parents, even if it's not anything that would be...
    Interviewer: Dodgy.
    Girl 2: Yes, dodgy or anything like that.

This often led to older children deliberately concealing what they were doing. The researchers described that 'in some households there appeared to be a guerrilla war going on where parents were secretly trying to find out what their children were doing, while children tried to prevent this' (2014,135).

Other reasons for not talking to parents about problematic situations that they encountered online were

- parents not believing explanations,
- fear of punishment,
- lack of trust,
- embarrassment.

Other family members and friends are often used by these young people as sources of information and support rather than parents/carers.

Reflection on the research

This part of the research indicates the potential conflict between children's rights and parents' duties to protect their children with the potential for mistrust from both sides.

What kind of issues relating to participation rights does this research cover?

What rights or duties of parents might be involved?

How do you think parents/carers and children might be able to deal with this potential conflict?

We have seen that the responsibilities of carers are complex and affected by many external factors. Chapter 1 cited Ruck and Storn who point to 'the influence on cultural values on young people's conceptions of rights and the tensions that arise between individuals' rights and prerogatives and cultural traditions, norms and practices' (2008, 691). For example, Female Genital Mutilation (FGM) is practiced in many African countries as well as in the Middle East and Asia by Muslims, Christians and traditional African religions usually on girls under the age of 18. It is also practiced by migrant communities in countries where it is seen as an unacceptable or illegal practice and in the United Kingdom it is considered to be a form of child abuse. However, the conflict between maintaining cultural practices and protecting young girls from this practice is evident in many families. An intercollegiate report from across medical associations in 2013 explained this.

> In the UK reasons for practising FGM may have adapted to their context, for instance, the use of FGM to curb sexuality and to preserve girls' cultural identity, even as prevention of FGM in the country of origin gains ground. Parents may also come under pressure from family and community members in the UK or abroad to have FGM performed on their girls, and need support to avert this. (RCM et al., 2013, 8)

The reasons for carrying out FGM, for example 'preservation of cultural identity', may even be used as an argument that it is in 'the best interests' of these girls and young women. This is, of course, without seeking the views of those girls and young women or addressing why 'cultural identity' would be more important in terms of 'best interests' than physical and mental health.

Engle (2006) points to the discrimination that takes place in some families because of gender, disability, birth order and physical attractiveness, and it would also be possible to add sexuality and religious belief to this list. In these cases parental attitudes to particular children may be such that the love, emotional security and affective support are lacking or removed because of the discrimination. Even when there isn't actual discrimination, some families have difficulty when there is a difference between children and their carers in their choice of lifestyle. The expectation of carers that children will conform to the values and cultural practices of the family is particularly difficult when there are pressures from outside the family to engage with a different lifestyle. The first piece of research investigated how young people experienced this 'double life'.

Example of research: leading a double life within and outside the family

Ahmad et al. (2008) worked with 36 young people between the ages of 11 and 21 to identify their experience of living with two different cultures. They found that while all the young people identified with the concept of a 'double life', 30 per cent felt they were trapped between the culture of their family and modern Western society. Some examples of the comments made are as follows:

*'My parents tell me to pray every day five times a day but I don't
want to.'*

*'Quite possibly with regards to marriage/marriage partners,
clothes, education and work opportunities. Parents may want their
children to act according to their culture and religion, while some
South Asian Young people may not feel as much obliged to follow
their culture, religion and family compared to their parents and may
feel more inclined to the Western society.'*

Equally they felt under pressure to conform to the accepted behaviour of the Western culture that they met outside the home, for
example,

*'Yes, it can, a person could be pressured by friends, and it can be
hard to say no as don't want to be left out.'*

*'Yes, because mates might want you to do something that you
don't want to do.'*

*'Yes, because it is difficult to say no to friends because then they
start back biting so you follow because you don't want that, you
want to be like everybody else.'*

*'Yes, they could be forced into smoking, boyfriends when you
don't want to.'*

*'Yes, because friends might force you to do something against
your religion and culture.'*

Unfortunately many of the young people felt unable to talk to their
family about the difficulties because of the following:

- Feeling of being judged
- Fear of parents
- Family might tell parents
- Fear of getting hit by parents
- Feeling they don't connect
- Generation gap
- Blackmailing by family, brothers and sisters
- Culture and religion – you have to have two different personali-
  ties to be able to cope with life today

As a result, the researchers identified a need for professional support
for young people in this situation to help them to explore these conflicts and how to deal with them.

Reflection on the research

The results of this research emphasize the difficulties that young South Asians face. This was a small-scale study and was carried out by researchers who were young South Asians themselves. How do you think this might have affected the research?

The researchers identified the need for professional support outside the family for the 30 per cent who felt trapped between the two cultures. How might the family be effectively supporting those young people who identified with the concept of 'a double life' but didn't feel trapped in the same way.

This research concentrated on young people from a culture that might be seen as very different from a Western culture. However, the same kinds of difficulties might be experienced by children and young people where there are differences in beliefs and values. Reynaert et al. (2009) consider that there is a danger that these difficulties may be viewed as conflicts between parental rights and children's rights. They review literature that identifies the difficulties that arise within a simplistic rights discourse when that discourse

- relies on a focus on individualism rather than relationships,
- needs legislation to resolve conflicts,
- generates a 'winner/loser mentality' (2009, 526) rather than debate and the desire to find a common solution.

Their concern is that the tensions that may arise within families because of different beliefs, and values can be exacerbated if views become polarized within a rights discourse that emphasizes individuality and conflict. An alternative discourse that seeks to engage all participants in debate and problem solving may be more productive as long as the 'powerful' participants are willing to acknowledge and relinquish their power as Brighouse (2002) suggests. This is acknowledged in the 'Fact Sheet on Participation' produced by UNICEF which states,

> The child's evolving capacity represents just one side of the equation: the other involves adults' evolving capacity and willingness to listen to and learn from their children, to understand and consider the child's point of view, to be willing to re-examine their own opinions and attitudes and to envisage solutions that address children's views. For adults, as well as for children,

participation is a challenging learning process and cannot be reduced to a simple formality. (2014, 2)

Key points: rights issues within families

- Carers have a very difficult task in enabling children to develop their own identity and beliefs while giving them the security of belonging within a family and community with its own culture and beliefs.
- Carers are faced with difficult decisions in attempting to protect children without restricting other rights including participation.
- While tensions exist in these areas it is possible that acknowledging the tension and using it as a source of debate and decision making involving all those involved may be a way forward.

What is the role of the state in relation to carers, children and their rights?

The role of the state in family matters was at the heart of the opposition to ratification of the UNCRC in the United States. The reasons for opposing the convention are that 'the best interests of the child' and 'the evolving capacities of children' will lead to the state, through the courts of law, deciding what these mean rather than parents (Parental Rights, 2017). This objection sees state intervention as interference in family life and has parallels with arguments about liberty rights that were discussed in Chapter 2. Archard (2015) explores this concern and identifies the 'liberal standard' that considers parents and carers know what is best for their children and have a right to bring up their children as they think fit. In this case the state should not interfere unless the child is in danger. He goes on to identify three elements:

- Commitment to the importance of 'the best interests of the child'.
- Parent and carers have the right to autonomy (freedom to bring up their children as they see fit) and privacy (no one can intrude in the family without consent).

- Clear conditions that help identify when it is appropriate for the state to intervene.

Within UK culture the last of these elements is usually in relation to children suffering abuse or neglect. When there is sufficient evidence that a child is 'at risk of significant harm' the state can interfere with the parents' or carers' rights to privacy and autonomy. However, the assumption explicit in The Children Act 1989 (Department for Health, 1989) and confirmed within the Children Act 2004 and The Children and Families Act 2014 is that the best place for a child to be is with their family.

This section will consider issues and tensions related to the role of the state in relation to

- the family and children's welfare rights,
- the family and children's rights to protection.

The state's role in supporting families' provision for children

In contrast to the liberal standard there is an expectation in the UNCRC that the state has a more positive role in supporting parents and carers in making adequate provision for their children. Fiscal policy, education services, welfare benefits and health and social services are all forms of state intervention but are generally seen as being there to support parents and carers in upholding children's provision rights. However, state provision is often influenced by political considerations that are as concerned with appearing to be tough on those who don't fit 'the norm' and economic prudence as with supporting children's rights to adequate support. This can lead to policies that appear to be supporting the child within the family setting but in reality have more negative outcomes; for example The Joint Parliamentary Committee on Human rights (2014) identified the disproportionate effects on children of austerity measures (see pages 44–5).

Burchardt (2008) identified the importance of time poverty as well as income poverty. She points out that while some parents work long hours in order to provide a good standard of living for their family, this may result in 'time poverty' where they don't have time to spend with their children. For many of these families there would be an option of reducing working time in order to have more time to spend with their children but that would be at a financial cost and would leave many families without enough income. Article 27 of the UNCRC identifies the right of the child to a standard of living that is sufficient to support their development with the state giving support where necessary. The following piece of research illustrates the complexity of how these tensions around working hours can affect families and how government policies can impact on families' ability to support children.

Example of research: time poverty and income poverty

Judge (2015), researching on behalf of the Child Poverty Action Group, asked 'How many hours should parents work (in order not to be poor)?' The research involved four phases:

1. A review of the evidence to identify current attitudes to parental employment.
2. A poll of a cross-section of the population to identify opinions about parental working hours.
3. Using the outcomes of the first two stages, these ideas, along with ideas about whether there should be different expectations for lower income parents, were explored with focus groups,
4. The views of employers on these results were investigated,

1. The review of evidence revealed that decisions about working hours are based on the values and individual circumstances of families. However, the economic situation of the family may limit the choices that can be made so low income families may feel increasing pressure to work longer hours.

The messages that families receive from the tax and benefits systems are contradictory. Lower income families receiving benefits are under pressure to work longer hours while the tax system for higher income, two-parent families encourages one parent to stay at home to care for children.

In addition, messages from think-tanks and government strategies reinforce the message that low income families can and should 'work their way out of poverty' and child care provision should be used to enable parents to go out to work earlier.

2. The poll of over 4,000 respondents asked what a reasonable expectation for any parent with respect to employment should be.

The results showed a very wide range of responses about what was a reasonable number of hours, when these should be, and commuting times with no real patterns emerging although there were higher expectations of lone parents for the number of hours worked and slightly lower expectations for commuting times.

3. The research then elicited the views of parents in two focus groups where they explored whether the different sets of rules for better off and lower income parents could really be regarded as 'fair'. The first focus group (Group 1) consisted of parents with lower incomes and the second group (Group 2) consisted of parent with higher incomes.

Both groups echoed the findings of the review of evidence that working hours were a matter of individual choice based on circumstances and values but also pointed to the lack of choice for those on lower incomes.

> It's about your own personal conflict and your value system, your belief system which is individual so you can't answer what is reasonable. (Couple parent, Group 2, 21)
> I don't think you can make choices based on what you'd like to do – a lot of it is dictated by money. There is no recognition that having children, that's hard work. It's more like, you have children – why should we as a society support you? Why should the workplace support you? (Couple parent, Group 1, 19)

In both focus groups it was clear that there was a tension between working sufficient hours to provide an adequate standard of living against being with their child and putting their best interests first.

> There are two expectations: if you're a parent you should be around for your kids... but by the same token there's an expectation that you will work. But at the centre of it there is still a child who needs support and love, however that takes place. (22)
> The question is very adult focused not child focused. I think a better question is what is a reasonable amount of time for a child not to have their parents around?

In contrast to the results of the poll there was an appreciation by both groups that there were additional pressures on lone parents that needed to be taken into account.

When asked explicitly if those on lower pay should have to work more hours than was 'reasonable' in order to get by, there was a strong sense from both groups that this simply was not 'fair'.

I think it is completely unreasonable to ask poor parents to work more. I say that as someone who used to work all the hours God sends and earned quite a low wage – we've got to balance things out much better. (Couple parent, Group 2, 24)

There was also a strong feeling from both groups that parenting wasn't valued

I also just feel that bringing up a child is working! Why is that not given the status? (Couple parent, Group 2, 24)

In addition the focus groups pointed to the importance of afford-able and good quality child care and the support of tax credit for those on low incomes. There were differences between the two groups in interpreting ideas about flexibility. Group 2 (higher income) parents appreciated flexibility as in general they were able to be in control of how this worked while Group 1 parents associated flexibility with unpredictability. Both groups agreed that employers needed to be more supportive of parents.

Employers need to think about how they can be flexible so that we can all have a less stressed, more caring environment – so that we can all feel we give the best to the next generation. The world needs to start thinking slightly differently [about working hours]. (Couple parent, Group 2)

4. The ideas about employer responsibility were picked up in the final phase of the research when businesses were interviewed and asked about hours, accommodating the needs of family life and the impact of policy on 'family-friendly' practice. They found that generally larger businesses were better able to manage family-friendly practice but for all businesses the 'business case' for any practice needed to be made.

Reflections on research

Activity 1

The research summarized and commented on the findings and iden-tified that in their decision making about working hours, pressures on families come from

- social, cultural and personal values and expectations,

- a tax and benefits system that incentivizes families to work in particular ways,
- employer behaviour.

They conclude that

> ... *all these pressures bear down on lower paid earners more strongly than they do on the better off. The gains from working more hours are much lower for low paid families than those higher up the income distribution...*
>
> *Rather than having their parental choices supported, low-income parents increasingly find themselves subject to subtle, and not so subtle, forms of coercion to work more hours than many consider reasonable. (Judge, 2015, 41)*

Look back at the results of the evidence review and identify these 'forms of coercion'.

Activity 2

They go on to say:

> *in-work poverty is the product of three variables: the level of pay; the level of in-work benefits; and the level of hours worked. Yet the agenda to address low pay and benefit levels is acutely political, as it needs to tackle vested interests and deeply ingrained ideological positions in business and government. Placing the emphasis on hours 'individualises' responsibility for in-work poverty: it is for parents to solve the problem through striving to work more and more hours (and they are failures if they do not do so). (41)*

- What do you think this says about the state's priorities in relation to working carers?
- What role do you think the state should have in relation to 'the level of pay; the level of in-work benefits; and the level of hours worked'?

Activity 3

Go back to the section in Chapter 2 that discusses the different ideologies around a rights discourse.

- What do you think the 'vested interests' and 'deeply ingrained ideological positions' might be?

- What could policy makers do to support carers in a way that would ensure that they have both the time and money to support their children?
- How would this be funded?
- What objections might be raised by those who believe that the state has a minimal role to play in family life?
- How do you think Article 27 should influence decisions about policy in this area?

Activity 4

The report suggests:

> For all parents, choice is regarded as paramount. They are the ones who know their children, are best placed to make decisions about the suitability of childcare and can judge how much they need to be at home to support them (including through the teenage years). Rather than coerce parents to work, then, policy should be premised on trust and should aim to facilitate, rather than compel, employment. (41)

Go back to discussions about the 'best interests' of the child (pages 61–2 and 208). Does current policy appear to have the child's 'best interests' at heart? How might a policy based on 'trust' and 'facilitating work' help with the idea of 'best interests'? What changes in 'ideological position' might need to take place before this can happen?

Interview with Lindsay Judge about the 'Round the Clock' research

Lindsay Judge, Resolution Foundation

Sue Welch: There seem to be some differences in interpretation of 'what hours should parents work?' that influenced the way people responded to this question. Could you say a bit more about this?

*Lindsay Judge: We spent a lot of time thinking about what was the right question: how many hours **should/ought** someone work rather than how many someone might **like** to work or how many is it **reasonable** to ask someone to work. We didn't want to explore preferences but instead wanted to explore norms (should/ought).*

We chose to say 'reasonable' because we thought we should temper the question a little. Another key distinction is that we wanted to know what people thought was reasonable for others, not just themselves which is what the preferences polling had picked up. The question we asked left it open to interpretation and this resulted in many 'don't knows' and we didn't expect this. This led to debate in the team about how many respondents genuinely didn't know and how many were really 'it depends' because of the different contingencies, for example leaving children in the care of others, financial situation and so on. It would seem that some interpreted it as a pragmatic question and this may explain some of the answers about lone parents: lone parents could have to work more hours because there's only one of them. The specifics of individual situations and the context of decisions make it difficult to have one answer. I'm not sure that a different construction would have led to fewer 'don't knows'.

Looking back it seems we asked a question that opened up ideas. It would have been interesting to have gone back and asked the question differently to see if there were different responses. In setting up the research we were expecting to find a consensual place to build policy from but got responses that reflected the complexity of the situation.

Sue Welch: One of the focus group parents thought that the question might have been rephrased to ask 'what is a reasonable amount of time for a child not to have their parents around?' How do you think this might have changed responses?

Lindsay Judge: This was a man and he was the first to speak in that focus group and his comment changed the tenor of discussion: the group kept coming back to it. In the other focus group there was a different type of discussion. It was clear that if the question was asked from a parent/household income/children point of view there would be a different answer. It shows the complexity of the issues involved and flushed out the 'trade-offs' that lower income families have to make. Flipping the question so the thinking starts from the respondent's own children and then move to scenarios with different priorities can lead to different answers. We may have set up the research in a way that takes people to the point of seeing the unfairness. We took them through the story to make them go through thought process so they had to think about who pays the cost – the child? It revealed uncomfortable tensions for

*example: 'Adults should be able to stand on their own two feet'
but when children came into the equation it gave a different slant.*

*Looking back it raises questions about the way we did the
research. We wanted to see if there was a norm that we could use
as a basis for pay and hours. If we had the time and resources it
would have been interesting to run different focus groups (made
up in the same way as the originals) but take them through in the
opposite direction to see if it made a difference. The key point here
is that the way you ask the questions is probably important – start
from 'the child' and you'd get a different set of responses from
start from 'the cost for the state'.*

*Sue Welch: In your review of evidence it's clear that there is a
difference in the expectations of the tax and benefits system for
low earning families and higher earning families and this makes it
appear that 'the best interests' of children are considered for higher
earning families but not those with lower incomes. Do you think
this true and, if so, why do you think this is the case?*

*Lindsay Judge: The context was a time of brutal cuts and caps
on benefit so if you lived in poverty it would be in the best interests
of the child to work. It is fundamentally difficult to work out the
'best interests' for the child. Parents go out to work to earn more
than when they're on benefits but the claw back in tax means that
it doesn't make much difference. However, there is a trade off to
staying sufficiently connected to employment further down line so
that it's possible to earn more in the future.*

*The benefits system tends to see recipients as failed individuals
and they are penalized and blamed for being poor. The trade offs for
low income parents are the time spent with their children against
the income they can earn through extra hours. We wanted to ask
'is it true?' Because there are so many considerations the parent
has to adjudicate rather than state. Concern about children and
how they are cared for are worries for all parents but there are extra
constraints for poorer parents that were seen as unreasonable
and there was a challenge to the notion that being with children
was a luxury. We had to be careful that we weren't implying one
was better than another and steer a line between the two: it was
about people making choices. Parents can be 'nudged' in particular
directions through government policy: carrot and stick. There are
changes to social norms so policy can change expectations. There
were assumptions about low income families and we wanted*

to say 'lets' take a breath' and not use a sledgehammer to push parents to work in ways that they're uncomfortable with as this can have a deleterious effect on child: support not coercion.

Sue Welch: One of the parents in the focus groups suggests that in the United Kingdom there is a less supportive approach to families in relation to employment than in other parts of Europe. Do you know if there is any research similar to your own that gives an idea of the situation in other countries?

Lindsay Judge: I think we were asking a question that hadn't been asked before so I'm not aware of any comparative research but I have personal observations, not based on literature.

Firstly I'm aware of a TV programme that showed that France and Germany had different approaches. I also have a Scandinavian friend from Sweden. When I had my child she was jealous that I did not have to go back to work. She felt that she had no personal choice as there was so much collective child care. She would have liked to have a nanny in her own home but this seems unreasonable when there is state funded child care. It was evident in the focus groups that there were different ethnic/cultural expectations of women leading to issues from rights perspective.

There has been more money in quality childcare support here so parents could go out to work but availability could mean it's not reasonable not to work. Is this less choice or more choice? There are tensions between the personal and the political. Cross-national studies would open up some interesting findings.

Sue Welch: Were there any results of your research that you found particularly surprising or interesting?

Lindsay Judge: The issue of flipping the question referred to earlier I found very interesting.

The finding I found most surprising was in the polling. I personally expected that lone parents would be expected to work fewer hours than Parent 2 in a couple. I was shocked to find they were expected to work more than Parent 2. Other members of the team who had done research in this area said it was quite a common punitive attitude: it's your fault you're in this position. However, another interpretation is that the interpretation of the question meant the respondents were saying you have to work more hours as a lone parent because there's only one income. There are probably a range of explanations. The focus groups were not punitive. They were more pragmatic about hours worked by lone parents out of necessity.

> *Sue Welch: Have you seen any changes in policies or rhetoric that suggest there may be a different approach to supporting families in in-work poverty?*
>
> *Lindsay Judge: The main changes have been the increase in national living wage and Universal Credit. There seems to be a growing sense that if benefits are cut back, pay has to improve. In terms of hours there is a natural boundary that anyone is able to work and this can't be crossed by those on low wages.*
>
> *The report seems to have struck a nerve and put ideas on the table. More than any other piece of research I've been involved with this has brought people back to talk. Everyone with children can relate to decision about leaving their child with someone else whilst working. The time-money trade off seems to have fallen on fertile ground. There are assumptions in the benefits system and we need to look at them and face up to the challenges.*

The interview with Lindsay Judge highlights many of the issues that are key to thinking about the state's role in helping families provide for children, some of which have been introduced earlier:

- social and cultural expectations about the role of parents and carers
- societal and cultural values

The following section develops this consideration of issues about social and cultural perspectives on children's rights, bringing in an additional angle on the analysis of the relationships between the state, family and child.

The state and protection and participation

Since ratification of the UNCRC, children's participation rights have gradually been given more consideration through the 1989 Children Act and, more recently, the 2004 Children Act. However, the state does not intervene in children's participation rights within the family unless there is a dispute between parents, as in divorce cases. As Qvortrup et al. (1994) point out, the needs of parents/carers and children are often seen as indivisible in the services that are provided by the state: so the relationship that the state has with children is nearly always through the family. This 'familialization' (Qvortrup et al., 1994) may account for the state's apparent lack of concern in children's participation rights within the family. Brannen and O'Brien (1996) suggest that this means that children are 'conceptually constrained by and substantively contained within, the social institutions of family and school' (1996, 1).

Protecting children from the actions of their parents and carers is probably the most controversial aspect of the relationship between families and the state. The very fine line between too little and too much 'interference' means that children may die through the actions of their carers, or may be taken from their carers unnecessarily. The judgements that have to be made in cases of suspected physical and sexual abuse are extremely difficult and may be made more complex when cultural factors come into play. For example, while Female Genital Mutilation is illegal and seen as a form of child abuse in the United Kingdom there have been no successful prosecutions to date. The intercollegiate report referred to earlier (RCM et al., 2013) cites research by Piwali (2013) which identified that one of the barriers to professionals reporting FGM is 'concern that they risk offending or stigmatizing people from BMER communities' (RCM et al., 2013, 14). Although reporting of FGM is now mandatory, this illustrates one of the many challenges that those acting on behalf of the state can experience when attempting to protect children from potential harm within the family.

This section of the chapter considers the role of the state in both protecting children and ensuring their participation as these two areas of rights are often seen to be in opposition to each other as seen in the previous section. However, as Cossar et al. (2016) suggest,

> The extent to which the tensions between children's right to participate and their right to protection are in opposition is debatable. Participation can be protective for vulnerable children, leading to increased confidence, self-efficacy and self-worth. (104)

Current guidance on safeguarding children (DFE, 2015) considers the following areas as relevant for intervention by the state:

- protecting children from maltreatment;
- preventing impairment of children's health or development;
- ensuring that children grow up in circumstances consistent with the provision of safe and effective care;
- taking action to enable all children to have the best outcomes.

The guidance stresses the importance of everyone concerned with children in need of protection being aware of and acting on the knowledge that children have said that what they want from their relationships with adults is:

- Vigilance: to have adults notice when things are troubling them
- Understanding and action: to understand what is happening; to be heard and understood; and to have that understanding acted upon
- Stability: to be able to develop an ongoing stable relationship of trust with those helping them
- Respect: to be treated with the expectation that they are competent rather than not
- Information and engagement: to be informed about and involved in procedures, decisions, concerns and plans
- Explanation: to be informed of the outcome of assessments and decisions and reasons when their views have not met with a positive response
- Support: to be provided with support in their own right as well as a member of their family
- Advocacy: to be provided with advocacy to assist them in putting forward their views

The following piece of research investigates children's response to service provision.

Example of research: participation and protection

Cossar et al. (2016) explored children's perspectives on the child protection process. This was a small-scale study involving 26 children aged 6–17 from 18 families all living at home with a child protection plan.

The study identified the following key factors in supporting or hindering children's participation and satisfaction with the process.

- The importance of trusting relationships between the child and social worker.

'Because if you're not honest with her she can't really help you and like it'll make things harder, if you lie about something it will make things harder, because she does try and help you with it and it it's not the truth and that it's not going to make things any easier

and she won't trust you either, because you've got to trust her and she's got to trust you. Otherwise there's no point.' (Louise aged 15)

- Children disliked their social worker being a remote figure, particularly when they knew that the social worker had a key role in decision making about their lives and they often felt intimidated by social workers 'interrogating' them and 'twisting words'.
- Level of understanding of the assessment process.

Older children (14–17) had a clearer understanding of the Child Protection process. Younger children only had a minimal or partial understanding and were trying to understand from pieces of information gleaned from a variety of sources. They could give a coherent account of some aspect of the process but not of the whole and the process had an emotional impact.

Involvement in the formal process

Again, older children reported being more involved than younger children by being invited to meetings and seeing or discussing reports. However, few felt listened to or able to ask questions. Only six had the results of the meetings explained to them.

Some of the comments from the children on their involvement in the process illustrate these negative experiences:

They just put it in the report and they don't even tell our family what they're going to write, so that's what I don't like about the social.

I'd rather go with someone from my family and my parents usually can't go. But they got angry and didn't like who I brought. I could tell they didn't want him there because of the way they looked at him. They wanted me to bring the headmaster instead but I wanted someone from my family.

Every time I went to speak, someone interrupted me and that really annoyed me so I was like right I'm going, I've got to get to school.

I didn't lie but there was a sense of awkwardness when you know you should say something but you don't want to say it in front of certain people.

I did go once but it was awful ... they were just all talking and I didn't understand what they were saying. It was about me. I didn't really enjoy it that much.

Reflection on the research

Activity 1

The study clearly shows that for this group of children and young people their understanding and level of participation in the process depended very much on the relationship with their social worker, the way that the process was explained to them and the way meetings were conducted to maximize their comfort and engagement.

Look at the things that children have identified as being important factors when they are in need of protection on page 226. How do the children and young people's experiences in this study compare with what children have said is important to them?

Why do you think there is a difference?

Activity 2

The role of the state in these circumstances is to make sure that the child is protected and this may mean protection from members of their family. One of the children suggested that taking a member of her family with her to the meeting was not a positive experience. Look back at what she said and think about why this person may not have been welcomed.

What issues does the emphasis on protection raise for families?

If there is a need for protection from one family member, how might that affect relationships within the family?

Why is it important to get the views of children in these circumstances? Should other family members be able to contribute to decisions?

In matters other than safeguarding children the main fears concerning the role of the state centre on children's participation rights and how the legal system might override parental decisions. Many of the concerns about children's provision and protection rights involve decisions being made by parents and carers 'in the best interests of the child'. Without the involvement of children themselves in making those decisions, it is unlikely that parents and carers can really determine what is in the child's best interests so participation rights become central to ensuring other rights too.

Although the UK government hasn't incorporated children's participation rights within the family into its laws, there are countries that have. Thomas (2002) identifies Scotland, Norway and Sweden as countries where these rights are incorporated in law and points out that the fears about increased litigation in response to doing this haven't materialized. Earlier discussion has pointed to the potential polarization of the rights of children and the wishes of parents when there is disagreement. Arneil (2002), in a similar vein to Reynaert et al. (2009), argues that an individual rights dialogue based on a liberal notion of rights may not be helpful to the child or carers and considers that more emphasis on our interdependence would create a less confrontational context. Thomas (2002) echoes this notion when he argues that 'How can we live together?' is a better question than 'Why should I not do exactly as I want?' as a basis for negotiating rights.

However, adults, and within the family, carers, have power over children. Our current society also views children as 'adults in the making' which reinforces this power differential between adults and children. Thomas (2000) questions whether adults will be willing to relinquish this power in order to acknowledge our interdependence and seek to find ways of living together.

Example of research: policy supporting children and families in the United Kingdom

Henricson and Bainham (2005) reviewed documents across family law, education, criminal justice, child protection and financial support to assess the relationship between child and family policy, and ways of balancing the interests of adults and children and supporting the family as a whole.

They found the following:

- Human rights commitments require the government to formulate policies that take account of the rights and needs of children and parents, but these needs are often competing.
- Progress in balancing individual and collective needs of different family members across policy areas varies.
- Children's welfare has dominated both the social exclusion agenda and issues of residence and contact. In both cases, this may have been to the detriment of the rights of parents and other adults.

- In education, the balance is in favour of parents' rights; children do not have rights to representation, consultation or choice.
- Tough youth justice measures promote the welfare of society above the rights and welfare of children and their parents. As such, they risk breaching the spirit, if not the letter, of the UN Convention on the Rights of the Child and the European Convention on Human Rights.
- The greatest balance has been achieved in managing commitments to universal family support alongside investment in child protection.

They conclude the following:

- The field would benefit from an overarching child and family policy that takes account of the separate and collective needs and rights of family members.
- Such a policy would need underpinning by a consideration of human rights to ensure that the entitlements of individuals are protected and balanced across the generations.

Reflection on the research

The research shows that there are some areas of policy that favour the needs of children over parents, some where parents are favoured over children and some where the state favours society as a whole.

Look back over the examples in this chapter and consider where the balance of the interests of child, carers and state lie.

How would the recommendations of this research help to resolve these imbalances?

It is clear that the role of the state in relation to families and children is complex and arises from the tensions around

- concepts of rights, duties and responsibilities
- concepts of childhood
- concepts of welfare rights and liberty rights

that were introduced in Chapter 2. The final section of this chapter attempts to identify how these tensions might be understood.

How can we understand the relationship between children, families and rights?

This chapter has considered the challenges that face families in economically developed and developing countries in supporting children's rights. It is clear that the extent to which children can be provided for and protected within their family depends on the family's economic, social and cultural circumstances and that the degree of child participation in decision making is influenced by the relationships within the family and the perceived status of children. These circumstances can be affected both positively and negatively by the policies and practices of the state through the services that they provide.

The tensions between welfare rights and liberty rights that were highlighted in Chapter 2 are paralleled in the relationships that exist between children and their families and children, families and state. In relation to children and families, there is a tension between how parents and carers protect and provide for children (welfare rights) while ensuring children participate as fully as possible in decisions that are made (liberty rights). The state can take a positive role in providing services that support the family's ability to provide for and protect children. However, in doing so they may be seen to be taking away some of the autonomy that parents and carers have. This relationship between family and state becomes particularly problematic when children's participation rights are concerned, as the relationship between the state and the child is usually mediated by the family. However, those working with children and families do have the opportunity to support all children's rights by ensuring that they listen and take into account the views of children and other family members in finding ways to provide for children's survival and development and protect them from exploitation and harm. If the relationship between the state and the family models the good practice of involving and negotiating ways forward, the possibility of changing relationships within the family to give children a position of respect where they are part of the decision making process is far more likely.

Activities

The following activities are designed to help you to reflect on the chapter as a whole:

Chapter activity 1

The first part of the chapter discusses the difficulties families might have in providing for and protecting children and enabling their participation. The second part of the chapter identifies some of the tensions around state involvement in family life.

How might a 'rights discourse' be the source of these tensions and how might it be used to find a way of resolving them?

Chapter activity 2

The chapter draws on Archard's influential commentary on rights in relation to the following:

- Commitment to the importance of 'the best interests of the child'.
- Parent and carers have the right to autonomy (freedom to bring up their children as they see fit) and privacy (no one can intrude in the family without consent).
- There are clear conditions that identify when it is appropriate for the state to intervene.

Consider the issue of the state's position of the 'best interests' of a child being made by parents or adults working with children in relation to the research by Jobe and Gorin on pages 260–1.

How do children's rights relate to their involvement or non-involvement in decisions made about the services they receive?

Summary

This chapter has

- considered how the external context might influence children's experience in families,
- discussed the rights issues that arise within families,
- examined the role of the state in relation to children, their carers and their rights,
- considered the relationship between children, families and their rights.

Further reading

Archard, D. (2015) *Children, Rights and Childhood*. Abingdon: Routledge.

Chapter 11, 'Family and State' explains the different philosophical positions regarding the relationship between the family and the state and how these influence ideas about rights within the family.

The Children's Society (2015) *The Good Childhood Report*. London: The Children's Society. Available online at: https://www.childrenssociety.org.uk/sites/default/files/TheGoodChildhoodReport 2015.pdf.

This large-scale research project has collected evidence from children and young people for over a decade and this report summarizes changes and trends including what children think about being part of a family.

Thomas, N. (2002) *Children, Family and the State: Decision-Making and Child Participation*. London: Macmillan.

Chapter 5, 'Children, Parents and the State' considers the kind of relationships between parents and children that need to exist in order to support children's rights.

Research details

Example of research: rights, families and education

Quennerstedt analyzed the UN Working Group's reports that show how the articles of the 1989 Convention were formed and identifies the challenge that emerged during this process in relation to the rights of parents and their children.

Quennerstedt, A. (2009) 'Balancing the Rights of the Child and the Rights of Parents in the Convention on the Rights of the Child', *Journal of Human Rights*, 8 (2) 162–176.

Example of research: discipline and abuse

Taylor et al. (2015) researched the experiences of ten deaf and disabled children and adults who had experienced abuse as a child.

Taylor, J., Cameron, A., Jones, C., Franklin, A., Stalker, K., and Fry, D. (2015) *Deaf and Disabled Children Talking about Child Protection*. Edinburgh: University of Edinburgh and NSPCC.

Example of research: poverty and child labour

This report draws on the work of Save the Children and other partner organizations to identify the experiences of children in various kinds of forced labour.

Save the Children (2007) *The Small Hand of Slavery*. London: Save the Children. Available online at:
https://resourcecentre.savethechildren.net/library/small-hands-slaverymodern-day-child-slavery

Example of research: the effects of poverty

In 2013, The Children's Society reviewed the available literature on children in poverty to establish the extent and effects of poverty on children.

Children's Society (2013) *A Good Childhood for Every Child? Child Poverty in the UK*. London: Children's Society.

Example of research: parents and online problematic situations for children

Smahel, D. and Wright, M.F. (eds) (2014). *Meaning of Online Problematic Situations for Children. Results of Qualitative Cross-Cultural Investigation in Nine European Countries*. London: EU Kids Online, London School of Economics and Political Science.

Example of research: leading a double life within and outside the family

Ahmad et al. worked with 36 young people between the ages of 11 and 21 to identify their experience of living with two different cultures. The researchers were young people themselves and the research was supported by the Young Researchers' Network and Barnardos.

Ahmad, S., Akbar, A., Akbar, H., Ayub, S., Batool, A., Batool, S., Hussain, B., Kiani, S., Mahmood, S. and Rauf, R.(2008) *'East Meets West – Why Do*

Some South Asian Young People Feel They Need to Lead a Double Identity and How Does Cultural and Religious Issues Affect Them?' Young Researchers Network. Available online at: http://childrensresearchcentre.open.ac.uk/research/Barnardo'sresearchreport. pdf.

Example of research: time poverty and income poverty

Research on behalf of the Child Poverty Action Group into the hours that people should work in order not to be poor, used an evidence review on current attitudes to parental employment, a poll of a cross-section of the population, focus groups of parents and views of employers and business groups.

Judge, L. (2015) *Round the Clock: In-work Poverty and the 'Hours Question'*. London: Child Poverty Action Group.

Example of research: participation and protection

The paper presents the findings from a qualitative study exploring the views of 26 children, aged 6–17 years, about their participation in the child protection system in England.

Cossar, J., Brandon, M. and Jordan, P. (2016) 'You've got to trust her and she's got to trust you': Children's views on participation in the child protection system', *Child & Family Social Work*, 21 (1), 103–112.

Example of research: policy supporting children and families in the United Kingdom

Research supported by the Joseph Rowntree Foundation reviews government policy in the context of international human rights commitments in order to stimulate debate about the tensions in family and child.

Henricson, C. and Bainham, A. (2005) *The Child and Family Policy Divide. Tensions, Convergence and Rights*. York: Joseph Rowntree Foundation.

7

Working with Children

Introduction and key questions

While working with children can be an extremely fulfilling occupation there are also problems and tensions and these are considered in this chapter. It considers some of the issues and debates around children's rights that have been introduced in earlier chapters and draws out their particular relevance for those working with children. Activities within the chapter ask you to refer back to previous chapters to support your understanding of the rights issues that those working with children experience in terms of the opportunities and the challenges they create in supporting the realization of children's rights. The key questions are as follows:

- In what kinds of contexts does work with children occur?
- What rights issues arise for those working with children?
- What can research tell us about developing positive, rights informed relationships between children and those who work with them?

In what kinds of contexts does work with children occur?

The range of occupations working with children is very varied. For example, workers may be concerned with supporting children's health, welfare, care or education or intervene in children's lives through the justice system or child protection. Others may be providing services such as sport, leisure or play facilities. Many jobs are part of services provided by the state and others may be with private companies or voluntary organizations. Their roles might be totally focused on children or have a wider focus with occasional interactions with children. They may be located within the Minority World or the Majority World. The following two examples are of workers in different parts of the world, both working with children as their main focus: one concerned with the education of refugee children and one concerned with child protection.

Example 1

Halima works for a voluntary organization, 'Children on the Edge', in their Lebanon 'tent school' for refugees who are escaping from conflict. This extract is from the webpage explaining what the 'tent schools' do.

There are currently 28 Syrian refugee teachers at the tent schools we support for refugee children in Lebanon. These people are trained up from within the refugee camps and they not only teach, but are a source of help and advice for parents and the wider community. They are a force for good despite living in a situation completely out of their control. 'The teachers here speak the same dialect of Arabic as their students (often they're from the same or the neighbouring camp as the children), they get their culture, so nothing gets by them. The teachers are motivated to learn, motivated to be useful, and motivated to be a changing force in their communities.' (Nadine, School's Co-ordinator)

Halima is a teacher who has taught with the tent schools for two years, and she also works as a trainer. She describes her experience:

Our work is very focused. We work wholesomely, not just to educate the kids but to help them grow into better, more well-rounded people. It's also been really good to learn how to support our student's growth in learning not to physically abuse each other, and learning about therapeutic methods to deal with what the kids have seen in war; learning about forgiveness. I've gained so much experience, and this job has encouraged me to grow not just as a teacher but also in my passions. I write stories and songs and poetry and use them to give the children more fun, creative resources to learn. As not just a teacher but also a mother to one of the students, I'm so glad that my son can read and write well, especially when I hear about other schools' poor levels of education. I really like that we teach the children to make conclusions instead of pointing everything out to them. (Children on the Edge, 2016)

Example 2

Polly is a social worker in a UK Local Authority. This is an extract from her letter to David Cameron (the UK prime minister at the time) urging him to be more supportive of social workers.

I am writing to you as a social worker with 30 years' experience of child protection work.

During that time, I have always done my best to keep the children I have worked with safe. Most of the time, I have succeeded. I am particularly proud of my involvement in a complex piece of work that uncovered a group of multiple perpetrators sexually abusing acutely vulnerable children across county borders.

Despite graphic disclosures from the children, none of the adults involved in the abuse were ever prosecuted. But care proceedings kept the children safe. When I meet up with two of the children concerned (who are now adults) they still ask me why the man that hurt them so badly never went to prison.

But I also know that I have made mistakes, as we all do. Risk is not always predictable or preventable. I have been involved with children who have been seriously hurt – this is tragic but almost inevitable in a long social work career. Even when we do everything right, we don't always know how to stop children getting hurt.

Because we are human, we don't always do everything right. The consequences are serious. As a human being, I am motivated by my wish to improve the lives of the children and families I work with. Nothing else is needed to ensure that I do my very best.

More money would not make me try harder and nor would the threat of prison. I already live with the risk of being vilified in the media if I make a mistake – or even if I don't, but something goes wrong anyway.

What might help is: smaller caseloads, more time to think, better supervision, less paperwork and more training. We know from international research that the best way to improve the lives of the most vulnerable children is to invest in the lives of all children.
(Children, Comment, Stand Up for Social Work, 2015)

Activity

Halima and Polly are working in very different circumstances although both are concerned about children who have had very difficult life experiences. Think about the challenges that face Halima and Polly and the children that they are working with in relation to issues raised earlier in the book:

1. What kind of rights is Halima likely to be most concerned with? How might these be similar to and differ from the rights Polly might be most concerned with? (Refer to Chapter 2, sections on liberty rights and welfare rights)

    Where might there be difficulties in each situation, for the adults and children, in addressing all the other rights that should be taken into consideration outside their main focus? Think about rights such as participation in decision making, freedom of expression, the right to rest, play and leisure.
2. Which of the following factors identified in Chapter 6 might be influencing the abilities of carers to provide for children's rights in each of these contexts?
    - absolute or relative poverty
    - children being seen and treated as economic assets
    - conflict, fear and political repression.
    - the consumer society
    - over- and under-employment (families where too little work results in too little money or too much work results in little time with children)

- the commodification of children as social and emotional assets
- the perception of danger and blame where children's activities might be restricted because carers are concerned about being blamed for putting their children in danger
3. What constraints might there be to children and young people being active agents in relation to their rights
4. Where does the funding for each context come from? Does this stem from legal or moral considerations? (Refer to Chapter 2)
5. What kind of factors might be 'silencing' the voice of children in each context? (Refer to Chapter 4)
6. What might Halima and Polly be able to do to support children's voices being heard? (Refer to Chapter 4)

Because there are so many different organizations concerned with children, there is the potential for fragmentation and difficulties in ensuring all aspects of a child's life are considered in a holistic way. For example, those who work in education may be less concerned with a child's health and well-being than someone working in the health service and vice versa. There may also be a number of different agencies working with a child or family – for example health, education, care, justice – each with its own focus and unaware of what other agencies are doing. In the United Kingdom this fragmentation has been of particular concern in the area of child protection when, in extreme cases, children have died or, particularly in the case of unaccompanied migrant children, have 'disappeared'. This has resulted in policies attempting to ensure that children don't 'fall through the net'. Working Together to Safeguard Children (DFE, 2015) gives guidance for all those who come into contact with children in a professional role on working collaboratively and taking a holistic view of the child. This should mean that, although professionals may have a particular specialist focus, this would be in the context of understanding the child in relation to their family, peers and community and within these contexts, understanding their rights and needs. We might therefore expect a seamless approach by all those working with children but this is clearly not the case. The next section addresses the complexity of rights issues that might provide challenges and explain the continued difficulties in providing a seamless service for children in the United Kingdom.

> ## Key points: the contexts of working with children
>
> The wide range of roles occurs within many different contexts, each with its own challenges and issues.
>
> The potential fragmentation of support for children raises issues about how those who work with children collaborate and view children in a holistic way.

What rights issues arise for those working with children?

Earlier chapters have drawn out the tensions and issues around children's rights and these are all relevant to those working with children. This section will consider four aspects of earlier discussions and the implications for those working with children:

- Issues concerned with the holistic ideal of children's rights.
- Issues concerned with the political, economic and social pressures that impact on rights.
- Issues concerned with the impact of inequalities on children's rights.
- Issues concerned with critiques of the UNCRC with regard to what rights children should have and who should decide what these are.

Issues concerned with the holistic ideal of children's rights

The basic tenets of the UNCRC point to the importance of all those who work with children being able to understand and support children's rights. As the UNCRC makes clear, while a service may have a particular focus on a particular right or group of rights, their other rights cannot be ignored. For example, a professional within the health service has a child's survival and development rights their key focus, but should also ensure that children's rights to protection and participation are also given equal consideration. However, this is within the context of children being part of a wider society that also has needs and rights that need to be taken into consideration. In addition, government policies, while ostensibly having children at the heart, are also concerned with the economic and social position of the state. Consequently those who work with children, particularly in services provided by the state, have to work within the framework of their particular service which will have its own priorities. These are reflected in Table 7.1.

Activity

1. The services in Table 7.1 will have norms concerning the space and time that is given to children being involved in decision making. Look back at the section titled 'Key points: spaces and norms in decision making (Chapter 5, page 156) and see how they fit in with the key focus for each service.
2. The key focus for each service and the implications for those working in the service are likely to reflect different ways of thinking about children and the kinds of relationships that exist between children and adults. Look back at Table 2.2, Rights and child–adult relationships (Chapter 2, page 52) and think about the kinds of relationship that are implicit in each of the services.
3. In Chapter 1 there is a discussion of research by Lyle (2014) about training teachers about the UNCRC. One of her findings was that it was commonly assumed children were incapable of forming their own views because they are not old enough; therefore, age becomes a key objection to the UNCRC in schools, especially in the early years and infant classroom (ages 4–7) (2014, 220).

   Why might the key focus for teachers mean that they think of children in this way. Are there other workers who might have similar ideas because of their key focus?

Issues concerned with the political, economic and social pressures that impact on rights

In 2015 the United Kingdom submitted its fifth periodic report to the CRC on the progress made on children's rights. This was considered by the CRC

Table 7.1 Services for children: key focus and possible tensions

Service sector	Working with individuals or groups	Key focus	Implications and possible tensions for those working in the service
Health	Individuals	Ensuring children are brought up in circumstances that support health and, when they are ill, providing appropriate healthcare.	Possible tensions in ensuring children's rights to be involved in decisions about treatment are considered alongside parents' legal duty to make these decisions.
Education	Groups	Ensuring that children have the knowledge, skills and attitudes that are necessary to be productive and responsible citizens.	Balancing the requirements of society, in the form of the curriculum and academic targets, with children's holistic development and participation. Ensuring children are treated as individuals not as a group.
Day care and 'wrap around' services	Groups	Ensuring children are cared for, usually while parents are working.	Ensuring children are treated as individuals not as a group.
Care and protection services	Mainly individuals	Ensuring children who are vulnerable are protected.	Balancing the need for protection with remaining in the family. Ensuring children are involved in decision making.
Justice	Mainly individuals	Ensuring children conform to the laws of society and dealing with them when they don't conform.	Balancing children's rights with the needs of the wider community.
Play and leisure	Groups	Providing opportunities for children to engage in play and leisure activities.	Ensuring children are treated as individuals not as a group.

alongside comments made by organizations and individuals concerned with children's rights. After interviews with all these parties, the CRC published a list of issues associated with the UK report. The following are extracts from the report (UNCRC, October 2015) that illustrate how national policies affect the context that those who work with children experience and influence the tensions

- between ensuring the individual rights of children are met and consideration of the rights and needs of the wider society,
- between the rights of the child and the wishes of their parents, and
- between children's rights to protection and to participation.

List of issues in relation to the fifth periodic report of the United Kingdom of Great Britain and Northern Ireland 2015

The CRC asked the UK government to provide clarification on a number of issues that were of concern. By asking for this clarification there is an implied criticism of the current situation. These related to:

- whether sex and relationship education is provided in all education settings (2015, 2);
- the measures taken to protect children, in particular Muslim children, from stigmatizing effects of the counter-terrorism measures (2015, 2);
- changes to welfare provision that could affect children and how the government will monitor these effects (2015, 3);
- how the best interests of the child are taken into account as a primary consideration in decisions involving migrant, asylum-seeking or refugee children (2015, 3).

Activity

It is clear from this list of issues that the CRC considers some current UK policies to be at odds with the spirit of the UNCRC. For those working with children these policies are likely to cause tensions between following national policies and acting in 'the best interests' of the children and young people they work with. Identify the tensions that those who work with children might face as a result of the identified concerns. Look at the examples in earlier chapters to extend your thinking:

- Counter-terrorism and liberty rights (Chapter 2, page 43)
- Welfare rights (Chapter 2, pages 44–5)
- Asylum-seeking children (Chapter 2, pages 53–4; Chapter 3, pages 96–9)
- Immigration centres (Chapter 3, pages 96–9)
- Safe school environments for LGBTI youth (Chapter 3, pages 87–8)

The above examples illustrate how policy in the United Kingdom can affect the context for those working with children but similar situations occur across the world where government policies can have an impact on children and their rights and those who work with them in positive and negative ways.

Example of research: the effects of health policy in Ghana

Hampshire, K., Porter, G., Owusu, S.A., Tanle, A. and Abane, A. (2011) 'Out of the reach of children? Young people's health-seeking practices and agency in Africa's newly-emerging therapeutic landscapes', *Social Science and Medicine*, 73, 702–710.

The research team were interested in how young people in Ghana, in urban and rural settings, sought out healthcare. They were particularly interested in young people's agency in the field of health in contrast to Western health systems that largely rely on adult control of health provision. Traditionally young people took a good deal of responsibility for their own healthcare but were restricted in what was available because of lack of resources and travel and limited information about effective treatments. The context in Ghana was of change in three areas:

- the introduction of a National Health Service through mutual aid groups where households paid an annual fee to gain access to health services;
- the growth in advertising of medicines in the media;
- the growth in access to mobile phones as an immediate means of communication between friends.

The research found that the introduction of the NHIS card gave young people with insurance access to better quality provision if they were in urban areas but less so in rural areas.

> *The doctor requested a laboratory test and then prescribed some drugs for me. I did not pay any money because of the NHS. I was also confident in going through the process because of the NHS. The scheme has allowed more children to go to health facilities alone because the authorities will not ask you to pay. It is a good scheme for us children. (Abigail, 15 years, urban)*

However, the growth in advertising and use of mobile phones, while increasing access to health information, also meant that young people were influenced by non-reliable sources of information.

> *I want to buy Pilex. I was convinced by the advert and I know someone who saw the advert and bought it and it was good. It is used to cure piles and visual impairment. The way they run the advert is convincing. (Kofi, 16 years, and not suffering from either piles or visual impairment)*

The research concluded that the positive impact of the NHIS card was limited because of location and resource issues and the impact of information gained through media and informal networks had negative as well as positive effects. In the absence of policies to increase NHS provision and regulate access to medicines and information, young people were not supported effectively in their health-seeking practices.

Reflection on the research

Activity 1

The comments of the young people indicate the positive aspects of the introduction of the NIHS card and some of the problems that arise. A number of workers will come into contact with these young people who are attempting to seek out appropriate healthcare, for example doctors, pharmacists and teachers.

> How might they be able to support Abigail?
> How might they be able to support Kofi?

Activity 2

The agency of these children in seeking out their own healthcare is much less regulated by carers than in the United Kingdom. What does this suggest about the image of children and young people in this society? (Look back at Chapter 2 and the interview with Kate Hampshire below).

What implications does this have for those working with children and young people?

What changes in policy might help both the young people and those who are trying to support them? After you have thought about this you might compare your ideas with those expressed by Kate Hampshire in the interview below.

Interview with Kate Hampshire about the research

Dr Kate Hampshire, University of Durham

> *Sue Welch: The young people's agency in seeking out healthcare is very evident. Do you know if the same degree of agency occurs in other areas of their lives?*
>
> *Kate Hampshire: Yes, but also with constraints, as in healthcare. For example, quite young children in Ghana may take considerable responsibility for contributing to household income and caring for younger children, among other things. Compared with children in the UK, Ghanaian children often move around independently from an earlier age – walking to school unaccompanied, for example, or to the market, although this does vary and in some cases girls' movement is more restricted than that of boys. However, as with healthcare, their ability to act optimally can be constrained through lack of resources, information, etc. For example, children who need to earn money to pay for their school expenses may end up working in exploitative conditions that can compromise their health and wellbeing.*
>
> *Sue Welch: Do workers who come into contact with children and young people have any role in supporting their healthcare choices?*
>
> *Kate Hampshire: Yes, they do, but children and young people come into contact with all kinds of 'workers' who may have very different degrees of knowledge/expertise and agendas. So a young person who takes her NHIS card to go to hospital may be well-supported by medical professionals, although in some cases young*

people complained that doctors talked down to them or didn't take their concerns seriously. On the other hand, small drug store owners or market traders who sell medicines over the counter may simply not be qualified to give appropriate advice, while some unscrupulous medicine sellers may try to take advantage of young people's relative lack of information/resources to make money.

Sue Welch: Did you do any work to find out what parent/carers views were? If so, what did you find?

Kate Hampshire: Yes, we did talk to parents and carers too. In rural areas in particular, many parents do not have any formal education and may also struggle to obtain appropriate healthcare for themselves or their children. In some cases, parents rely on their children, who may be better able to read than their parents, to help them interpret instructions on medicines, etc. In general, parents wanted to support their children's healthcare choices but were not always well equipped to do this effectively.

Sue Welch: How has the situation developed since your research report?

Kate Hampshire: Probably the biggest change is the rapid expansion of mobile phones, including 3G internet-enabled phones. While a few young people had access to these during our study, this has grown enormously since then. We did a follow-up study in the same communities and found that, whereas in our 2006–2009 study, 17% of 9–18-year-olds in our study sites had used a mobile phone in the preceding week, by 2012–2014, this had increased to 42%. We have written another paper in Social Science and Medicine (Hampshire et al., 2015) about the ways that young people are making use of mobile phones in their quest for healthcare, and at some of the opportunities and risks that this new technology brings.

Sue Welch: What policies do you think are needed to support children and young people in their health choices?

Kate Hampshire: First, and most crucially, policy makers need to realize that children and young people in Ghana (and many other parts of the world) are active agents in healthcare seeking and therefore they need to work to create conditions that enable young people to seek healthcare safely and effectively, rather than basing decisions on assumptions about what children should or should not be doing. So, if children and young people are self-medicating without professional advice, or being sold inappropriate medicines, health education in schools needs to extend beyond the usual

> health promotion messages to cover safe and appropriate use of medicines. This needs to be coupled with expansion in the quality, accessibility and affordability of youth-friendly health services in the formal sector and extending youth-focused training to informal healthcare providers, much frequented by young people. This should include training in medicine use (dosage, indications and contraindications) for local shopkeepers, who are often the first port of call for young people. The Ghanaian shopkeepers we interviewed were often unsure about the legality of prescribing and selling various medicines to under-18s, indicating an important information gap. And, crucially, it involves working closely with parents and wider families, who are crucial partners in young people's quests for healthcare.

Activity

Look back at the earlier sections of this chapter and compare what Kate Hampshire is saying about the issues for those that work with children and young people with the tensions described in those earlier sections.

Issues concerned with the impact of inequalities on children's rights

In addition to the issues considered in the previous section, those who work with children need to address equality issues. All those working with children need to ensure that

- stereotypes are challenged (e.g. seeing some children as 'disabled' rather than having abilities),
- issues relating to identity are addressed (e.g. consideration of cultural practices that may be different from those of the worker),
- access to resources (for children who come from low income families are not disadvantaged) are considered.

This may be particularly difficult when working with groups of children where the tendency is to focus on the group rather than the individual, but all workers have a duty to ensure that children's rights are upheld 'without discrimination of any kind, irrespective of the child's or his or her parents' or legal guardian's race, colour, sex, language, religion, political or other opinion, national, ethnic or social origin, property, disability, birth or other status' (UNCRC, 1989, Article 2). Summarizing issues around the 'social exclusion' aspect of the 'rights agenda', Chapter 1 points to:

> the need to ensure that rights do not become an isolated arena, that the complex forces at work that exclude, silence and disenfranchise children are recognized and addressed. The child rights agenda is one that needs to engage with areas of 'social, economic and political' concerns in a way that promotes inclusion and equity. (page 27)

Those who work with children have powerful positions that can mean that their own interests and values take precedence over the rights of children. A good example of this comes from Chapter 1 (page 12) in research from 'See it, say it, change it' (2015) where one of the interviewees said,

> Coming from a deprived area in London and growing up in poverty, I feel like I am not treated with respect and equality but instead I am dismissed and pushed aside due to my class background. I feel this in all aspects of my life. I feel like the current political system is apathetic towards my views and needs based purely upon my place in society. (Female, 17) (2015, 12)

This shows the impact of discrimination that can occurs because of the values of those who create and implement policy.

When children communicate their thoughts and feelings in ways that are different to the adults who work with them (e.g. in a different spoken language or through sign language) their rights to participation may be diminished unless a solution is found. This is illustrated through the following research extract that has already been considered in relation to families in Chapter 6.

Example of research: the effects of discrimination

Taylor et al.'s (2015) research looked at the accounts of ten deaf and disabled adults who had experienced abuse in childhood in order to identify barriers to disclosure and support. One significant factor was communication difficulties. A major concern raised by two deaf participants was the use of (abusive) parents or foster carers as facilitators of communication. This provided parents/carers with opportunities to conceal abuse. One deaf participant who was abused by her mother and the mother's partner said:

> ...I remember the social worker interviewing me but my mother was there... No, I didn't have any access to sign language, I didn't know any other deaf children...yeah, everything was through [my mother]. (Maggie 10FA, 31)

In contrast, Paul was eventually able to disclose at the age of 18 after ten years of abuse when police found him in an abusive relationship. The police were deaf aware: one officer had basic signing skills which reassured him. Paul asked for a qualified interpreter whom he knew and trusted and this was provided before the police interviewed him. Following this Paul received good support from the police, social worker, counsellor and interpreter. There was consistency in the support he received with, for example, the policeman who discovered him remaining at Paul's side during the hospital examination and during the court case and his social worker visiting him at home every day during the initial phases. This level of support was provided for a year until he was ready to move on. Paul had the same BSL interpreter throughout this whole period and this person supported him through counselling. He reports that he is stronger now and trying to get on with his life (2015, 33). Paul commented,

> It was good to see a policeman who could sign. I felt comfortable straightaway. I felt a candle was being lit and felt warm. I was not frozen with worry. It was calm. When the qualified interpreter came, I felt more comfortable. It meant that I was able to give information with no communication problems. It went smoothly. Correct information was conveyed to the police. The statement I read was correct. (Paul, 3MA, 34)

While Paul was positive about his experience of using an interpreter the report points to the ethical and professional issues for interpreters whose role is primarily to facilitate communication.

Reflection on the research

Activity 1

Consider the experiences of Maggie and Paul and the implications for those who are involved with the lives of deaf children. The limited communication approaches of the adults around them prevented both Maggie and Paul disclosing their abuse at an early age.

How were their other rights affected because of this?

Why might Maggie's social worker have relied on Maggie's mother to translate? What alternatives might the social worker have used?

Why was Paul's experience at 18 much more positive?

What issues for those working with children does Paul's experience raise?

Activity 2

Maggie and Paul had difficulties communicating because the contexts they lived in did not respond to their situation of being deaf and disabled. Other children may have other experiences of communication difficulties. What might these be?

Whose responsibility is it to make sure all children have a voice and are listened to? Think about the different levels of this responsibility – within a setting of service provision such as a school or care context or at national policy levels, for example.

Chapter 4 (pages 142–3) discusses research by MacNaughton et al. (2007) that challenged adult-orientated ways of communication and involvement in participation. How might this improve the experiences of children and young people who are in danger of being silenced through social exclusion?

In considering equality issues, it is important to identify areas that might be a source of discrimination. While the UNCRC has a list of areas, it isn't comprehensive.

Activity

The UNCRC Article 2 lists areas of discrimination that might affect children's rights. Chapter 3 identifies sexual orientation and gender identity as a further area that the UNCRC has neglected to include. Look back at Chapter 3 pages 86–90 and identify equality issues for those working with children in relation to

- stereotyping,
- identity,
- access to resources.

How might the fragmentation of services and/or national policies affect workers' ability to support LGBTI children?

How might a worker's own biases affect their relationships with these children? For example, think about the worker's own sexuality and their religious beliefs.

Issues concerned with critiques of the UNCRC

Chapter 2 identified issues that have arisen since the large-scale adoption of the UNCRC by the majority of states. One of these concerns was the 'top-down' nature of the UNCRC and the fear that the compromises and tensions in the UNCRC are ignored and that a rights dialogue becomes confrontational and legalistic around the implementation of the UNCRC rather than a discursive dialogue with children and adults about the nature and processes of rights issues. The implications for those working with children relate to the ways that children are educated about their rights through and by those who interact with them. Reynaert et al. (2010) focus on the implications of this for social work and identify two approaches to rights education.

The first model sees children being educated about their rights through making them aware of the UNCRC and is a knowledge-based learning process. The assumption behind this model is that informed children will be able to realize their rights and those working with children will work to bridge the gap between the ideal of the UNCRC and the reality of children's lives. The following research exemplifies this approach.

Example of research: rights education

Rebecca Webb (2015) investigated the process of rights education in a primary school by involving herself in all aspects of school life and taking notes on the rights issues that arose. She used the notes to help her to look critically at the place of rights within the school. These are extracts from her notes and discussion:

Rights – they appear everywhere, both concretely, as well as, somehow, floating in the ether – not so much on their own – but coupled with 'respect', dressed up as 'responsibility': they're on the

walls in UNICEF brightly coloured poster form; as 'home-made' school
charters on the walls of corridors, classrooms, hallways, outside in
the playground, on newsletters home, reminders of what can be
expected ('you have the right to be heard', and 'you have the right to
work' (and 'you have the responsibility to listen'...' and to 'let others
get on with their work'...); in passing remarks between teachers and
pupils, 'remember, it's lovely that we have the right to go out into the
sunshine to play, but we have the responsibility not to disturb other
children inside...' They feel invested in, by many, and in such a range
of spaces within the school. They are a garment, not so much worn
lightly, as with a mark of distinction...they are asking to be recognised
and valorised. This is Top Hill Primary saying, 'Hey, this is what we're
about...sit up and take notice.' (Rebecca's notes, October 2011)

Webb describes how she was involved in a group discussion where children had been asked, 'Tell me something about your Rights Respecting School'. Initially the discussion lacked enthusiasm until 'one child announced that "Toilet Charters" had started to appear on the doors to the junior school toilets. He pronounced this as, 'a joke'. He didn't know where they came from or who made them. Another child remarked that she thought that someone had flushed one of the Toilet Charters, 'down the loo'. This was greeted with barely contained delight by the assembled group, and a different child suggested glee-fully: 'I mean...some of them [the statements on the Toilet Charter] are just so funny ...' 'You have a right to feel safe and secure in the toilet'... 'It doesn't really happen so often [that someone doesn't feel safe] that you need to put a charter up!'

Another child added, 'It sounds like a joke but they – the teach-ers – mean it to be really serious. But like we could ask the builders to mend the doors so – like – no one can mess with them: maybe we could ask them when they're here doing other stuff?' (293)

Reflection on the research

Webb's analysis of the situation in the school points to the way that the rights agenda is being used, unintentionally, by the school to get children to conform to what the school perceives to be expected and accepted norms. While the children showed superficial acceptance of the charters and posters, the conversation about the 'toilet charter'

where children became animated and involved showed their awareness of a veneer of rights within the school.

Look back to Chapter 1 (pages 10–13) where the issue of educating
children in the United Kingdom about their rights is discussed. How
does this compare with the children in Webb's research? Think about
the concept of a 'rights veneer' that is discussed in Chapter 1. The
school in Webb's research really wanted children to be aware of their
rights so why might this 'rights veneer' be happening?

Reynaert et al. (2010) look critically at this 'top-down' model of rights education and point to the following assumptions:

- It presupposes a consensus on what we mean by children's rights rather
  than multiple interpretations.
- Interpretations can be based on particular views of the child that not
  all (probably very few) children fit, for example being autonomous,
  having access to resources, coming from particular backgrounds.
- In this way, interpretations accept existing power relationships and
  therefore are disadvantageous to children as a group and more vulnerable children in particular.

In this model, children who don't fit the 'ideal' view of the child (having autonomous agency, access to resources and coming from secure,
emotionally supportive backgrounds) can be seriously disadvantaged.
Recent accounts of sexual exploitation in the United Kingdom indicated
that children who were 'groomed', often children in care, were seen as
problems rather than children in need. As long ago as 1995, reporting
on the sexual exploitation of children. Kelly et al. (1995) identified that
' individuals and agencies have frequently failed to respond appropriately to cases of sexual abuse, often blaming the victim and excusing the
offender' (10).

One of the survivors, reflecting on her life said,

A lot of people assume that women and girls like me consent to this abuse.
Consent, however, is not a possibility for a girl who was delivered into the
hands of organized crime figures in New Jersey. (Evelina Giobbe, 6)

This kind of response illustrates the point made by Reynaert et al. that
assuming the autonomy of young people, and also adults, in these

Table 7.2 Two models of rights education

	Model 1 A top-down teaching practice where children learn about rights from more knowledgeable others	Model 2 An interactive open learning process involving individual and collective learning
Children	Learn about rights as a set of norms and values that are objective and uncontested. Act as autonomous, rational rights holders who can advocate and enforce their rights.	Learn about rights through their experiences by constructing rights in interaction with others. Become aware of the power relationships and the implicit rules and norms that exist and challenge these.
Workers	Inform children about their rights and find the best ways of realizing their rights.	Attempt to understand, working alongside children, what rights might mean in different contexts and for different children and what this means for their relationships. Identify the power relationships and the implicit rules and norms that exist and challenge these.
Rights	Established in the UNCRC and incorporated into legislation within states. States focus on implementing those rights through legal procedures and policies.	UNCRC is used as a basis for principles that need to be interpreted and discussed at every level.

situations is inappropriate and brings into question the effectiveness of this first model of rights education. What is lacking is the acknowledgement that, for individuals in many different kinds of difficult circumstances and unequal power relationships, just learning about rights is not enough. They need to learn what a rights dialogue means to them and how to engage with it, and they need to challenge existing assumptions and power relationships.

Table 7.2 shows how Reynaert et al. offer a second model of rights education that, while maintaining a voice for children, is more sensitive to individual circumstances and challenges accepted ideas and practices that can accentuate children's vulnerability.

Activity

The model of rights education advocated by Reynaert et al. (model 2) makes the role of those working with children much more open. They can't simply follow a set procedure but would need to negotiate with and involve children in different ways according to their circumstances and experience.

How might the school in Webb's research have acted differently if this alternative model of rights education was implemented?

Look at the research examples in Chapter 4 (pages 10–13). How does this relate to this model of Rights Education?

How might these ways of interacting have children supported Evelina (page 256)?

What challenges might this way of working cause for those working with children?

The term 'rights education' may imply that this only concerns workers in the education system but Reynaert et al. consider that all those who are concerned with children need to give this attention as it is fundamental to the way interactions with children occur. The next section looks in more detail at the types of relationships that children would like to have with those who work with them.

Key points: rights issues for those working with children

Those working with children are subject to tensions that can arise from

- the fragmented nature of services and provision for children and the different priorities that each service has;
- competition for resources and policies that are influenced by economic, social or political factors rather than the 'best interests' of children;
- ensuring that the many different lives that children lead are understood and taken into consideration;
- the complexity of rights issues and the ways we engage with children to support their understanding and actions.

What can research tell us about developing positive relationships between children and those who work with them?

The discussion of rights issues in the earlier sections of this chapter have highlighted some of the difficulties that those working with children might experience due to external factors. This section considers research that identifies what children and young people want from those who work with them and where, and why there might be differences between what they want and how workers relate to them.

Chapter 6 referred to the guidance in 'Working Together to Safeguard Children' (DFE, 2015) that identifies a number of factors that children say they need in their relationships with those who work with them:

- Vigilance: to have adults notice when things are troubling them.
- Understanding and action: to understand what is happening; to be heard and understood; and to have that understanding acted upon.
- Stability: to be able to develop an on-going stable relationship of trust with those helping them.
- Respect: to be treated with the expectation that they are competent rather than not.
- Information and engagement: to be informed about and involved in procedures, decisions, concerns and plans.
- Explanation: to be informed of the outcome of assessments and decisions and reasons when their views have not met with a positive response.
- Support: to be provided with support in their own right as well as a member of their family.
- Advocacy: to be provided with advocacy to assist them in putting forward their views.

All these factors identified in the guidance need to be addressed by all those working with children and young people but research shows that children's experience of seeking and receiving support doesn't always live up to these expectations.

Research example: what children want from those who work with them

Jobe and Gorin (2013) carried out face-to-face interviews with 24 young people in six different local authority areas and represented a range of ethnic backgrounds and ages. The purpose of their research was to find out young people's understandings, perceptions and feelings about two things: seeking help and receiving help

In terms of seeking help they found that trust was the most important factor in who they chose to disclose to. While friends and family members were most commonly approached first, when young people did talk to professionals it was most often teachers.

> *It's all about trust isn't it – some people you get on with and some people you don't like – some people you can trust and some people you can't so I don't know really just keep trying to be approachable and then people would probably go to you. (Lisa, aged 15)*

Other important elements for disclosure of abuse were confidence in themselves and feeling safe to speak out. For example on confidence and safety, one respondent noted:

> *That's the only reason why I didn't speak out for nine months because of low self esteem and I was terrified. Have to have the confidence and they have to have a big safety net around them 'cos if kids don't feel safe they don't do anything. (Emma, aged 14)*

In terms of receiving help their relationships with social workers were central. Again, young people valued having a consistent relationship with a professional they felt they could trust: they spoke positively about their social workers when they had regular meetings with them and when social workers had time to work with young people and build relationships:

> *I think one of the main things is that when a social worker is designated, you should keep that social worker for as long as possible...I really think that they should try and keep that same social worker with that child for as long as possible, so then a relationship can get built up, the trust can get built up... I think if they expect children to tell them things and put trust in them, then you need to put the work in and be with them for a long period of time, and just make a relationship with them. (Anna, aged 17)*

Some young people felt that they had not been listened to, that their views had not been taken into account and they did not feel informed of what was happening to them and raised issues of confidentiality.

> *Interviewer: Did you understand what was happening or what people were doing?*
>
> *Fatima: No, it all it felt like whatever I told them they would go and tell my mum … so I would just stop telling them.*
>
> *Interviewer: What did you expect to happen or what did you want to happen?*
>
> *Fatima: I thought that they were going to help me and not tell my mum when I told them stuff…*
>
> *Interviewer: Do you feel that they listened to what you had to say?*
>
> *Fatima: No, they listened to what my mum had to say.*

The research concluded thus:

> *It is apparent from the young people we interviewed that the current system does not always meet the needs or expectations of young people who are in need of safeguarding. From young people's perspectives this is because the current safeguarding system does not always allow for the development of relationships which can facilitate disclosures and/or provide protection.*

Reflection on the research

Look back at the list of things that the 'Working Together' suggested children wanted. How far does this fit with the findings of Jobe and Gorin?

In Chapter 6 there is a discussion of research by Cossar et al. that includes children's relationships with those who work with them (pages 226–7). They concluded,

> *The findings suggested a trusting relationship could offer opportunities to promote confidence, feelings of safety and self-efficacy.*

What are the similarities between the findings of Cossar et al. and Jobe and Gorin?

Both are concerned with social workers and children in need of care and protection. Do you think the findings would be different if the context was children in school and their teachers?

Unfortunately, the ideal and reality don't always meet, and research can give us insight into why this might be the case. A number of research studies, from different parts of the world, have investigated why those who work with children, particularly social workers, appear to be unwilling to engage the children they work with in decision-making processes. Chapter 5 has already looked at the work of Alfandari (2015) and Van Bijleveld et al. (2014) in some detail. Here we summarize the findings that are concerned with effective relationships.

Examples of research: children and decision making

Israel, Alfandari (2015)

By following 21 case studies of families involved in care proceedings, this research evaluated a reform that was designed to reinforce children's participation in child protection decision making. It found that although structures and processes included positive features such as informed preparation, opportunities to attend committee meetings and several options for communication, children's voices were neither heard nor taken seriously into account. They found this was due to

- social workers' lack of skill and time,
- organizational messages about practice priorities,
- social workers' paternalistic views of the roles and capabilities of children and adults.

The research concluded that

- Organizations need to provide enabling conditions for workers, such as time, skills and professional guidance, to work directly, consistently and effectively with children in order for meaningful participation to be achieved.
- Participation will occur when practitioners truthfully understand the need to be open to, and influenced by, the views and wishes

of the people, both adults and children, who know best what is wrong in their lives and experience the impact this has on them.
- Policy makers need to stop simply telling workers what to do, and direct effort towards establishing systems that enable them to do it.

Norway (Vis et al., 2012)

The researchers used questionnaires to establish the views of case managers and social work students on children's participation in the decision-making process. They found that although child participation is mandatory through regulations in the Norwegian Child Welfare Act, there were three main reasons for not engaging children in decision making.

- Some social workers fear they will harm children in the process.
- Some believe participation is necessary but have difficulty achieving effective participation in the context of child protection case processing.
- Some may feel that they do not have the communication skills needed to engage children and that organizational barriers will sometimes not allow them to develop the necessary relationships.

They concluded that communication skills training and guidance is necessary and argue that in order to reduce barriers towards child participation, social work training and guidance should also put greater emphasis on ways of working with children in participation processes rather than 'hearing' children for the sake of decision making. There was also a need to look into ways of making case processing more 'child-friendly' in order to overcome organizational barriers.

Norway (Bae, 2010)

Reviewing research on children in kindergartens and their ability to participate and make their views known, Bae identifies how capable children are from a very young age to find ways of expressing themselves when in the company of sensitive, skilled adults. However, her review also indicates that many working with children don't enable or encourage participation because of

- their perceptions of young children's capabilities and perceptions of adult–child relationships that emphasize traditional roles;

- lack of knowledge of workers, managers and trainers of ways of communicating effectively with young children and encouraging positive relationships and questioning traditional perspectives.

She concludes,

By meeting adults who are willing to challenge their own thinking and to interpret children's rights in local settings, children might have experiences in kindergarten that contribute to a sense of participating on one's own terms from very early on in life.

Instead of isolating oneself within segregated theoretical islands excluding one's opponents and/or looking negatively at others who work with different perspectives and methods, it seems more fruitful to venture into dialogue and be challenged by people and ideas that seem foreign. This might liberate mental energy and enhance collaboration, which is needed to deal with some of the structural constraints (pressures on static measures of quality, testing of children etc.) that threaten to narrow the space for participation on the part of both the children and the adults working with them.

Netherlands (van Bijleveld et al., 2014)

Through interviews with Child Protection Case Managers and young people under the Care and Protection Service, the researchers identified significant differences in the perception and expectations of the two groups in relation to the participation of young people in the protection process.

They found that

- case managers see participation as important, but generally this is only because it is a means to ensure the child's cooperation;
- young people want to be heard, informed and taken seriously.

They concluded thus:

Because of the different perceptions there is no meaningful dialogue between the case manager and the young person. Despite evidence that children and young people can contribute meaningfully, the knowledge and experiences of young people are not valued, taken seriously, or acted upon in the process of youth care.

They consider that efforts need to be made in order to change perceptions of case managers.

Reflection on the research

Activity 1

There seem to be common themes in the research that have been considered in earlier chapters:

- contexts
- perception of the meaning of 'participation'
- perceptions of child–adult relationships

Look back at the earlier section in this chapter on rights issues for those working with children and identify some of the external pressures that might influence how workers interact with children. How do these relate to the findings of these research examples?

Activity 2

Look back at Chapter 2 and examples of participation. How do these relate to the findings of these research examples?

Activity 3

Look at the different models of child–adult relationships in Chapter 6. How do these relate to the findings of these research examples?

Most of these examples are concerned with the relationships between children and social workers, often in the difficult context of intervention in family situations. Chapter 5 also looks at research in the areas of child cancer care (Coyne et al., 2014) and Youth Courts in Ireland (Kilkelly, 2008) where similar issues arise. In all these cases it is clear that although the relationship between the child and the worker is crucial it is affected by factors outside the control of either. Chapter 5 refers to four elements of a 'jig-saw':

- Culture
- Structure
- Practice
- Review

All four are important features of the way organizations work that can influence how well children and young people are supported in their participation and decision making. It is important to consider how each of these might be supporting or inhibiting relationships in the research examples above.

Key points: what research can tell us about developing positive relationships between children and those who work with them

While children and young people have a clear view of what 'effective practice' is and this is often embedded in guidance and policies, many of those working with children have difficulties forming positive working relationships with them. Sometimes this is due to external constraints of national policies or local working practices and sometimes it is due to personal beliefs and constructs that are fundamental to how they perceive their role.

In a more positive example of working with children, Alison Clark describes how the well-developed 'Mosaic Approach' to working with young children can enable children to participate in decision making.

Example of research: positive example of working with children – spaces to play

Alison Clark (2005) reports how young children were involved with parents, practitioners and planners in a project funded by Learning through Landscapes to develop an outside play area. They used the Mosaic Approach to find out what was important to young children and reflected, with the young children, on what they found to develop the play area. The Mosaic Approach to listening to young children was developed as part of a research process but has evolved to be used in practice in Early Years settings so practitioners can see things from the point of view of the young children. The elements of this approach are as follows:

- Multi-method: the different 'voices' or languages of children are recognized by using e.g. interviews, photography, book-making, tours and 2D and 3D representations made by children.
- Participatory: children are treated as experts and agents in their own lives.
- Reflexive: children, practitioners and parents are involved in reflecting on and interpreting the evidence collected through the different methods.
- Adaptable: the methods can be applied in a variety of early childhood institutions.

- Focused on children's lived experiences: the methods can be used for a variety of purposes including looking at lives lived rather than knowledge gained or care received.
- Embedded into practice: it can become a framework for listening that has the potential to be both used as an evaluative tool and to become embedded into early years practice.

In this particular study the following methods/tools were used to listen to children:

- Qualitative observation accounts
- Short structured interviews conducted one to one or in a group
- Children's photographs of 'important things' and books
- Tours of the site directed and recorded by the children
- Map making using children's own photographs and drawings
- Informal interviews with practitioners and parents
- A 'magic carpet' slide show of familiar and different places

These were used to gather children's and adults' perspectives. These were then reviewed by all involved and used to make decisions about the play area. Each of the tools was discussed in turn in order to reveal emerging themes. Discussions centred around two main questions:

- Which places do children see as important in this outdoor space?
- How do the children use these places?

The results of these discussions were mapped out on a large plan. Similar ideas were linked and conflicting meanings noted. Four categories of place in the outdoor space were identified through the review process: places to keep, places to expand, places to change and places to add. This resulted in the expansion of the house, adaptation of the fence to make it more attractive and the addition of digging and seating areas.

Analysis of case studies of individual children's involvement showed the importance of the Mosaic Approach in helping children express their thoughts and be part of the decision making. Clark gives the following example of four-year-old Rees:

Rees had been able to convey important features of his experience at the preschool. These included the pleasure of being with other children but with no particular friend, his liking for the playhouse and the pram and an interest in mechanical objects. Rees had conveyed these 'ways of seeing' through the Mosaic Approach, using a range of languages and learning styles. This in turn led to Rees displaying an interest in communicating through developing graphic skills as well as entering into more conversations with the researcher. However, had the study relied solely on the interview he would have been another invisible child and Rees would not have had the opportunity to engage with the question 'what does it mean to be in this place?' and perhaps more importantly 'what does it mean to be me here?' (36)

Clark identifies three areas that are important in making this approach work

1. Power relationships: The Mosaic Approach includes an element of role reversal for the adults involved. Children participate as document-ers, photographers, initiators and commentators. Children play an active role, taking the lead in which ideas, people, places and objects are given significance.

2. The many languages of children: The Mosaic Approach requires adults to relearn other languages they may be unfamiliar with using in an educational context or to acquire new skills, for example using observation, discussing photos and drawings with children to identify and confirm what is important.

3. Making the findings visible: By displaying both the evidence of what children are 'saying' and reflections on this evidence the capabilities of young children can be made visible and show the wide applications, not only within a learning environment but also in altering the expecta-tions and the role that young children can play in the wider community.

Reflections on the research

Activity 1

Clark shows how young children are able to express their views and be part of decisions that affect them when the adults who work with them adapt their ways of listening.

How does the idea of shifting power relationships fit with the model of Rights Education put forward by Reynaert et al.?

How might the appreciation of 'many languages' have helped the children in the research by Taylor et al. (2015) (pages 197–8)?

Activity 2

Look at the examples of research by

- Harcourt and Hägglund (2013) in Chapter 1 (pages 15–17) and Chapter 2 (pages 72–4).
- Wickenden and Kembhavi-Tam (2014) in Chapter 4 (page 134–6).
- MacNaughton et al. (2007) in Chapter 4 (pages 142–3).

What are the similarities in approach between these examples and the Mosaic Approach?

Activity 3

In Chapter 5 (page 154) Franklin and Sloper (2006) make the distinction between decision making on 'children's issues' and 'higher level' decisions. The focus for this research was concerned with involving young children in decisions about a play area that might be considered a 'children's issue'. Do you think similar methods could be used to involve children of all ages in other types of decisions for example their education, care, health?

Activity 4

The research referred to earlier in this chapter identified the apparent difficulties social workers have in forming positive relationships with children and young people. The common themes identified were

- contexts
- perception of the meaning of 'participation'
- perceptions of child–adult relationships

The elements of the Mosaic Approach include 'adaptability' and 'embedded into practice'. Thinking about the reasons for social workers' difficulties in forming positive relationships, how well do you think the Mosaic Approach might be adapted to social work situations and become embedded in social work practice?

How might the context of social work practice affect the incorporation of this approach? Think about the reasons for the difficulties and the constraints that Polly referred to in her letter to David Cameron (page 239) and those identified in the section on rights issues (pages 242–58).

Even though there clearly are positive aspects of listening to children and young people and encouraging their participation in decision making, Moss (2006) urges caution that adults working in this way need to be sure that

- they are aware of the unequal power relationships that might exist so, even in the Early Years setting some children might be more vocal than others and their voice may take priority;
- 'listening to children' can be tokenistic unless there is a willingness to act on what is heard;
- even more dangerously, by asking children about what they think and feel, there is the potential to use this information in ways that don't have benefits for the children: a means of manipulating children.

Activity

These pointers echo those that are made in Chapter 4 Table 4.1 (page 122) on 'Silence and Voice', and 'Key points: voice and participation rights' (page 124), concerning children's voices and participation in decision making. Think about those who work with children and how all these factors might need to be taken into consideration. What challenges might workers face in dealing with these issues?

Chapter 4 also identifies how to avoid some of these 'traps':

- involve children and young people in the earliest stages of planning;
- start slowly, proceed carefully and draw on pilot projects;
- take time and ensure there are the relevant resources;
- recognize and enable the wider changes in attitudes, behaviour and power required;
- provide consistent support and staff development for steady progress to spread (The National Youth Agency, 2005).

How might this advice help those who work with children and young people?

How might it help those who manage services for children and young people?

What implications does this have for the government that funds these services?

Activities

The following activities are designed to help reflect back over the book as a whole. key themes are identified with activities that relate to the theme in a number of chapters.

Theme 1 – the children's rights agenda: silencing and voice

Chapter 4 identified three particular ways that can be helpful in considering the complex factors silencing children when working with children. These were as follows:

1. The worth of children's voices.
2. The ways that social exclusion silences children.
3. The dominance of adult-orientated ways of communicating and decision making.

The following activities ask you to review the research examples in relation to these three kinds of factor.

1. The first factor was described as: 'the tendency has been to link the worth and validity of a child's voice to adult opinions about appropriate "levels" of competency and capability' (page 120).

Review the following examples of research and identify how the right to participate was engaged with positively or negatively in terms of ideas of worth, judgement, maturity, capability and power:

- Chapter 4: 'Child's voice and age'– Perez-Expósito (2015) (pages 129–31).
- Chapter 5: 'How children become invisible in child protection work' – Ferguson (2016) (pages 160–1).
- Chapter 6: 'Participation and protection' – Cossar et al. (2016) (pages 226–7).
- Chapter 7: 'Rights education' – Webb (2015) (pages 254–5).

2. The second was described as 'the ways in which a variety of factors to do with *social exclusion* interconnect in the silencing of children. These concern how people are excluded within society, and these are additional forces which add to the ways in which children are not given voice. Such factors include the ways in which poverty, class, gender, race, sexuality or disability affect children's lives' (page 120).

Review the following research examples and identify how poverty, class, gender, race, sexuality or disability have affected the way children's voices have been listened to:

- Chapter 3: Stonewall and University of Cambridge (2012) (pages 87–8).
- Chapter 4: 'Ask us too!' (2014) (pages 134–6).
- Chapter 7: Taylor et al. (2015) (pages 197–8).

3. The third was described as 'the assumption that *adult modes of communicating* are the only way that participation can be valid. This is embedded in many aspects of most societies: communication, consultation and decision making are made through the adult-orientated written word or speech. Here 'voice' is seen as something that is *articulate* only in particular ways and that articulacy is given to a certain status: the position of the adult' (page 121).

Review the following examples of working with children and identify how the right to participate was affected by the ways adults engaged with children and young people. Identify possible barriers to communication and how they were addressed.

- Chapter 4: MacNaughton et al. (2007) (pages 142–3).
- Chapter 7: Taylor et al. (pages 197–8).
- Chapter 7: Clark (2005) (pages 266–8).

Theme 2 – rights-informed approaches to relating to children: decision making

Chapter 5 discussed the Social Care Institute for Excellence's guide to enabling the participation of children and young people in work concerning social care. They proposed that even when an organization says that it is committed to a culture of participation, they do not always change their ways of working as a result. Their argument includes the idea that unless children and young people can influence decision-making processes their right to participate will not be effectively realized. They proposed four areas to assist in organizations review. Chapter 5 summarized the elements that combine to enable decision making:

Culture: the ethos of an organization, shared by all staff and service users, which demonstrates a commitment to participation;

Structure: the planning, development and resourcing of participation evident in an organization's infrastructures;

Practice: the ways of working, methods for involvement, skills and knowledge which enable children and young people to become involved;

Review: the monitoring and evaluation systems which enable an organization to evidence change affected by children and young people's participation.

Re-examine the following two examples of research into ways of working with children:

- Chapter 4: MacNaughton et al. (2007) (pages 142–3).
- Chapter 7: Clark (2005) (pages 266–8).

Does the example indicate whether the culture demonstrates a commitment to participation? If it does – how does it do that? If not, how do you think change could be effected to create such a culture? In reflecting on this, think especially about the organizational structures that are in place, or that could be changed.

Does the example include effective practice – ways of working or methods – that enables children and young people to be involved? If it does – how does it do that? If not, how do you think change could be effected to create methods? In reflecting on this think especially about whether there is effective involvement of children in reviewing the organization.

Theme 3 – tensions, spaces and relationships: state, family, best interests and rights

Chapter 1 discussed the idea that an emerging theme within children's rights concerned tensions 'between the different spaces and relationships within which children live their lives. One of this book's key themes concerns the tensions between children's experiences of spaces where rights informed policies and laws operate and where they do not'. Chapter 6 discussed a key aspect of this tension, concerning the relationship between children's rights, children's position in their family and the role of the state. It talks about the relationship between the concept of 'best interests' and the role of carer in the following way.

When put against the concept of 'the child's best interests' this makes it clear that carers need to be aware of the power relationship that they have with the child and acknowledge that their personal interests may be in conflict with the child's. Knowing the child's thoughts on the matter can only be beneficial in trying to make the best decision.

The main implication of these ideas is that in order for carers to act in the best interests of the child they need to be aware of and respect the views of the child. This doesn't mean that the child will always do exactly what he or she wants but he or she will participate in discussions about what actions might be best. Interestingly, Thomas's (2002) research into children's participation in decision making found that 'what they wanted was above all the opportunity to take part in dialogue with adults, not for either themselves or the adults to determine the outcome' (2000, 152).

Look back at the examples:

- Chapter 5: 'Decision making and participation rights in education' (pages 162–6).
- Chapter 6: 'Example of research – Cossar et al.' (2016) (pages 226–7).
- Chapter 7: 'Example of research – Jobe and Gorin' (2013) (pages 260–1).

What ideas about 'the best interests of the child' emerge from the adults and children in the examples?

How are children's views of what they think is in their 'best interests' taken into account?

How might the dialogue between adults and children concerning what is 'in the child's best interests' be supported in each example?

The UNCRC makes it clear that the 'best interests' principle also needs to be at the heart of states' policies and legislation but this is often secondary to political and economic factors. Review the following examples of UK policies and identify how well 'the best interests' principle has been taken into account. What other economic and political factors have been important in developing the policies in the following examples?

- Chapter 2: Smyth (2013a, 2013b) on asylum seekers (pages 53–4).
- Chapter 3: The treatment of children at Yarl's Wood Immigration Removal Centre (pages 96–9).
- Chapter 6: Judge (2015) on parents' working hours (pages 216–18).

Theme 4 – critiques of the UNCRC: power relationships, agency and a 'bottom-up' approach to rights

Chapter 2 identified issues that have arisen since the large-scale adoption of the UNCRC by the majority of states. One of these concerns was the 'top-down' nature of the UNCRC and the fear that the compromises and tensions in the UNCRC are ignored. In contrast, Chapter 1 pointed out that the 'lived experiences' of children often don't match up with the idealized notion of rights implementation. It discusses how Harcourt and Hägglund (2013): 'looked at very young children's experience of rights'. Their work was informed by what some call a *bottom-up perspective* (Katz, 1992; Harcourt and Keen, 2012), which involves 'recommending critical indices of quality from the child perspective that could serve to inform adults and policy-makers through the evidence provided by the child experience'.

Another concern is the degree of agency that is assumed of both children and adults in being able to realize their rights. Tisdall and Punch (2012) list some of the areas where researchers have attributed agency to children as an alternative to helpless victims: child soldiers, child prostitutes and street children. They challenge the degree of agency that children actually have in these circumstances. It is clear that this tension is in need of further investigation so that vulnerable children are not marginalized because of the wider context beyond their control.

Chapter 4 discusses how:

adults are in positions of power in areas such as decision making and responsibility, and children are excluded from holding and using power. Their exclusion can be termed as having no 'voice' or power in making decisions. This absence of voice and power is seen within large-scale decisions in government through to children's everyday lives at school or at home. (page 120)

This combination of power relationships and lack of agency can be seen in many of the examples throughout the book. Review the following examples and consider the power relationships, issues of agency and how children and young people's experience of rights in their everyday lives may be influenced.

- Chapter 3: Dowty (2008) on rights, protection and privacy (page 108).
- Chapter 4: Kilkelly et al.(2005) on school and voice (page 125).
- Chapter 5: Coyne et al. (2014) on children, participation and decision making during cancer care (pages 168–70).
- Chapter 6: Smahel and Wright (2014) on online problematic situations for children.(pages 209–10).
- Chapter 7 Hampshire et al. (2011) on the effects of health policy in Ghana (pages 246–7).

Summary

This chapter has

- explored the contexts of working with children and the different challenges that are posed;
- identified rights issues that arise for those working with children in relation to
  - the holistic ideal of children's rights,
  - the political, economic and social pressures that impact on rights,
  - the impact of inequalities on children's rights,
  - to what rights children should have and who should decide what these are;
- discussed how research can inform us about different perceptions between children and some of those who work with them about children's participation;
- given a positive example of working with children that encourages their participation through positive relationships.

Further reading

Jones, P. and Walker, G. (eds) (2011) *Children's Rights in Practice*. London: Sage.
   Walker, G. (2008) *Working Together for Children: A Critical Introduction to Multi-agency Working*. London: Continuum.

Research details

Example of research: the effects of health policy in Ghana

This research was undertaken in Ghana after the introduction of a version of a National Health Service. It is concerned with identifying how young people make use of the services available.

Hampshire, K., Porter, G. Owusu, S.A., Tanle, A. and Abane, A. (2011) 'Out of the reach of children? Young people's health-seeking practices and agency in Africa's newly-emerging therapeutic landscapes', *Social Science and Medicine*, 73, 702–710.

Example of research: the effects of discrimination

This research was commissioned by the NSPCC to investigate the experiences of deaf and disabled children when they were involved in the child protection system.

Taylor, J., Cameron, A., Jones, C., Franklin, A., Stalker, K., and Fry, D. (2015) *Deaf and Disabled Children Talking about Child Protection.* Edinburgh: University of Edinburgh and NSPCC.

Example of research: rights education

As part of a PhD study, Webb investigated how one school that was committed to improving children's rights tackled Rights Education.

Webb, R. (2015) 'Negotiating the "3Rs": Deconstructing the politics of "rights, respect and responsibility" in one English primary school', in T. Dragonas, K. Gergen, S. McNamee and E. Tseliou (eds) *Education as Social Construction: Contributions to Theory, Research and Practice*. Chagrin Falls, OH: WorldShare (e-book). Available online at: http://www.taosinstitute.net/education-as-social-construction.

Example of research: what children want from those who work with them

This research involved face-to-face interviews with 24 young people from a range of backgrounds in order to find out young people's understandings, perceptions and feelings about seeking help and receiving help from social services.

Jobe, A. and Gorin, S. (2013) 'If kids don't feel safe they don't do anything': Young people's views on seeking and receiving help from Children's Social Care Services in England', *Child & Family Social Work* 18, 429–438.

Examples of research: children and decision making

A number of research studies from different countries looked at the effectiveness of social workers' relationships with children and young people and the possible reasons for difficulties.

Alfandari, R. (2015) 'Evaluation of a national reform in Israeli child protection practice designed to improve children's participation in decision making', *Child & Family Social Work*, June 2015. Available online at: https://www.researchgate.net/publication/284243972.

Vis, S.A., Holtan, A. and Thomas, N. (2012) 'Obstacles for child participation in care and protection cases – Why Norwegian social workers find it difficult', *Child Abuse Review*, 21, 723.

Bae, B. (2010) 'Realizing children's right to participation in early childhood settings: some critical issues in a Norwegian context', *Early Years: An International Research Journal*, 30 (3) 205–218.

van Bijleveld, G.G., Dedding, C.W.M. and Bunders-Aelen, J.F.G. (2014) 'Seeing eye to eye or not? Young people's and child protection workers' perspectives on children's participation within the Dutch child protection and welfare', *Child and Youth Services Review*, 47, 253–259.

Positive example of working with children: spaces to play

Clark describes how the Mosaic Approach to working with young children enabled them to take part in decision making in improving their play area.

Clark, A. (2005) 'Ways of seeing: Using the Mosaic Approach to listen to young children's perspective', in A. Clark, A. Kjørholt and P. Moss, (ed) *Beyond Listening: Children's Perspectives on Early Childhood Services*. Bristol: Policy Press, pp. 29–49.

Appendix: UNICEF's Summary of the Rights under the Convention on the Rights of the Child

Article 1 (Definition of the child): The Convention defines a 'child' as a person below the age of 18, unless the laws of a particular country set the legal age for adulthood younger. The Committee on the Rights of the Child, the monitoring body for the Convention, has encouraged States to review the age of majority if it is set below 18 and to increase the level of protection for all children under 18.

Article 2 (Non-discrimination): The Convention applies to all children, whatever their race, religion or abilities; whatever they think or say, whatever type of family they come from. It doesn't matter where children live, what language they speak, what their parents do, whether they are boys or girls, what their culture is, whether they have a disability or whether they are rich or poor. No child should be treated unfairly on any basis.

Article 3 (Best interests of the child): The best interests of children must be the primary concern in making decisions that may affect them. All adults should do what is best for children. When adults make decisions, they should think about how their decisions will affect children. This particularly applies to budget, policy and law makers.

Article 4 (Protection of rights): Governments have a responsibility to take all available measures to make sure children's rights are respected, protected and fulfilled. When countries ratify the Convention, they agree to review their laws relating to children. This involves assessing their social services, legal, health and educational systems, as well as levels of funding for these services. Governments are then obliged to take all necessary steps to ensure that the minimum standards set by the Convention in these areas are being met. They must help families protect children's rights and create an environment where they can grow and reach their potential. In some instances, this may involve changing existing laws or creating new ones. Such legislative changes are not imposed, but come about through the same process by which any law is created or reformed within a country. Article 41 of the Convention points out the when a country already has higher legal standards than those seen in the Convention, the higher standards always prevail.

Article 5 (Parental guidance): Governments should respect the rights and responsibilities of families to direct and guide their children so that, as they grow, they learn to use their rights properly. Helping children to understand their rights does not mean pushing them to make choices with consequences that they are too young to handle. Article 5 encourages parents to deal with rights issues 'in a manner consistent with the evolving capacities of the child'. The Convention does not take responsibility for children away from their parents and give more authority to governments. It does place on governments the responsibility to protect and assist families in fulfilling their essential role as nurturers of children.

Article 6 (Survival and development): Children have the right to live. Governments should ensure that children survive and develop healthily.

Article 7 (Registration, name, nationality, care): All children have the right to a legally registered name, officially recognized by the government. Children have the right to a nationality (to belong to a country). Children also have the right to know and, as far as possible, to be cared for by their parents.

Article 8 (Preservation of identity): Children have the right to an identity – an official record of who they are. Governments should respect children's right to a name, a nationality and family ties.

Article 9 (Separation from parents): Children have the right to live with their parent(s), unless it is bad for them. Children whose parents do not live together have the right to stay in contact with both parents, unless this might hurt the child.

Article 10 (Family reunification): Families whose members live in different countries should be allowed to move between those countries so that parents and children can stay in contact, or get back together as a family.

Article 11 (Kidnapping): Governments should take steps to stop children being taken out of their own country illegally. This article is particularly concerned with parental abductions. The Convention's Optional Protocol on the sale of children, child prostitution and child pornography has a provision that concerns abduction for financial gain.

Article 12 (Respect for the views of the child): When adults are making decisions that affect children, children have the right to say what they think should happen and have their opinions taken into account. This does not mean that children can now tell their parents what to do. This Convention encourages adults to listen to the opinions of children and involve them in decision making – not give children authority over adults. Article 12 does not interfere with parents' right and responsibility to express their views on matters affecting their children. Moreover, the Convention recognizes that the level of a child's participation in decisions must be appropriate to the child's level of maturity. Children's ability to form and express their opinions develops with age and most adults will naturally give the views of teenagers greater weight than those of a preschooler, whether in family, legal or administrative decisions.

Article 13 (Freedom of expression): Children have the right to get and share information, as long as the information is not damaging to them or others. In exercising the right to freedom of expression, children have the responsibility to also respect the rights, freedoms and reputations of others. The freedom of expression includes the right to share information in any way they choose, including by talking, drawing or writing.

Article 14 (Freedom of thought, conscience and religion): Children have the right to think and believe what they want and to practice their religion, as long as they are not stopping other people from enjoying their rights. Parents should help guide their children in these matters. The Convention respects the rights and duties of parents in providing religious and moral guidance to their children. Religious groups around the world have expressed support for the Convention, which indicates that it in no way prevents parents from bringing their children up within a religious tradition. At the same time, the Convention recognizes that as children mature and are able to form their own views, some may question certain religious practices or cultural traditions. The Convention supports children's right to examine their beliefs, but it also states that their right to express their beliefs implies respect for the rights and freedoms of others.

Article 15 (Freedom of association): Children have the right to meet together and to join groups and organizations, as long as it does not stop other people from enjoying their rights. In exercising their rights, children have the responsibility to respect the rights, freedoms and reputations of others.

Article 16 (Right to privacy): Children have a right to privacy. The law should protect them from attacks against their way of life, their good name, their families and their homes.

Article 17 (Access to information; mass media): Children have the right to get information that is important to their health and well-being. Governments should encourage mass media – radio, television, newspapers and Internet content sources – to provide information that children can understand and to not promote materials that could harm children. Mass media should particularly be encouraged to supply information in languages that minority and indigenous children can understand. Children should also have access to children's books.

Article 18 (Parental responsibilities; state assistance): Both parents share responsibility for bringing up their children, and should always consider what is best for each child. Governments must respect the responsibility of parents for providing appropriate guidance to their children – the Convention does not take responsibility for children away from their parents and give more authority to governments. It places a responsibility on governments to provide support services to parents, especially if both parents work outside the home.

Article 19 (Protection from all forms of violence): Children have the right to be protected from being hurt and mistreated, physically or mentally. Governments should ensure that children are properly cared for and protect them from violence, abuse and neglect by their parents, or anyone else who looks after them. In terms of discipline, the Convention does not specify what forms of punishment parents should use. However any form of discipline involving violence is unacceptable. There are ways to discipline children that are effective in helping children learn about family and social expectations for their behaviour – ones that are non-violent, are appropriate to the child's level of development and take the best interests of the child into consideration. In most countries, laws already define what sorts of punishments are considered excessive or abusive. It is up to each government to review these laws in light of the Convention.

Article 20 (Children deprived of family environment): Children who cannot be looked after by their own family have a right to special care and must be looked after properly, by people who respect their ethnic group, religion, culture and language.

Article 21 (Adoption): Children have the right to care and protection if they are adopted or in foster care. The first concern must be what is best for them. The same rules should apply whether they are adopted in the country where they were born, or if they are taken to live in another country.

Article 22 (Refugee children): Children have the right to special protection and help if they are refugees (if they have been forced to leave their home and live in another country), as well as all the rights in this Convention.

Article 23 (Children with disabilities): Children who have any kind of disability have the right to special care and support, as well as all the rights in the Convention, so that they can live full and independent lives.

Article 24 (Health and health services): Children have the right to good quality health care – the best health care possible – to safe drinking water, nutritious food, a clean and safe environment, and information to help them stay healthy. Rich countries should help poorer countries achieve this.

Article 25 (Review of treatment in care): Children who are looked after by their local authorities, rather than their parents, have the right to have these living arrangements looked at regularly to see if they are the most appropriate. Their care and treatment should always be based on 'the best interests of the child'.

Article 26 (Social security): Children – either through their guardians or directly – have the right to help from the government if they are poor or in need.

Article 27 (Adequate standard of living): Children have the right to a standard of living that is good enough to meet their physical and mental needs. Governments should help families and guardians who cannot afford to provide this, particularly with regard to food, clothing and housing.

Article 28: (Right to education): All children have the right to a primary education, which should be free. Wealthy countries should help poorer countries achieve this right. Discipline in schools should respect children's dignity. For children to benefit from education, schools must be run in an orderly way – without the use of violence. Any form of school discipline should take into account the child's human dignity. Therefore, governments must ensure that school administrators review their discipline policies and eliminate any discipline practices involving physical or mental violence, abuse or neglect. The Convention places a high value on education. Young people should be encouraged to reach the highest level of education of which they are capable.

Article 29 (Goals of education): Children's education should develop each child's personality, talents and abilities to the fullest. It should encourage children to respect others, human rights and their own and other cultures. It should also help them learn to live peacefully, protect the environment and respect other people. Children have a particular responsibility to respect the rights their parents, and education should aim to develop respect for the values and culture of their parents. The Convention does not address such issues as school uniforms, dress codes, the singing of the national anthem or prayer in schools. It is up to governments and school officials in each country to determine whether, in the context of their society and existing laws, such matters infringe upon other rights protected by the Convention.

Article 30 (Children of minorities/indigenous groups): Minority or indigenous children have the right to learn about and practice their own culture, language and religion. The right to practice one's own culture, language and religion applies to everyone; the Convention here highlights this right in instances where the practices are not shared by the majority of people in the country.

Article 31 (Leisure, play and culture): Children have the right to relax and play, and to join in a wide range of cultural, artistic and other recreational activities.

Article 32 (Child labour): The government should protect children from work that is dangerous or might harm their health or their education. While the Convention protects children from harmful and exploitative work, there is nothing in it that prohibits parents from expecting their children to help out at home in ways that are safe and appropriate to their age. If children help out in a family farm or business, the tasks they do should be safe and suited to their level of development and comply with national labour laws. Children's work should not jeopardize any of their other rights, including the right to education, or the right to relaxation and play.

Article 33 (Drug abuse): Governments should use all means possible to protect children from the use of harmful drugs and from being used in the drug trade.

Article 34 (Sexual exploitation): Governments should protect children from all forms of sexual exploitation and abuse. This provision in the Convention is augmented by the Optional Protocol on the sale of children, child prostitution and child pornography.

Article 35 (Abduction, sale and trafficking): The government should take all measures possible to make sure that children are not abducted, sold or trafficked. This provision in the Convention is augmented by the Optional Protocol on the sale of children, child prostitution and child pornography.

Article 36 (Other forms of exploitation): Children should be protected from any activity that takes advantage of them or could harm their welfare and development.

Article 37 (Detention and punishment): No one is allowed to punish children in a cruel or harmful way. Children who break the law should not be treated cruelly. They should not be put in prison with adults, should be able to keep in contact with their families, and should not be sentenced to death or life imprisonment without possibility of release.

Article 38 (War and armed conflicts): Governments must do everything they can to protect and care for children affected by war. Children under 15 should not be forced or recruited to take part in a war or join the armed forces. The Convention's Optional Protocol on the involvement of children in armed conflict further develops this right, raising the age for direct participation in armed conflict to 18 and establishing a ban on compulsory recruitment for children under 18.

Article 39 (Rehabilitation of child victims): Children who have been neglected, abused or exploited should receive special help to physically and psychologically recover and reintegrate into society. Particular attention should be paid to restoring the health, self-respect and dignity of the child.

Article 40 (Juvenile justice): Children who are accused of breaking the law have the right to legal help and fair treatment in a justice system that respects their rights. Governments are required to set a minimum age below which children cannot be held criminally responsible and to provide minimum guarantees for the fairness and quick resolution of judicial or alternative proceedings.

Article 41 (Respect for superior national standards): If the laws of a country provide better protection of children's rights than the articles in this Convention, those laws should apply.

Article 42 (Knowledge of rights): Governments should make the Convention known to adults and children. Adults should help children learn about their rights, too (see also Article 4).

Articles 43–54 (Implementation measures): These articles discuss how governments and international organizations like UNICEF should work to ensure children are protected in their rights. https://www.unicef.org

References

Action Aid (2011) *Action Aid Bangladesh Annual Report 2011.* Available online at: http://www.actionaid.org/sites/files/actionaid/aab_annual_report_2011.pdf.

Ahmad, S., Akbar, A., Akbar, H., Ayub, S., Batool, A., Batool, S., Hussain, B., Kiani, S., Mahmood, S. and Rauf, R. (2008) 'East meets West – Why do some South Asian young people feel they need to lead a double identity and how does cultural and religious issues affect them?' *Young Researchers Network.* Available online at: http://childrensresearchcentre.open.ac.uk/research/Barnardo'sresearchreport. pdf.

Alanen, L. and Mayall, B. (2001) *Conceptualizing Child-Adult Relations.* London: Routledge/Falmer.

Alderson, P. (2008) *Young Children's Rights: Exploring Beliefs, Principles and Practice.* London: Jessica Kingsley Publishers.

Alderson, P. and Montgomery, J. (1996a) *Health Care Choices: Making Decisions with Children.* London: Institute for Public Policy Research.

Alderson, P. and Montgomery, J. (1996b) 'What About Me?' *Health Services Journal,* 11 (1) 22–24.

Alfandari, R. (2015) 'Evaluation of a national reform in Israeli child protection practice designed to improve children's participation in decision making', *Child & Family Social Work,* June. Available online at: https://www.researchgate.net/publication/284243972.

Alston, P. and Tobin, J. (2005) *Laying the Foundations for Children's Rights.* Florence: Innocenti Research Centre.

Anderson, K. (2008) 'Sidelined: The marginalisation of children's voices in education', *Child Right, Journal of Law and Policy Affecting Children and Young People,* October, 18–21.

Archard, D. (2015) *Children, Rights and Childhood.* Abingdon: Routledge.

Archard, D. and Skivenes, M. (2010) 'Deciding best interests: General principles and the cases of Norway and the UK', *Journal of Children's Services* 5 (4) 43–54.

Arneil, B. (2002) 'Becoming versus being: A critical analysis of the child in liberal theory', in Archard, D. and Macleod, C. (eds) *The Moral and Political Status of Children.* Oxford: Oxford University Press.

Bach, M. (2002) 'Social inclusion as solidarity: Rethinking the child rights agenda'. *Perspectives on Social Inclusion Working Papers Series.* Toronto: The Laidlaw Foundation.

Bae, B. (2010) 'Realizing children's right to participation in early childhood settings: Some critical issues in a Norwegian context', *Early Years: An International Research Journal*, 30 (3) 205–218.

Balagopalan, S. (2008) 'Memories of tomorrow: Children, labor and the panacea of formal schooling', *The Journal of the History of Childhood and Youth*, 1 (2) 267–285.

Barton, L. (2003) *Inclusive Education and Teacher Education: A Basis for Hope or a Discourse of Delusion?* London: Institute of Education.

Benhabib, S. (2011) *Dignity in Adversity in Troubled Times*. Cambridge, MA: Polity Press.

Bhana, D. (2014) *Under Pressure: The Regulation of Sexualities in South Africa Secondary Schools*. Braamfontein: MaThoko's Books.

Bird, S. (2011) 'Consent to medical treatment: The mature minor', *Australian Family Physician*, 40 (3) 159–160.

Brannen, J. and O'Brien, M. (1996) *Children in Families: Research and Policy*. London: Falmer Press.

Brighouse, H. (2002) 'What rights (if any) do children have?', in Archard, D. and Macleod, C. (eds) *The Moral and Political Status of Children*. Oxford: Oxford University Press.

British Medical Association (2010) *Children and Young People Toolkit*. London: BMA.

Brummelman E., Thomas S., Slagt M., Overbeek G., de Castro B.O. and Bushman B.J. (2013) 'My child redeems my broken dreams: On parents transferring their unfulfilled ambitions onto their child. *PLoS ONE* 8 (6) e65360. doi:10.1371/journal.pone.0065360.

Bühler-Niederberger, D. (2010) 'Defining the state of the art and ensuring reflection', *Current Sociology*, 58 (2) 155–164.

Burchardt, T. (2008) *Time Poverty and Income Poverty: CASE Report 57*. London: London School of Economics and Political Science.

Carr, M., May, H., Podmore, V., Cubey, P., Hatherly, A. and Macartney, B. (2002) 'Learning and teaching stories: Action research on evaluation in early childhood in Aotearoa-New Zealand', *European Early Childhood Education Research Journal*, 10 (2) 115–125.

Charles, A. and Haines, K. (2014) 'Measuring young people's participation in decision making: What young people say', *International Journal of Children's Rights*, 22 (3) 641–659.

Children, Comment, Stand Up For Social Work (2015) '*I Already Live* with the *Risk of Being Vilified*': *A Social Worker's Letter to David Cameron*. Available online at: http://www.communitycare.co.uk/2015/03/19/already-live-risk-villified-social-workers-letter-david-cameron/.

Children on the Edge (2016) *Tent Schools for Syrian Refugee Children in Lebanon:-A Teachers view* Available online

at: http://www.childrenontheedge.org/latest-stories/
-tent-schools-for-syrian-refugee-children-in-lebanon-a-teachers-view.

Children's Rights Alliance of England (2008) *Survey Children's Rights.*
London: Children's Rights Alliance for England.

Children's Rights Alliance of England (2013) *The State of Children's Rights in
England: Review of Government Action on United Nations' Recommendations
for Strengthening Children's Rights in the UK.* London: Children's Rights
Alliance for England.

Children's Rights Alliance of England (2015) *See It, Say It, Change It.*
Available online at: www.crae.org.uk/media/78664/crae_seeit-sayit-
changeit_web.pd.

Children's Rights Alliance of England (2017) Children's rights and the
law: What are children's rights? Available online at: http://www.crae.org.uk/
childrens-rights-the-law/what-are-human-rights/.

The Children's Society (2015) *The Good Childhood Report.* London: The
Children's Society. Available online at: https://www.childrenssociety.org.uk/
sites/default/files/TheGoodChildhoodReport 2015.pdf.

Clark, A. (2005) 'Ways of seeing: Using the Mosaic Approach to listen to young
children's perspective', in Clark, A., Kjørholt, A.T. and Moss, P. (eds) *Beyond
Listening: Children's Perspectives on Early Childhood Services.* Bristol: Policy
Press, pp. 29–49.

Coram Children's Legal Centre (2015) *Home Office Consultation 'Reforming
Support for Failed Asylum Seekers and Other Illegal Immigrants.* Available
online at: http://www.childrenslegalcentre.com/userfiles/Home%20
Office%20consultation%20on%20support%20for%20failed%20asylum%20
seekers_FinalSep2015.pdf.

Coram Children's Legal Centre Response, September 2015.

Cossar, J., Brandon, M. and Jordan, P. (2016)' 'You've got to trust her and she's
got to trust you': Children's views on participation in the child protection
system', *Child & Family Social Work*, 21 (1). doi: 10.1111/cfs.12115.

Council of Europe. (1950) *The European Convention on Human Rights.*
Available online at: www.hri.org/docs/ECHR50.html.

Covell, K.R., Howe, B. and McGillivray, A. (2017) 'Implementing
children's education rights in school', in Ruck, M.D., Peterson-Badali,
M. and Freeman, M. (eds) *Handbook of Children's Rights: Global and
Multidisciplinary Perspectives.* London: Routledge.

Coyne, I., Amory, A., Kiernan, G. and Gibson, F. (2014) 'Children's
participation in shared decision-making: Children, adolescents, parents and
healthcare professionals' perspectives and experiences', *European Journal of
Oncology Nursing*, 18 (3) 273–280.

Criminal Justice and Courts Act (2015) http://www.legislation.gov.uk/ukpga/
2015/2/section/42.

Dalacoura, K. (2014) 'Homosexuality as cultural battleground in the Middle East: Culture and postcolonial international theory', *Third World Quarterly*, 35 (7) 1290–1306.

Dalrymple, J. (2005) 'Constructions of child and youth advocacy: Emerging issues in advocacy practice', *Children & Society*, 19 (1) 3–15.

Davey, C. (2008) *What Do They Know? Investigating the Human Rights Concerns of Children and Young People Living in England*. London: Children's Rights Alliance for England.

Davey, C., Burke, T. and Shaw, C. (2010) *Children's Participation in Decision-making: A Children's Views Report*, London: Children's Rights Alliance of England, National Children's Bureau, Office of the Children's Commissioner and Participation Works.

Department for Education (2004) *Children Act*. Available online at: http://www.legislation.gov.uk/ukpga/2004/31/contents/enacted.

Department for Education (2014) *Children and Families Act*. Available online at: http://www.legislation.gov.uk/ukpga/2014/6/contents/enacted.

Department for Education (2015) *Working Together to Safeguard Children*. London: Department for Education.

Department for Health (1989) *Children Act*. Available online at: http://www.legislation.gov.uk/ukpga/1989/41/contents/enacted.

Ehlers, L. and Frank, C. (2016) 'Child participation in Africa', in Sloth-Nielsen, J. (ed.) *Children's Rights in Africa: A Legal Perspective*. Oxon: Routledge.

Engle, P. (2006) '*Comprehensive Policy Implications of Children's Rights*' in United Nations Committee on the Rights of the Child, United Nations' Fund and Bernard van leer Foundation (eds) '*Implementing Child Rights in Early Childhood: A Guide to General Comment 7 Implementing Child Rights in Early Childhood*'. The Hague: Bernard van leer Foundation.

Equality and Human Rights Commission (2015) *Children's Rights in the UK Equality and Human Rights Commission Submission to the United Nations Committee on the Rights of the Child on the United Kingdom's Implementation of the Convention on the Rights of the Child*. London: Equality and Human Rights Commission.

Eurochild (2012) *Consultation with Eurochild members and Other Interested Organisations on Participatory Methods with Children and Young People*. Available online at: http://www.eurochild.org/fileadmin/public/05_Library/Thematic_priorities/05_Child_Participation/Eurochild/Consultation_on_Participatory_Methods_with_Children_Young_People.pdf.

European Commission (2011) *Children's Rights, as They See Them*. Luxembourg: Publications Office of the European Union.

Ferguson, H. (2016) 'How children become invisible in child protection work: Findings from research into day-to-day social work practice', *British Journal of Social Work*, 46 (1) 153–168.

Franklin, A. and Sloper, P. (2006) 'Participation of disabled children and young people in decision making within social services departments', *British Journal of Social Works*, 36 (5) 723–741

Freeman, M. (2000) 'The End of the Century of the Child?', *Current Legal Problems*, 58(1), 505–558.

Gov.uk (2016) *Parental Rights and Responsibilities*, Directgov. Available online at: https://www.gov.uk/parental-rights-responsibilities/what-is-parental-responsibility.

Guasp, A. (2012) *The School Report, The Experiences of Gay Young People in Britain's Schools in 2012*. Cambridge: Stonewall and the University of Cambridge.

Hampshire, K., Porter, G. Owusu, S.A., Tanle, A. and Abane, A. (2011) 'Out of the reach of children? Young people's health-seeking practices and agency in Africa's newly-emerging therapeutic landscapes', *Social Science & Medicine*, 73, 702–710. Hampshire, K., Porter, G., Owusu, S.A., Mariwah, S., Abane, A., Robson, E., Munthali, A., DeLannoy, A., Bango, A. Gunguluza, N. and Milner, J. (2015) 'Informal m-health: How are young people using mobile phones to bridge healthcare gaps in Sub-Saharan Africa?', *Social Science & Medicine*, 142, 90–99. Available online at: http://www.sciencedirect.com/science/article/pii/S0277953615300496.

Harcourt, D. and Hägglund, S. (2013) 'Turning the UNCRC upside down: A bottom-up perspective on children's rights', *International Journal of Early Years Education*, 21 (4) 286–299.

Harcourt, D. and Keen. D. (2012) 'Learner engagement: Has the child been lost in translation?', *Australasian Journal of Early Childhood*, 37 (3) 71–77.

Henricson, C. and Bainham, A. (2005) *The Child and Family Policy Divide: Tensions, Convergence and Rights*. York: Joseph Rowntree Foundation.

HM Government (2011) *Prevent Strategy*. Norwich: TSO. Available online at: https://www.gov.uk/government/uploads/system/uploads/attachment_data/file/97976/prevent-strategy-review.pdf.

Ignatieff, M. (2003) *Human Rights as Politics and Idolatry*. Princeton NJ: Princeton University Press.

Inter-Parliamentary Union (2012) *Youth Advisory Forum*. Available online at: https://beta.ipu.org/our-work/youth.

Jackman, M. and McRae, A. (2013) *Medical Decision-Making and Mature Minors*. Available online at: http://www.royalcollege.ca/portal/page/portal/rc/common/documents/bioethics/section1/case_1_5_2_e.html.

Jensen, A. (2003) 'For the children's sake', in Jensen, A. and McKee, L. (eds) *Children and the Changing Family*. London: Routledge/Falmer.

Jobe, A. and Gorin, S. (2013) ' "If kids don't feel safe they don't do anything": young people's views on seeking and receiving help from

Children's Social Care Services in England', *Child & Family Social Work*, 18 (4) 22–35.

Johnson, R. (2015) 'Strengthening the monitoring of and compliance with the rights of the African child', *The International Journal of Children's Rights*, 23 (2) 365–390.

The Joint Parliamentary Committee on Human Rights (2014) *The UK's Compliance with the UN Convention on the Rights of the Child Eighth Report of Session 2014–15*. London: The Stationery Office.

Judge, L. (2015) *Round the Clock: In-work Poverty and the 'Hours Question'*. London: Child Poverty Action Group.

Katz, L.G. (1992) 'Early childhood programs: Multiple perspectives on quality', *Childhood Education*, 69 (2) 66–71.

Kellett, M. (2005) *How to Develop Children As Researchers*. London: Paul Chapman.

Kelly, L., Wingfield, R., Burton, S. and Regan, G. (1995) *Splintered Lives: Sexual Exploitation of Children in the Context of Children's Rights and Child Protection*. Ilford: Barnardos.

Kilkelly, U. (2008) 'Youth Courts and Children's Rights: The Irish experience', *Youth Justice*, 8 (110) 39–56.

Lansdowne, R. (1996) *Children in Hospital: A Guide for Family and Carers*. Oxford: Oxford University Press.

Lowden, J. (2002) 'Children's Rights: A decade of dispute', *Journal of Advanced Nursing*, 37 (1) 100–107.

Lundy, L. (2012) 'Children's rights and educational policy in Europe:T implementation of the United Nations Convention on the Rights of the Child', *Oxford Review of Education*, 38 (4) 393–411.

Lundy, L., Kilkelly, U., Byrne, B. and Kang, J. (2012) *The UN Convention on the Rights of the Child: A Study of Legal Implementation in 12 Countries*. Belfast: Unicef/Centre for Children's Rights School of Education.

Lyle, S. (2014) 'Embracing the UNCRC in Wales (UK): Policy, pedagogy and prejudices', *Educational Studies*, 40 (2) 215–232.

MacNaughton, G., Hughes, P. and Smith, K. (2007) 'Young children's rights and public policy: Practices and possibilities for citizenship in the early years', *Children & Society*, 21 (1) 458–469.

McCarry, M. (2012) 'Who benefits? A critical reflection of children and young people's participation in sensitive research', *International Journal of Social Research Methodology* 15 (1) 55–68.

Mill, J.S. (1859) *On Liberty*. London: Parker and Son.

Ministry of Social Development (2016) *Involving Children: A Guide to Engaging Children in Decision-making*. Available online at: http://www.msd.govt.nz/documents/about-msd-and-our-work/publications-resources/archive/-involving-children.pdf. Accessed 9 November 2016.

Moorehead, C. (1997) 'Despite Safeguards, Children's Rights are Still Ignored'. Press Release. 26 March. Available online at: http://pangea.org/street_children/world/unconv3.htm.

Moss, P. (2006) 'Listening to young children – Beyond rights to ethics', in *Perspectives: A Series of Occasional Papers on Early Years Education: Let's Talk about Listening to Children: Towards a Shared Understanding for Early Years Education in Scotland*. Scotland: Learning and Teaching Scotland.

National Youth Agency (2005) *Involving Children and Young People – An introduction*. London: National Youth Agency.

O'Keeffee, A. (2008) 'Their right to liberty', *New Statesman*. Available online at: www.newstatesman.com/uk-politics/2008/12immigration-detention-children.

O'Neill, O. (1984) 'Paternalism and partial autonomy', *Journal of Medical Ethics*, 10, (1) 173–178.

Organization of African Unity (OAU) *African Charter on the Rights and Welfare of the Child*, 11 July 1990, CAB/LEG/24.9/49 (1990). Available online at: http://www.refworld.org/docid/3ae6b38c18.html.

Parental Rights (2017) *The State of Parental Rights 2017*. Available online at: http://www.parentalrights.org/vertical/Sites/%7BC49108C5-0630-467E-9B9B-B1FA31A72320%7D/uploads/SOPRA17.pdf.

Parsapoor, A., Parsapoor, M., Rezaei, N. and Asghari, F. (2014) 'Autonomy of children and adolescents in consent to treatment: Ethical, jurisprudential and legal considerations', *Iranian Journal of Pediatrics*, 24 (3) 241–248.

Pérez-Expósito, L. (2015) 'Scope and quality of student participation in school: Towards an analytical framework for adolescents', *International Journal of Adolescence and Youth*, 20 (3) 346–374.

Playday (2013) *Playday Opinion Poll*. Available online at: http://www.playday.org.uk/2013-opinion-poll/.

Potgieter, C. and Reygan, F. (2012) 'Lesbian, gay and bisexual citizenship: A case study as represented in a sample of South African Life Orientation textbooks', *Perspectives in Education*, 30 (4) 39–51.

Prout, A. (2000) 'Children's participation: Control and self-realisation in British Late Modernity', *Children and Society*, 14, 304–315.

Quennerstedt, A. (2009) 'Balancing the rights of the child and the rights of parents in the convention on the rights of the child', *Journal of Human Rights*, 8 (2) 162–176.

Quennerstedt, A. and Quennerstedt, M. (2014) 'Researching children's rights in education: Sociology of childhood encountering educational theory', *British Journal of Sociology of Education*, 35 (1) 115–132.

Qvortrup, J., Bardy, M., Sgritta, G. and Wintersberg, H. (1994) *Childhood Matters*. Aldershot: Avebury.

Raby, R. (2014) 'Children's participation as neo-liberal governance?' *Discourse: Studies in the Cultural Politics of Education*, 35 (1) 77–89.

Radford, L., Corral, S., Bradley, C., Fisher, H., Bassett, C., Howat, N. and Collishaw, S. (2011) *Child Abuse and Neglect in the UK Today*. London: NSPCC.

RCM, RCN, RCOG, Equality Now, UNITE (2013) *Tackling FGM in the UK: Intercollegiate Recommendations for Identifying, Recording, and Reporting*. London: Royal College of Midwives.

Reading, R., Bissell, S., Goldhagen, J., Harwin, J., Masson, J., Moynihan, S., Parton, N., Pais, M., Thoburn, J. and Webb, E. (2008) 'Promotion of children's rights and prevention of child maltreatment', *The Lancet*, 10, 1016

Reynaert, D., Bouverne-de-Bie, M. and Vandevelde, S. (2009) 'A review of children's rights literature since the adoption of the United Nations Convention on the Rights of the Child', *Childhood*, 16 (4) 518–534.

Reynaert, D., Bouverne-de-Bie, M. and Vandevelde, S. (2010) 'Children, rights and social work: Rethinking children's rights education', *Social Work and Society International Online Journal*, 8 (1) 60–69. Available online at: http://www.socwork.net/sws/article/view/23/63.

Rivers, I. and Cowie, H. A.(2006) 'Bullying and homophobia in UK schools: A perspective on factors affecting resilience and recovery', *Journal of Gay and Lesbian Issues in Education*, 3 (4) 11–43.

Ruck, M. D. and Storn, S. (2008) 'Charting the landscape of children's rights', *Journal of Social Issues*, 64 (4) 685–699.

Save the Children (2007) *The Small Hand of Slavery*. London: Save the Children. Available online at: https://resourcecentre.savethechildren.net/library/small-hands-slaverymodern-day-child-slavery.

Save the Children (2012) *Untold Atrocities: The Stories of Syria's Children*. Available online at: http://www.savethechildren.org.uk/sites/default/files/docs/untold-atrocities.pdf.

Scottish Government (2010) *Deciding Which School You Would Prefer Your Child to Go to*. Available online at: http://www.gov.scot/Publications/2010/11/10093528/2.

Simmons, B. (2010) 'Treaty Compliance and Violation', *Annual Review of Political Science*, 13 (1) 273–296.

Sinclair, R. (2004) 'Participation in practice: Making it meaningful, effective and sustainable', *Children & Society*, 18 (1) 106–118.

Smahel, D. and Wright, M.F. (eds) (2014) *Meaning of Online Problematic Situations for Children. Results of Qualitative Cross-Cultural Investigation in Nine European Countries*. London: EU Kids Online, London School of Economics and Political Science.

Smith, A. (2011) 'Respecting children's rights and agency', in Harcourt, D., Perry, B. and Waller, T. (eds) *Young Children's Perspectives: Ethics, Theory and Research*. London: Routledge.

Smith, A. B. (2016) *Children's Rights: Towards Social Justice*. New York: Momentum Press.

Smyth, C. (2013a) 'Is the right of the child to liberty safeguarded in the Common European Asylum system?' *European Journal of Migration and Law*, 15 (2) 111–136.

Smyth, C. (2013b) *The Common European Asylum System and the Rights of the Child: An Exploration of Meaning and Compliance*. Doctoral Thesis, Leiden University. Available online at: https://openaccess.leidenuniv.nl/handle/1887/20462.

Social Care Institute for Excellence (2006) *SCIE Guide II: Involving Children and Young People in Social Care*. Available online at: www.scie.org.uk/publications/guides/guide11/index.asp

Tasioulas, J. (2012) 'Towards a philosophy of human rights', *Current Legal Problems*, 65 (1) 1–30.

Taylor, J., Cameron, A., Jones, C., Franklin, A., Stalker, K., and Fry, D. (2015) *Deaf and Disabled Children Talking About Child Protection*. Edinburgh: University of Edinburgh and NSPCC.

Thomas, N. (2002) *Children, Family and the State: Decision-Making and Child Participation*. Bristol: Policy Press.

Thomas, N. (2011) *Children's Rights: Policy into Practice. Centre for Children and Young People Background Briefing Series, no.4*. Lismore: Centre for Children and Young People, Southern Cross University.

Tisdall, K. and Punch, S. (2012) 'Not so 'new'? Looking critically at childhood studies', *Children's Geographies*, 10 (3) 249–264.

Tomasevski, K. (2004) *Manual on Rights Based Education*. Bankok: UNESCO.

Tomlinson, P. (2008) 'The politics of childhood', in Jones, P., Moss, D., Tomlinson, P. and Welch, S. (eds) *Childhood: Services and Provision for Children*. London: Pearson.

UNICEF (2014) *Eliminating Discrimination against Children and Parents Based on Sexual Orientation and/or Gender Identity*. UNICEF Position Paper 9, November 2014, Accessed 20 October 2016. Available online at: https://www.unicef.org/videoaudio/PDFs/Current_Issues_Paper_Sexual_Identification_Gender_Identity.pdf.

UNICEF *Fact Sheet: The Right to Participation*. Available online at: https://www.unicef.org/crc/files/Right-to-Participation.pdf.

United Nations (1948) *Universal Declaration of Human Rights*. Available online at: www.un.org/ Overview/rights.html.

United Nations (1989) *Convention on the Rights of the Child, Geneva*. Washington, DC: Office of the United Nations High Commissioner for Human Rights. Available online at: www.unhchr.ch/html/ menu3/b/k2crc.htm.

United Nations Committee on the Rights of the Child (2002) *Concluding Observations: UK of Great Britain and Northern Ireland.* Available online at: www.unhcr.org/refworld.

United Nations Committee on the Rights of the Child (2003) *General Comment No. 5: General Measures of Implementation of the Convention. On the Rights of the Child (Parts 4, 42 and 44).* Available online at: www.unhcr.org/refworld.

United Nations Committee on the Rights of the Child (2006) *General Comment No. 9: The Rights of Children with Disabilities,* 27 February 2007, CRC/C/GC/9. Available online at: http://www.refworld.org/docid/461b93f72.html.

United Nations Committee on the Rights of the Child (2008) *'Day of general discussion on "the right of the child to education in emergency situations". Recommendations'* Available online at: http://www.ohchr.org/EN/HRBodies/CRC/Pages/DiscussionDays.aspx

United Nations Committee on the Rights of the Child (2008) *General Comment No. 1: The Aims of Education.* Available online at: www.unhcr.org/refworld.

United Nations Committee on the Rights of the Child (2013) *General Comment No. 14: On the Right of the Child to Have His or Her Best Interests Taken as a Primary Consideration (Art. 3, Para. 1),* 29 May 2013, CRC /C/GC/14. Available online at: http://www.refworld.org/docid/51a84b5e4.html.

United Nations Committee on the Rights of the Child (2013) *General Comment No. 15: On the Right of the Child to the Enjoyment of the Highest Attainable Standard of Health (Art. 24),* 17 April 2013, CRC/C/GC/15. Available online at: http://www.refworld.org/docid/51ef9e134.html.

United Nations Committee on the Rights of the Child (2015) *List of Issues in Relation to the Fifth Periodic Report of the United Kingdom of Great Britain and Northern Ireland,* 11 November 2015, CRC/C/GBR/Q/5. Available online at: http://www.refworld.org/docid/573d76574.html.

United Nations General Assembly (2000) *Optional Protocol to the Convention on the Rights of the Child on the Involvement of Children in Armed Conflict,* 25 May 2000. Available online at: http://www.refworld.org/docid/47fdfb180.htm.

United Nations General Assembly (2001) *Optional Protocol to the Convention on the Rights of the Child on the Sale of Children, Child Prostitution and Child Pornography,* 16 March 2001, A/RES/54/263. Available online at: http://www.refworld.org/docid/3ae6b38bc.html.

United Nations General Assembly (2010) *The Right to Education in Emergency Situations: Resolution/Adopted by the General Assembly, 27 July 2010,* A/RES/64/290. Available online at: http://www.refworld.org/docid/4c6241bb2.html.

United Nations General Assembly (2015) *The Girl Child: Report of the Secretary-General,* 4 August 2015, A/70/267. Available online at: http://www.refworld.org/docid/55f673844.html.

United Nations High Commissioner for Refugees (2016) *Vulnerability Assessment of Syrian Refugees in Lebanon 2016.* Available online at: http:// www.refworld.org/docid/586f59c94.html.

United Nations Human Rights Committee (HRC) (2004) *General Comment no. 31 [80]: The Nature of the General Legal Obligation Imposed on States Parties to the Covenant,* 26 May 2004, CCPR/C/21/Rev.1/Add.13. Available online at: http://www.refworld.org/docid/478b26ae2.html.

United Nations Human Rights Office of the High Commissioner (2016) *Committee on the Rights of the Child Reviews the Report of the United Kingdom.* Accessed 20 September 2017. Available online at: http://www.ohchr.org/EN/NewsEvents/Pages/DisplayNews. aspx?NewsID=20007&LangID=E.

United Nations Human Rights Office of the High Commissioner. *Fact Sheet No.10 (Rev.1), The Rights of the Child.* Available online at: http://www.ohchr. org/Documents/Publications/FactSheet10rev.1en.pdf.

van Bijleveld, G.G., Dedding, C.W.M. and Bunders-Aelen, J.F.G. (2014) 'Seeing eye to eye or not? young people's and child protection workers' perspectives on children's participation within the Dutch child protection and welfare', *Child and Youth Services Review,* 47, 253–259.

Vis, S.A., Holtan, A. and Thomas, N. (2012) 'Obstacles for child participation in care and protection cases – Why Norwegian social workers find it difficult', *Child Abuse Review,* 21, 723.

Wade, A. and Smart, C. (2003) 'As fair as it can be?: Childhood after divorce', in Jensen, A. and McKee, L. (eds) *Children and the Changing Family.* London: Routledge/Falmer.

Walker, G. (2008) *Working Together for Children: A Critical Introduction to Multi-agency Working.* London: Continuum.

Webb, R. (2015) 'Negotiating the "3Rs": deconstructing the politics of "Rights, Respect and Responsibility" in one English Primary School', in Dragonas, T., Gergen, K., McNamee, S. and Tseliou, E. (eds) *Education as Social Construction: Contributions to Theory, Research and Practice.* Chagrin Falls, OH: WorldShare (e-book). Available online at: http://www.taosinstitute.net/ education-as-social-construction.

Webber, F. (2016) *Prevent and the Children's Rights Convention.* Institute of Race Relations. Available online at: http://www.irr.org.uk/wp-content/ uploads/2016/01/IRR_Prevent_Submission.pdf.

Welsh Government (2004) *Children and Young People: Rights to Action.* Available online at: http://www.wales.gov.uk/assemblydata/pdf.

Welsh Government (2011) *Rights of Children and Young Persons (Wales) Measure.* Available online at: http://www.legislation.gov.uk/cy/mwa/2011/2/ contents.

White, S. (2007) 'Children's rights and the imagination of community in Bangladesh', *Childhood*, 14, 505–520.

Wickenden, M. and Kembhavi-Tam, G. (2014) 'Ask us too! Doing participatory research with disabled children in the global south', *Childhood*, 21 (3) 400–417.

Willow, C. (2002) *Participation in Practice: Children and Young People as Partners in Change*. London: Save the Children.

Index